TEAMS
UNLEASHED

Praise for *Teams Unleashed*

"The drive to deliver team performance is relentless. The tools to get there are few. Now with *Teams Unleashed*, Sandahl and Phillips have given us a clear, practical map—a readable resource for more productive team results and truly engaged team culture—an exceptional resource for those who work with or lead teams."

—**Marshall Goldsmith**, *New York Times* **#1 bestselling author of** *Triggers, Mojo,* **and** *What Got You Here Won't Get You There*

"Team coaching is becoming an established discipline and needs practical guides to good practice from highly experienced practitioners—which is exactly what this book provides!"

—**David Clutterbuck, author of** *Coaching the Team at Work*

"A valuable resource for team coaches and team leaders alike. *Teams Unleashed* provides practical coaching questions and frameworks, filling a palpable need for team performance in today's ever-changing context."

—**Jennifer J. Britton, MES, PCC, CHRL, author of** *From One to Many: Best Practices for Team and Group Coaching* **and** *Effective Virtual Conversations*

"This relevant and timely guide poses the coaching questions every business team needs to address before the zombie apocalypse!"

—**Darelyn 'DJ" Mitsch, MCC, author of** *Zombies to Zealots—Reawaken the Spirit at Work,* **and creator of** *Team Advantage—the complete guide for team transformation*

"Still far too many teams at all levels in organizations are performing at less than the sum of their parts. Phillip Sandahl and Alexis Phillips have provided teams and team leaders with a rich panoply of methods and examples that teams can use to liberate their potential, resolve conflicts, and become more creative. Easy to follow and apply, I wish this book was around when I was first a team leader."

—**Professor Peter Hawkins, author of** *Leadership Team Coaching,* **and** *Leadership Team Coaching in Practice,* **global thought leader in systemic team coaching**

"Given the shifting and uncertain landscape of our current world, it is vital that we learn to work together ever more effectively. In *Teams Unleashed*, authors Phillip Sandahl and Alexis Phillips provide a ground breaking, proven and accessible approach to freeing the phenomenal power and potential of teams. A wonderful book and a great approach to working with teams of people!"

—**Karen and Henry Kimsey-House, Cofounders, The Co-Active Training Institute and coauthors of** *Co-Active Coaching: The Proven Framework for Transformative Conversations at Work and in Life*

"*Teams Unleashed* is a must read for anyone who is leading or supporting a team in any capacity. As the definitive voices in team coaching, Phillip Sandahl and Alexis Phillips have brought together a simple but powerful framework that will transform how organizations approach developing their teams. As a global business leader, I have seen the successful application of this approach to teams across the world, and personally can attest to the power that these principles have across regions, languages, and cultures. This book not only provides guidance on how to drive greater performance in teams, but more importantly provides the blueprint for what makes people function better as human beings."

—**Mazher Ahmad, Global Head of Talent Acquisition, Organizational Development, Culture and D&I / Leading Life Sciences Company**

"Building high performance teams has become more and more critical for leaders who face business challenges in today's VUCA world. *Teams Unleashed* provides a structured and tangible framework to address team high performance from a fundamentally human level and system view. I believe this book will be beneficial for HR and team leaders to build new strengths on teams. It will bring in new perspectives on team dynamics and clear factors on where to focus for team success. It provides practical guidance for those new to team coaching and experienced coaches as well for conscious development of in-depth team coaching competences and skills."

—**Xie Xue, Talent Development Expert,
Bayer (China) Limited**

"*Teams Unleashed* is an essential guide for any practitioner, team leader or team member who is serious about team coaching and maximizing team performance. Sandahl and Phillips approach the complexity of teams with insight and practical guidance drawn from a life time of engagements with real teams from around the world. They share their wisdom and experience in clearly articulated and compelling language and models that make this book both extremely useful and a pleasure to read."

—**Alexander Caillet, CEO—Corentus, Inc.,
Cor (Heart) + Eventus (Results)**

"In an age when organizations struggle to make the dramatic shift from individual to truly team-centric designs in order to survive, let alone thrive, *Teams Unleashed* couldn't be more timely. Sandahl and Phillips have curated a treasure trove of insights and practical tools for teams, team leaders and team coaches to navigate this often-times perilous yet ultimately fruitful journey."

—**Krister Lowe, PhD, Founder, Team Coaching Zone**

"Phillip Sandahl and Alexis Phillips offer practical wisdom for individuals who want to sharpen their skills in the work of developing team performance. In *Teams Unleashed* they share invaluable insights and lessons—from identifying teams that are ready for coaching, to creating supportive structures for elevating team practice—about how team coaches can help teams build and sustain great performance over time."

—**Ruth Wageman, PhD, coauthor of *Senior Leadership Teams***

"It is an everlasting topic for every organization: how to create high performing teams continuously. As an HR partner we never stop looking for a better approach that will support business leaders to make their teams great. This book provides practical guidance on how team coaching can unleash the team's potential and enable teams to achieve sustainable, outstanding results."

—Maggie Shen, Armstrong World Industries (China) Limited, Asia HR Head

"High performing individuals are diverse and don't always work together well. It's a significant challenge for leaders to turn a group of great minds into a cohesive, high performing team. *Teams Unleashed* gives team leaders the practical tools they need to bring diverse talent together in a powerful way."

—Sherman Chen, Armstrong World Industries (China) Limited, General Manager, North Asia

TEAMS UNLEASHED

How to Release the Power and Human Potential of Work Teams

By Phillip Sandahl
Cofounder of Team Coaching International

and Alexis Phillips
Cofounder of Team Coaching International

NICHOLAS BREALEY
PUBLISHING

BOSTON • LONDON

First published in 2019 by Nicholas Brealey Publishing

An imprint of John Murray Press

An Hachette UK company

24 23 22 21 20 19   1 2 3 4 5 6 7 8 9 10

A CIP catalogue record for this title is available from the British Library

Library of Congress Cataloging-in-Publication Data
Names: Sandahl, Phil, author. | Phillips, Alexis, author.
Title: Teams unleashed : a coaching framework to release the power and human potential of work teams / by Phillip Sandahl, Co-founder of Team Coaching International, and Alexis Phillips, Co-founder of Team Coaching International.
Description: Boston, MA : Nicholas Brealey Publishing, 2019. | Includes bibliographical references and index.
Identifiers: LCCN 2018055785 (print) | LCCN 2018059710 (ebook) | ISBN 9781529337068 (ebook) | ISBN 9781529337075 (library ebook) | ISBN 9781529337044 (pbk. : alk. paper)
Subjects: LCSH: Teams in the workplace—Management. | Employees—Coaching of.
Classification: LCC HD66 (ebook) | LCC HD66 .S258 2019 (print) | DDC 658.4/022—dc23
LC record available at https://lccn.loc.gov/2018055785

ISBN 978-1-5293-3704-4
US eBook ISBN 978-1-5293-3706-8
UK eBook ISBN 978-1-5293-3705-1

Printed and bound in the United States of America.

John Murray Press policy is to use papers that are natural, renewable, and recyclable products and made from wood grown in sustainable forests. The logging and manufacturing processes are expected to conform to the environmental regulations of the country of origin.

John Murray Press Ltd
Carmelite House
50 Victoria Embankment
London EC4Y 0DZ
Tel: 020 3122 6000

Nicholas Brealey Publishing
Hachette Book Group
53 State Street
Boston, MA 02109, USA
Tel: (617) 263 1834

www.nbuspublishing.com

Contents

Acknowledgments

Our gratitude begins with our fellow pioneers in this important and still-emerging coaching field: Alexander Caillet; David Clutterbuck; Peter Hawkins; Patrick Lencioni; Ruth Wageman; and especially, for sharing their wisdom and the wisdom of teams, Jon Katzenbach and Douglas Smith. For those who contributed to a deeper understanding of teams and systems, Arnold Mindell and Peter Senge, thank you for the insight.

We want to acknowledge the thousands of teams around the world who have stepped into the team coaching process, sometimes courageously, sometimes reluctantly. They taught us everything we know about what works and just as much about what doesn't work. Behind those teams, our gratitude goes to the organizations that often took a chance on a relatively unknown process. They deserve to be acknowledged for their vision and a commitment that includes the bottom line but goes deeper than that by recognizing the value of team development on a fundamentally human level.

We also extend our gratitude to the early adopters who joined us in our mission by bringing our work into their country and in many cases, provided the translation to bring it to life locally. They put the "international" in Team Coaching International (TCI) and confirmed that, although there are important local cultural differences, the model resonates with teams around the world. In that vein, we want especially to recognize our partners in China, Jane Zhang, Jessie Feng, and Mandy Liu, for their vision and their commitment to high professional standards.

We learned a great deal about teams by being one, especially in those start-up days. Paul Sherman played a key role in our growth, and

Shelly Recchio over the years has worn all the hats on the shelf. They have our gratitude.

For the worldwide, purpose-driven TCI faculty, for their dedication to teams and organizational effectiveness, and for the hundreds of ways they have contributed creativity, innovation, and common sense to the training of team coaches, we are grateful. For more than a dozen years they have been at the forefront, carrying the torch and shining the light.

A special thank you to Marita Fridjhon and Faith Fuller for the valuable training they have created to illuminate and support relationship systems work, and to Gracia Maioli and Jeanine Kenigstein for their pioneering commitment to team coaching in Latin America.

Finally, we would certainly be remiss if we did not acknowledge our coaching roots with the Co-Active Training Institute and the founders, Karen Kimsey-House, Henry Kimsey-House, and Laura Whitworth. We are honored and humbled to believe our work stands on the shoulders of what CTI created as a foundation.

Phillip Sandahl and Alexis Phillips

Introduction

The purpose of this book is to share a model and methodology that can unleash the power and human potential of teams. The need has never been more acute. Work teams at every level in the organization are under pressure to perform in a world where work stress is epidemic and the landscape is constantly changing. In this increasingly competitive, demanding, and uncertain world, teams struggle to live up to their potential. It is a global phenomenon affecting teams at every level in every imaginable industry segment. Our goal is to provide a framework and process that can consistently change the environment and support teams to work together more effectively. The key, we believe, is to create a cycle of action and learning that enables teams to achieve outstanding results and create a culture that is empowering and sustainable. This is a practical coaching approach based on years of experience and the results from thousands of teams worldwide.

The Gap

Our data shows that fewer than 10 percent of teams rate themselves as high-performing.[1] That means nearly nine out of 10 teams fall short. In a way, it's not too surprising. These are challenging times for teams. The pressure is on to do more with fewer resources—on every team, in every organization we've seen, around the world. The speed of change continues to accelerate. Contact time shrinks while expectations grow. That imperative drives teams to form, perform, and reform at an astonishing rate.

Organizations have rightly identified teams as a means to improve productivity. That's where the leverage is. The diversity of strengths and experience on a team means teams, acting together, can do things that individuals acting alone simply can't. Today the workplace is a maze of nested teams: intact, cross-functional, networked, project, agile, matrix, cross-cultural, and virtual. It's no wonder teams are underperforming. In fact, according to a recent Gallup poll, 85 percent of employees are not engaged or are actively disengaged, which accounts for approximately $7 trillion in lost productivity across the globe.[2] The financial impact alone should get every organization's attention.[3] The human costs—stress, turnover, a culture of indifference—are incalculable.

The strategy to put more emphasis on teams makes sense, but it is crippled by an assumption that is simply not true—that team members naturally know how to work collaboratively. The thinking goes, "We all know what a team is. We've all been on teams. I do my job, you do yours, and everything will be okay." Unfortunately, working together effectively is not the sum of individual efforts, even when the individual performance is stellar. We have all seen or been on a team of high-performing individuals who couldn't function at a high level as a team.

No doubt you've been on a great team too, or observed one in action. It's inspiring. Here's the point: almost without exception they were created by accident. It was a combination of the right people, the right chemistry, the right time, and the right purpose. If it can happen once, randomly, surely there must be a way to create a repeatable process for that. Yes, there is most certainly a way, or we wouldn't be writing this book. There is a proven process to improve team performance, deliver real business results, and create committed, engaged, empowered teams. There is a way to unleash the power and human potential in teams.

What You Will Learn

There are three sections in the book. In part 1, we look first at the qualities that make great teams great. What do high-performing teams do better than other teams? What is that template? The team effectiveness model we describe has two fundamental dimensions for team performance: conditions necessary for teams to get the job done—Productivity strengths—and conditions necessary for teams to work together effectively—what we call Positivity strengths.

This leads naturally to a detailed description of the seven Productivity factors and seven Positivity factors that make up the two dimensions. Each factor is a unique and essential contributor to team effectiveness. We show the role that each factor plays in team performance and provide suggestions, tips, and exercises you can use with teams to build those team-effectiveness muscles. There are clear distinctions made to distinguish team building, group facilitation, group coaching, and team coaching. You will also learn about the different roles in a team coaching process, and the contribution and responsibility for each. In chapter 5 we describe a three-phase team coaching process and include insight into the important differences between individual coaching and team coaching. As a process for change, coaching is an ideal methodology for building new strengths on teams.

Part 2 describes the five key team coaching competencies and how together they form a constellation of ways to work with the team. We provide a description of team coaching skills associated with each of the five competencies. These are skills drawn from the larger glossary of coaching skills, and they have been adapted to teams. You will find unique team coaching skills as well. As you can imagine, one of the fundamental differences between individual coaching and team coaching is simply the awareness that there is so much going on, on so many levels. It is happening all at once and changing constantly. These are the skills and competencies we have learned and honed over years of working with teams and training team coaches around the world.

Part 3 brings together a number of important considerations related to an effective team coaching process and approach. For example:

- Best candidates for team coaching
- Coaching the virtual team
- A close-up look at the special role of the team leader
- The crucial and often overlooked relationship between team and the stakeholder network

We close with a view of the mission and vision for this work with teams, including a look at why we believe the work is so important beyond the obvious benefit to bottom-line results.

Who Should Read This Book?

This is a book for people who work with teams. That includes a wide range of professionals searching for a practical, repeatable process to support sustainable team performance improvement. It is a coaching approach, but people from a variety of functional backgrounds play the "team coach" role. That would include team coaches of course, but executive, business, and leadership coaches too. In addition, basically all professionals who work with groups and teams will benefit: organizational consultants, HR business partners and organizational development professionals, facilitators, learning and development specialists, and team-building practitioners. It would quickly become cumbersome to repeat that list each time we mention the role, so for simplicity's sake the book uses the term "team coach" to refer to all those who work with teams to improve performance.

This is also a book for team leaders and, in fact, any team member who wants to learn more about how to support a team to reach its potential. In our model, that means a team that grows in both dimensions—Productivity and Positivity—and develops strengths in all 14 of the Team Performance Indicators.™

Summary

As we noted earlier, in organizations today the pressure is on to do more with less and do it faster. For employees, managers, and leaders, that atmospheric pressure is the air they breathe every day, and it is a global phenomenon. There is a relentless search for the next best way to improve productivity and be more competitive. In the face of that challenge, more organizations turn to teams as the engines that drive business results. Teams provide an ideal resource to meet that challenge because of the team's diversity of strengths and the power that comes from shared connection, working together with a common purpose and vision.

The key to meeting the business challenges will be teams that have learned how to work effectively in that interconnected world. We have seen the results, and they are inspiring. We see teams that set and meet—even exceed—their most challenging goals. Just as importantly, we see teams that are changing the quality of life at work. That's the underlying purpose for this book and our mission.

There is a need for a clear, practical, repeatable process. A random approach to teams will yield only one out of 10 that is high-performing. As a wise person once said, "Accidental success is not a viable business strategy." We believe every team has the potential to be a great team. In this book we outline a proven approach that can unleash the power of teams.

PART 1

How to Consistently Create High-Performing Teams

O ur data from more than 10 years of team-assessment results tells us two things—and these two things are related.

First, as we noted in the introduction, our data shows that fewer than 10 percent of teams rate themselves as high-performing. A survey of executives by McKinsey & Company found only 20 percent thought their team was a high-performing one.[4] Pick your statistic, that is still an alarming revelation, and it ought to be a resounding call to action.

Second, even with no special training or development work with the team, one in 10 teams *do* rate themselves high-performing. And if one in 10 can do it with no help, imagine what would be possible if we simply figured out what those high-performing teams do well. That would lay the groundwork for a process designed to transfer that know-how to other teams. That's the focus for the first five chapters of the book.

We start by distilling the essential attributes of high-performing teams. Out of that exploration we build a team-effectiveness model—a template any team can emulate. You will see how those attributes sort easily into two primary dimensions: qualities that optimize a team's ability to get the job done and qualities that optimize the team's ability to collaborate.

A viable model is a great start, but it's not sufficient when the outcome we want is a process that will help any team work more effectively. If the goal is growth and development, like learning any new skill, it takes more than reading a book, attending a workshop, or—for teams—having an engaged conversation. Change—real change—takes place over time by practicing new behavior. That is why a coaching methodology is ideal for this purpose. In fact, a coaching model not only provides a structure to practice new ways of interacting, it holds the team accountable for that behavior to help ensure change is integrated into life at work.

In this section we will look at each of the 14 team effectiveness factors that make up the two dimensions. This section will show team coaches or team leaders how to explore those factors with a team in engaging ways. We describe the change/coaching process for teams and what distinguishes it in comparison to other modalities. You will discover the key differences between individual and team coaching and see the guiding principles on which this team coaching methodology is based.

The coaching process begins by putting a pin in the map, as a team, and saying, "We are here." That awareness leads naturally to a team conversation about "Where we want to be" and "How we will get there." The model provides a compass for the team development journey, and coaching provides the means to stay on course.

CHAPTER 1

The Model for Great Teams

The central question is this: What makes great teams great?

If we knew the answer to that question, we would be a long way ahead in helping teams work together more effectively. It's a question that has been widely studied, so there is a vast amount of research available.[5] And there is another, simpler way to get to the heart of the matter right now without digging into the published research. For the purposes of simplicity, do this exercise, tapping into your own experience.

Take a moment and think about a really great team you've been on. Scan back in your memory for a team that really stands out. It could be a work team, or a sports team. It could be an experience from theater or music. It could be a current team you're on, or a recent team, or a team from your youth, but that team stands out in your memory. *That* was a great team.

Relive for a moment what it was like to be on that team. Remember the people you were with, what you accomplished, maybe even what you had to overcome. Recall a special moment with that team. What did it feel like? Savor that experience.

We've done this exercise with dozens of teams, hundreds of team members. The stories they tell are uplifting. One story after another—very different teams and circumstances but the energy created by these memories is inspiring: A school sports team, perennial underdogs, with grit and spirit stronger than their individual talents, wins the state championship. A new team, pulled together under impossible project deadlines and limited resources—long hours, late nights, and many pizza boxes later they deliver, and what they remember most is the laughter. The stories aren't all about overcoming great odds. Sometimes it is simply the unexpected magic and personal connections that last years after the team has dispersed to other organizations and other lives.

In each remembrance you can feel the unique spirit of that team. The stories remind us of the commitment people felt for one another and the commitment to the team's goal or mission. You can see it on the faces of the storytellers. There was a powerful feeling of "we were in this together." Those teams that stand out in the storytelling are teams that were truly alive, engaged, and empowered by a common purpose and spirit.

Teams like that, *that's* what's possible. You know that's possible because, if you're like nearly every team member who has ever participated in this "best team" exercise, you've been on a team like that.

Now ask yourself this question: What were the qualities that made that team a great team? What sets that team apart from other teams you've been on? Here is a sample list of qualities we consistently hear from team members:

- Clear roles. Everyone knew what their job was.
- Support. I've got your back, you've got mine.
- Clear goals
- Fun—despite the pressure
- We had a great mix of personalities, skills, and experience.
- People were accountable.
- Mutual respect
- We didn't always agree—it sometimes got heated—and that was okay. We worked things out.
- People cared. They cared about the project and they cared about each other.
- Even when things looked the worst, *we* knew we could do it.
- We were unstoppable. Nobody thought we could do it, and we *did*.

From your own experience of being on teams, what qualities of great teams would you add to the list? When you study the list of attributes, over time a structure emerges. You begin to see that the list can be sorted into two categories. Here is how we sorted them.

The Productivity Dimension

We start with a fundamental premise, that teams exist to produce results. That's the ground on which we stand. There is no other reason for an organization to put a team together. That premise then leads us to a very obvious question: What are the conditions necessary for teams to get results; to get the job done; to be productive?

Those "productivity" attributes are there in the list of "best team" qualities. From a long list of possibilities, we settled on seven that we believe—and research supports—are essential for teams and, by the way, where high-performing teams excel. These are the Productivity strengths. In chapter 2 we will go into more detail about each of these Productivity factors and how they show up as strengths on teams. We will also include activities to help teams improve in each of the seven areas. For now, here is an overview.

Seven Productivity Strengths

- **Team Leadership**
  The team leader's role is clear. The team leader is supportive of the team as a whole. There is also a strong sense of *team* leadership; team members step up as the need for leadership arises, and that leadership is empowered. In one sense, everyone on the team is responsible for leadership.[6]

- **Resources**
  This is not about the quantity. We have yet to meet a team that says, "Resources? Oh, we have plenty, thank you." Instead, it's about the ability to effectively manage what the team has. Think of resources broadly: material resources, skills, training, time, team capacity, human capital.[7]

- **Decision Making**
  The team has clear and efficient decision-making processes and is adept at applying different processes to different situations. Excellence in decision making is both the ability to make timely and effective decisions and the commitment to learn from decisions that are made.[8]

- **Proactive**

  A proactive team is a team that takes initiative—rises to the challenge. Some teams are satisfied with "good enough." As Jim Collins pointed out in his book, *Good to Great*, these days "good enough" is no longer good enough. Teams that are proactive show it by being creative and innovative and by embracing change.

- **Accountability**

  When we look at accountability through a team lens, we see that it is more than a high level of individual accountability. On high-performing teams, team members hold one another to a higher *team* standard and actively support each other to meet that standard.[9]

- **Goals and Strategies**

  The team has set challenging objectives; targets and outcomes are clear and reinforce a strategic vision.

- **Alignment**

  There is a sense of common mission and purpose. The team values cooperation, cohesion, and interdependence. Team members are all pulling in the same direction.[10]

These seven are like different muscles. Each one is distinct and serves a particular function, and they are all important in order for the team to function as a whole. Some teams are very strong when it comes to these seven attributes. They would be "High Productivity" teams. Some teams are not, and they would be somewhere lower on the Productivity scale. Notice that we keep looking through the lens of "the team." Every team member will have their own unique contribution to these attributes; our primary focus is on how the team as a whole functions.

When taken together, these seven attributes define the team's capacity to be productive. That word "capacity" is important. It doesn't mean that a team that scores well in those seven areas *will* be productive by whatever business measures are relevant to that particular team. But it does mean the team has the ability to be productive.

The Positivity Dimension

We also know that the culture of a team exerts tremendous influence on the ability of team members to work together collaboratively.[11] The Positivity dimension represents the relationship infrastructure of the team; these factors form the environment in which the work gets done. A team culture can be enormously empowering and supportive, and it can be a toxic fog that sabotages the team's ability to work together.[12] You know this from your own experience on teams. The team morale and the prevailing team attitude—whether it's sunny and smooth or a cautious walk through a potential minefield—affects every team member and the team's ability to perform.

This is the team experience—the invisible cloud, the air that the team breathes every day. It can be invigorating and it can be poisonous. This awareness that there is a powerful cultural aspect to every team leads to the next obvious question: What are the conditions necessary for team members to work effectively together? This dimension looks at how team members relate to one another—how the team creates an environment of support and performance. There are many examples of teams of star performers who were simply incapable of working as a cohesive team. They were missing key aspects of this dimension in their work together.

These qualities make up the second dimension. We call this dimension Positivity, a word we borrowed from Daniel Goleman's work in emotional intelligence many years ago.[13] It's a word that sometimes needs a little clarifying for teams. When we describe these seven factors as "Positivity strengths," there are times when we can see team members smirking as if they were thinking, "Oh, yeah, right. From now on we're going to be a 'happy team.' Good luck on that."

Of course, Positivity does not necessarily mean "happy," although it could include happy, or fun. When there seems to be resistance to the word, we tell teams they can substitute the word "engagement" to describe those attributes of a great team culture. So a variation on the Positivity question would be, What are the attributes necessary in order for a team to be fully engaged? We've worked with teams that were absolutely, 100 percent engaged, but at that moment they were not wearing their party hats. Maybe you have had that experience too.

Seven Positivity Strengths

In chapter 3 there will be additional details about each of the Positivity factors along with activities to help teams improve. For now, here is an overview of the seven.

- **Trust**

  Team members would say, "We can be open and honest with each other without fear of reprisal. There is a sense of safety on this team even when conversations are challenging. We can count on each other."

- **Respect**

  There is an atmosphere of mutual respect and genuine positive regard. Respect is extended to team members; it is part of the bond that upholds a sense of mutual value for each team member.

- **Camaraderie**

  This is the social aspect of being on a team. There is a strong sense of belonging and when present, it reinforces the sense of identity as a team. "This is who we are. We are in this together." There is an underlying quality of mutual support. "I've got your back, you've got my back."[14]

- **Communication**

  Clear and efficient communication is valued and practiced. When communication is a strength on teams, it shows up in both the commitment to clarity of the message and in awareness of the impact. In the description of this factor, it is also important to emphasize that communication is not just about *sending* effectively or about sending *more*. Communication is a two-way loop that includes sending *and* receiving. Great teams are great listeners.

- **Constructive Interaction**

  The team understands that they have the ability to wholeheartedly disagree for the sake of something important to the team. Team members would say, "We know how to work things out. Even when the conversation is heated, the attention is on the issue—not the people." On the best teams, healthy conflict is constructive; it contains the seeds for new thinking and new action.

- **Diversity**
  A team that values diversity recognizes the strength that comes from differences. Teams can do much more than individuals operating alone because of the diversity of talent, experience, perspective, expertise, and the individual styles and strengths of each team member.[15]

- **Optimism**
  The team is forward looking and appreciative of each other. Even on the darkest days, this is a team that believes "we can do it."

If the model is a compass, these 14 are the points of the compass that help provide direction to the team. They represent the natural and obvious experience of being on a team where collaboration is necessary in order to fulfill the team's mission. They capture the everyday language teams already use when they talk about issues such as how things are going, what's working, and what's not working. Together, these two dimensions of Productivity and Positivity create a dynamic balance that helps teams understand where they stand in the moment and creates the opportunity for conversation about where the team wants to focus in order to improve.

The Intersection of Productivity and Positivity

It is possible to graphically map the intersection of these two core dimensions of Productivity and Positivity. To do that, we put Productivity on a horizontal axis. Teams that score high on the Productivity factors will be on the right side of that line; low-Productivity teams will be on the left. We put Positivity on the vertical axis, with high-Positivity teams in the upper half and low-Positivity teams below, forming a familiar four-quadrant matrix.

The ideal position for a team is in the upper-right corner: a balance of Productivity and Positivity. The best of both worlds. But in addition to showing the aspiration for teams, this matrix reveals the inherent power that team culture creates and the impact of that culture on how the team works together, what the team values, and what the ground rules are for success or failure.

FIGURE 1-1: Productivity and Positivity: Quad Diagram

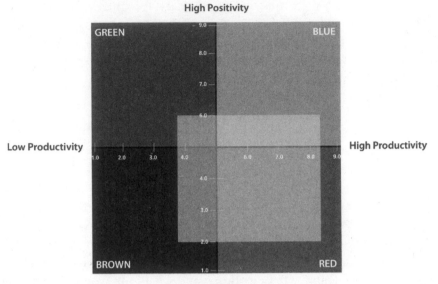

High Productivity – Low Positivity

For example, start in the lower right corner: High Productivity and Low Positivity. This is the "red" corner of the world. This is typically the area that the organization prizes above all others. The incentives are all designed around "get results" at any cost, sometimes even human cost. This is the "drive" corner. Just get the job done. You've probably been on a team like this.

In this world, relationship is sacrificed over meeting personal goals. "I got my job done. I hope you got yours done." Here, relationships are based on functional roles. On a cross-functional team, the team member from manufacturing views the team member from marketing as a role, not a person—and sometimes as a competitor for resources. Silos are prevalent.

Results drive this team. Teams like this often show great pride and high energy. Celebration of the team's ability to produce results should be encouraged. And there are natural consequences. It's no coincidence that the color in this corner is red. Red for the heat of stress and pressure. Red for the fires that suddenly ignite and must be put out. Red for burnout. Red for alarms going off.

This is a "me first" world where individual team members are generally more concerned about their personal success than they are about team success. Sometimes they are simply unaware of the impact of their solo behavior. Sometimes they are consciously making sure of their own success at the expense of others. Under pressure and stress to achieve performance goals, competition within the team can become rampant and destructive to team performance. Pressure to produce results in this culture can also mean sacrificing quality, customer relationships, or even ethical behavior. While we all agree that getting results is essential, this is a team environment that is simply not sustainable.

Worth noting: There are times when a focus on high productivity is normal and essential. For example, when a competitor comes to market with a new product or service and your team or organization is caught off guard. There is a necessary urgency to address the issue. But it doesn't mean the team has to abandon the Positivity dimension. In fact, the opposite is true. An important challenge is an opportunity to pull the team together, balancing the best of both Productivity and Positivity.

A director of sales brought us in to work with his team, much to the surprise of the team. "But we're hitting our numbers," some said. It was true. The team had historically top-performing sales figures and a steadily growing market. They also had historically high turnover and historically low employee engagement scores. They were all paying a price for their success. Simply rotating new people onto the team as others burned out meant starting new customer relationships, additional time and investment in training, and relentless pressure to hit targets. The costs may be hidden but they are real.

High Positivity – Low Productivity

High Positivity teams feel good. These are teams that have created unspoken agreements around maintaining the "it feels good" atmosphere. Disagreements are avoided, handled discreetly, or processed, often over long periods of time with little actual resolution. On High Positivity – Low Productivity teams there is a drive to consensus in decision making even when it is not the most effective or necessary decision-making approach.

This team places a high value on ensuring that everyone is heard, acknowledged, respected, and included. The team is generally very sensitive to the emotional climate. In meetings, you are more likely to hear the question "How do you feel about this?" than "What do you think?"

On a High Positivity – Low Productivity team, process is valued over production. How the issue is addressed is more important than timely results. These are teams that typically lack a sense of urgency. Keeping an "even keel" is a high priority. Risk taking is taboo because it's likely to be disruptive and might lead to conflict. Low Productivity is often seen as the result of circumstances beyond the team's control.

There are times when a team might end up in this quadrant as a natural result of the team's life cycle. For example, a team that worked hard and achieved a major success might rest here for a while to enjoy the afterglow, putting team performance on cruise control for a time. That would be normal, but if it's more than a brief "push the pause button," this will be a team in trouble because hanging on here is also not sustainable. Someone will surely notice that the team is not producing results. Over time, this lack of productivity is a strain on team members who value getting things done and take pride in accomplishment. It may feel good to visit here, but as a team culture it is disabling if the goal is to be a high-performing team.

Low Productivity – Low Positivity

Teams that find themselves in this corner of the world are missing both motivation and connection. It can feel stagnant and isolating. There is a pessimistic, helpless air around these teams. When we talk to team members on teams in this quadrant and ask them what it feels like, we hear reports with words like "It feels hopeless." "What's the point?" "I'm going to fly under the radar here and hope nobody notices." Or sometimes you might hear "I'm the only one working hard here."

The responses are a combination of somber, angry, or frustrated. There is a definite energy created here. The color is muted, brownish, lifeless, and featureless. There is a mood on teams like this that is contagious. Like a bad cold, it gets passed around and around until everyone is infected. When people recall what it was like when they were on Low Productivity – Low Positivity teams, they also talk about what it was like at home during those times—and they do not paint an uplifting picture.

On some Low-Low teams there is little desire to change. If they are getting by, it is less risky and potentially less painful to maintain the current system than to make changes. In that case the team is basically saying, "Leave us alone." As a coach who invites change, you become the enemy of the status quo and their stable, if unfulfilling, way of life.

Over time, a sense of powerlessness begins to grow on teams in this quadrant. The circumstances feel insurmountable as well as being the explanation for all the trouble and strife. Defensiveness and blame contribute to the toxic atmosphere. Teams begin to believe they have zero control over their lives and work. It feels hopeless and helpless. These teams don't need cheering up. They need help finding a way out of the dark.

High Productivity – High Positivity

No doubt the team you remembered when this chapter opened was one of these High Productivity and High Positivity teams, and it qualified as a truly great team even if you didn't win the championship or break the sales record. Great accomplishments happen with teams in this corner, but what teams mostly recall is how they performed at the top of their game when they worked together.

- There was a feeling of unquestionable support.
- People could disagree and that was okay.
- People rose to the challenge.
- There was deep appreciation for the diversity on the team.
- People could ask for help in a judgment-free atmosphere.

It wasn't always a smooth ride, but it was a meaningful and memorable ride the team created together. High-performing teams like this are also typically restless. They're always looking to raise the bar.[16] There is much to celebrate with teams in this quadrant.

If the team you're working with is one of those 10 percent teams that starts in this High-High corner, congratulations. Teams that find themselves in this corner are rare and deserve to be acknowledged. And that leads to the next obvious questions for this team: What did you do to get here? and What's next?

Be aware that sometimes high-performing teams become protective of what they have created or achieved. There can be an underlying attitude of "Don't rock the boat!" Collusion begins to seep in; there may be examples of tolerating what was once intolerable. For example, on teams that attain High-High status, one of the keys was likely the ability to take risk or engage in tough conversations, calling each other to accountability. They may start to back away from the very strengths that carried them to that high level of performance. Integrating new team members can also be a challenge. There may be a subtle evaluation period or hazing to make sure this new team member is up to the team's standard.

The Goal: Dynamic Balance

The matrix is a window into the way team culture influences team results. It is a simple and compelling way to recognize the impact of these four combinations of Productivity and Positivity. Note that it would be rare for a team to fit neatly into one of the four corners at the start of a team coaching engagement. The picture teams create is more likely to be a range of both Productivity and Positivity. In the Productivity dimension, for example, a team might be strong when it comes to being proactive—moving forward, getting into action—and not so strong when it comes to making good decisions. The same is true for the Positivity dimension. A team might show respect freely but might not communicate well. The result will be a range depending on the culture and character of the team.

Every team is unique, but the influences on the picture are common to all teams. Teams are influenced by the organization's culture, of course. An organization that places high value on bottom-line results will breed teams that work to that model. That's where the rewards are. Team members have influence on the qualities, personality, and

Figure 1-2: Four worlds of team culture

LOW PRODUCTIVITY/ HIGH POSITIVITY	HIGH PRODUCTIVITY/ HIGH POSITIVITY
Collegial, comfortable Value for consensus and connection Lack of effective focus Insufficient sense of urgency Change resistant: "Don't rock the boat" Commitment to relationship over results Tolerate incompetence Avoid disagreement and conflict	Competent, successful Flow, synchronicity Up to the challenge Inspiring vision Mutual support Open, direct communication Proactive: "What's the next level?" Balance of business results and relationship care
LOW PRODUCTIVITY/ LOW POSITIVITY	HIGH PRODUCTIVITY/ LOW POSITIVITY
Atmosphere of criticism, blame, and cynicism "Firefighting" short-term orientation Turf protection Self-protection over team results Uncertainty, fear of job loss Helpless to change the circumstances Cliques and covert conversations Hide under the radar	Results driven, bottom-line focus High pressure, high stress Burnout, turnover Silos and solo operators Competitive within the team Guarded "Just do it"

priorities of the team—especially what gets appreciated and what gets discouraged. New team members can affect the mix of team capabilities and skills and bring new perspectives to the team. The team leader has a major impact on the team by setting and reinforcing priorities.[17] Each of these separate influences helps shape the team's culture and the team's ability to deliver results. They add brushstrokes to the portrait of each team.

Figure 1-3: Average scores from more than 3,000 teams from the TCI Team Diagnostic™ database, 2008-2017.

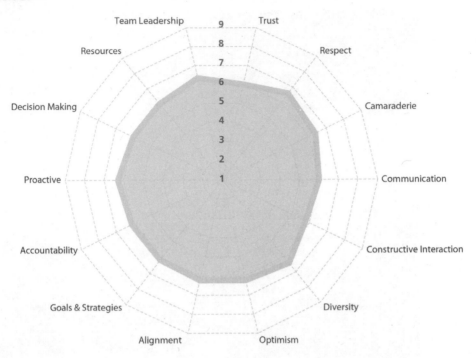

The "state of teams." Average scores for more than 3,000 teams from the TCI Team Diagnostic™ database, 2008-2017 (Figure 1-3). In Chapters 2 and 3 we will show more detailed comparisons between high-performing teams and low-performing teams. Even with this simple graphic showing average teams, it is clear there is ample room for team development—improvement that will make a difference to the organization in measures that matter.

Summary

We started this chapter with a question: What do high-performing teams do better than the rest? We looked at the qualities of best teams, those attributes that set great teams apart. The answer to that fundamental question is, high-performing teams excel at both dimensions, Productivity and Positivity, and all 14 factors.

It's likely that this description of what makes great teams great sounds familiar. It confirms your own experience and observations. There are no surprises. When we do the "best team" exercise with teams, that's what they report. This synthesis simply puts it all together in one place, in a simple model that gives teams, team coaches, and team leaders a shared and familiar language.

It's that language—in particular the 14 factors of Productivity and Positivity—that will be the focus of the next two chapters. Our intention is to see these common attributes in the context of what they mean in team behavior. Ultimately, it is how these qualities show up in the everyday interaction between team members that will determine the relative strength or weakness of that particular quality in the team's performance. A clear understanding of what we mean when we refer to these factors is the starting place for coaching interaction.

For Team Coaches

❑ Think about teams you have worked with or teams you've been on. Pick a team that stands out for its success. Focus on the atmosphere that existed with that team. Make a few notes about the quality of the environment on that team and the energy it created. Look for images or metaphors that evoke that experience. What was the breathing like on that team? Easy? Rapid? Tight? Expansive?

❑ Then pick a team that was 180 degrees in the other direction. Ask yourself the same questions. Both examples provide clues to the culture of those teams. The clues are symptoms that point to expectations on that team and the conditions created by team norms. The symptoms are actually vital signs that give us information about the health of the team.

For Team Leaders

❑ Take some time to recall your personal experience on excellent teams—use any sort of team from any time in your life. What are the qualities that stand out? What are a few words that describe the attitude of those great teams? What were the outstanding strengths? How did they behave under stress or failure? What is one trait from those excellent teams you would like to implant in every team? Maybe especially the team you currently lead?

❑ On teams that were dysfunctional or simply not performing up to standard, where was the breakdown? It's always easy to point to the impact of specific team members as the reason things didn't go well, and to some degree that is likely true. But looking beyond individual personalities, what was a team behavior that was present or missing that undermined team success?

CHAPTER 2

7 Keys to Maximize Productivity

In the previous chapter we made the assertive and maybe obvious declaration, "Teams exist to produce results." A roomful of teams would all respond with a resounding "Yes" to that, or the organization certainly would. But after the affirmation there is work to be done, so the next obvious question would be: What are the key contributors to team productivity—the conditions necessary to get results? That's what this chapter is about. In this chapter, we will:

- Go into a deeper description of each of the seven factors introduced briefly in chapter 1
- Look at the ways each factor influences team productivity
- Provide suggestions for how you might work with that factor with your team

This Productivity dimension includes the team strengths that are key to getting the job done. There is a strong sense of "this is what we *do*" in this half of the team wheel. You can hear it in the sentences "We set goals. We make decisions. We hold each other accountable. We take initiative." Although the "we" refers to the team, within that plural there is a strong sense of the individual's role, contribution, and responsibility.

When attention begins to focus on the need for team improvement, these seven factors get most of the attention because they are easy to see. The impact of not doing them well gets attention, and there are things teams and individual team members know how to do to improve. These seven make sense to teams. They are regarded as essential to the team's ability to get work done. They have been the subject of vast amounts of training investment and are often the context for performance management evaluation. They

> Team Leadership
> Resources
> Decision Making
> Proactive
> Accountability
> Goals & Strategies
> Alignment

are spoken of as the "real" skills necessary for team performance, especially compared to the so-called "soft skills" that show up in the Positivity dimension.

In this chapter and the next, we will look at each of the 14 Team Performance Indicators (TPI) and its contribution to team performance. For this book, they are described sequentially, but the sequence does not imply importance or priority. Using the polar diagram as a graphic

Figure 2-1: Seven Productivity strengths on the left side from Team Leadership to Alignment. Seven Positivity strengths on the right side from Trust to Optimism.

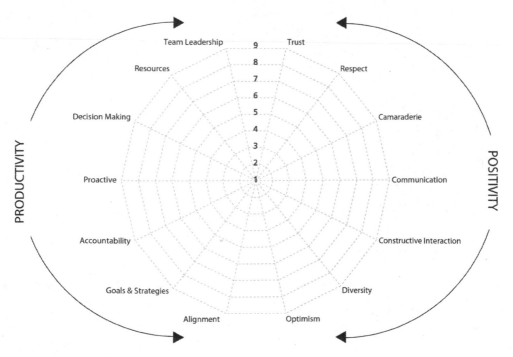

In this chapter and the next, as we describe each of the Team Performance Indicators, we will also include questions that team coaches or team leaders might use as conversation starters to explore that factor as it applies to the team's everyday experience.

The goal is to deepen an understanding of each factor and, more importantly, look at how it shows up on this team. Shining a light on the factor might lead to an interesting and thoughtful conversation. We want the team to address the question, So what? What does that mean on our team?

We will also provide suggestions for activities to support awareness of the role this factor plays on the team. The more aware teams are of the state of these productivity contributors, the more likely there will be action to improve.

example, the 14 factors surround the team; they form a constellation of potential strengths.

We begin the exploration by looking at the seven Productivity TPI. Not because they are more important than the Positivity TPI but because they are familiar and highly prized in organizations.

Productivity strengths support the team to accomplish tasks and stay on course to reach goals and objectives. Each of the factors is a facet of the whole. It is valuable to look at each one individually. This helps the team come to a common understanding of each one as well as how that factor shows up in behavior on the team. In the end, the team's definition of each factor is more important than a book definition.

Coming to a clear understanding of what each factor means to the team will bring to the surface assumptions, expectations, and the opportunity to clarify and align. The discussion will create heightened awareness of that aspect of team behavior; the conversation will also create more ownership by the team and motivation to strengthen that area.

1. Team Leadership

The team leader's role is clear and supportive of the team as a whole. There is also a strong sense of team leadership; team members take initiative to provide leadership as the need arises. Leadership is seen as the responsibility of every team member and is empowered by the team.

There was a time when team leadership was a simple matter of knowing "who's the boss." The role for the team leader was clear and well established. There was a certain comfort in the structure. There was consistency and predictability. People knew their place.

Those days are gone. Imagine a scrapbook of team photos that goes back about 20 or 30 years. Look back at that team photo from a few decades ago. Notice what that typical team looks like. Probably all men in dark suits and ties with somber faces. They likely have similar education and social status. The team leader had tenure. He—almost certainly "he"—was the most experienced in that functional area or had the most prestigious credentials. Direction came from him. That was the seat of authority and decision making. It was customary to escalate challenges up the ladder to the boss.

Now flip to a page in the scrapbook for this year. You'll see a multigenerational team, male and female, and in many cases multicultural as well. The person with the most expertise on this team might be the 25-year-old in the corner. The pace of work has dramatically accelerated, and with it the demand on teams to be much more responsive. Decisions need to be made quickly, and often the person in the best position to make that decision is the one closest to the internal or external customer. The world is becoming less vertical and more horizontal, with fewer hard lines of reporting and more dotted lines.

How teams are organized and how they work within the organization is changing too. In that picture of the team in the past, you see an intact team that is likely to be together for years. Even if personnel change, the function of that team is expected to remain consistent over time. One team with one leader.

In today's world, people are often on multiple teams and might live in different parts of the country or different corners of the world, connected only by technology. The workplace is a maze of assorted team forms, all under pressure to get results.

Clearly, the role of team leadership is changing, trying to stay relevant in this changing world. What has served in the past—that traditional hierarchy—is not going away. It's just not sufficient to meet the needs of today. Teams can't rely on the geometry of the org chart to ensure effective team leadership. With authority and decision making being pushed further out into the organization, there is an emerging sense that leadership is everybody's responsibility.

Working with a project team years ago, we saw firsthand how leadership on teams is a team effort, not the sole responsibility of the person holding the title of team leader. This particular team's mandate was to complete phase two of a major capital improvement project that was already behind schedule and over budget. The daunting goal the team was given: complete the project on time and on budget. We attended the team's first full meeting and listened to the project manager set the expectations. Everyone in the room knew the challenge ahead.

Here is how the team leader spoke about the crucial role of leadership. "You were each chosen for your leadership. If you are waiting for me to tell you what you already know is right, we will fail. We simply must empower whoever is standing on the critical path." You could feel every member of the team sit up a little straighter in their chairs. This was a true call to team leadership. The project was completed on time and on budget.

There is still an essential and important role for the team leader, but that role is more multifaceted and not as predictable as it once was.[18] The ability to operate with a leadership milieu that is more complex and often requires dealing with ambiguity, still at high speed—that is the hallmark of teams that excel at team leadership.[19]

Conversation starters:

- Review with the team critical situations or turning points and investigate the role of leadership. Who was leading when? What was the value of that contribution? How did other team members contribute to the leadership of the team?
- What are ways that new team members take on the role of leadership within a team they have just joined?

Suggested team activity:

- Have the team look for specific examples of leadership on the team—especially from those who are not "team leader." Set a time frame such as "this week." Ask the team to notice different people taking on the role of leadership and to think about how it was empowered—or not. Report on the impact.

2. Resources

The team clearly requests and manages resources to meet its objectives. There is sufficient expertise to accomplish the team's objectives. This factor, "resources," is not about the quantity; it's about the ability to effectively manage what the team has.

Like a song with a refrain that repeats over and over and over...listen to almost any team in any organization anywhere in the world and you will hear that mournful song. "Resources. We don't have enough—not nearly enough."[20] Mostly, teams are referring to not enough people to complete the job that's expected of them; sometimes it's the lack of training, but the theme of the song is the constant lack of money, time, and talent.

The pressure is on teams to do more with less. It's a race, a highly competitive and global race that has no finish line. This relentless pressure is a breeding ground for frustration, competitiveness, hoarding, silos, and communication breakdowns. People become more isolated. That's a short summary of conditions that are destructive to the team's ability to achieve team results. And it stems from the pressure to do more with less. The truth is, there is a great deal that the team simply does *not* have control over. If the team's attention focuses on what they don't have and what they can't get, a feeling of helplessness sets in.

On high-performing teams, the question shifts to, What *do* we have control over? That shift in perspective, from what we don't have to what we do have, opens up possibilities and the ability to take action.

When teams start looking at the potential instead of the self-defeating conclusion that "we are helpless and therefore doomed," possibilities arise. Teams find a broader definition for "resources" and see more ways they can manage what they have. In addition to the material resources, they find ways to share the load, become more supportive, be aware of the energy that is generated, and learn how to use that to the team's advantage. There may not be a way to acquire more resources, but there is definitely a way the team can be more resourceful.

Conversation Starters:

❏ What will make this team more resourceful?

❏ What are the intangible resources of this team? How can they be maximized/leveraged?

❏ When it comes to resources, clearly there are some things the team does not have control over. What *does* the team have control over? Think outside the box. What else?

Suggested Team Activity:

❏ Invite the team to recall a project or initiative where at least one of the severely limiting barriers to success was a lack of resources. Look for all the ways the team was resourceful in addressing a lack of resources. What lessons can the team learn from that experience?

3. Decision Making

The team has clear and efficient decision-making processes and is adept at applying different processes to different situations. Excellence in decision making is both the ability to make timely and effective decisions and the commitment to learn from decisions that are made.[21]

There was a time when the person at the head of the table—or at the desk in the corner office—made the decisions. That's what bosses did. That was inherent in the role; that's the authority that came with the title. The way teams have changed and the way work gets done today means decision making looks quite different. The team leader is still the final decision maker for critical decisions; that hasn't changed and won't. What has changed are the variations on the "who" and "how" of decision making on teams.

As the speed that decisions need to be made increases, and as responsibility for decisions becomes more distributed, the chances for chaos and miscue grow exponentially. The key to effectively managing this tension is *clarity,* which is too often missing in the process. Fundamental questions don't make it to the table. Questions such as Who is making the decision? Who is involved in providing input? Team members need to know their role in the process.[22]

In the face of that persistent pressure, there is often a strong desire to slow things down and put more structure, more controls in place, with sometimes disastrous results. Yes, there are times when a codified process adds to clarity and efficiency; process controls can be invaluable. At the same time, tightening down the decision making or forcing it into too rigid a form can lead to unnecessary complexity and procedures that drag teams down. They actually get in the way of clarity and efficiency.

The intention is on target. Teams are always looking for more effective ways to make decisions that optimize time and talent requirements. In fact, there are many decision-making models and variations on those models that provide structure when structure is called for. At the same time, it is vital to recognize the tension between the need for structure and the need for flexibility and agility. More than ever, teams today need the ability to make decisions and move forward, even in an environment of ambiguity. Remember that snapshot of yesterday's teams and today's teams? Today, with matrix teams for example, there will be more than one person in a designated leadership role, which can create conflicting priorities in an environment where decisions still need to be made efficiently and rapidly.

In this critical factor affecting team performance, high-performing teams have awareness and practice that sets them apart. There is a respected willingness to test assumptions, question the process,

Decision-making effectiveness will depend on a variety of factors, including the nature of the decision and the roles of those involved, among others. We worked with a team of regional VPs whose team decision making scored low. At first, when they saw the scores, there was defensiveness on the part of the team. "We make decisions that affect our vertical areas. We don't make many decisions among the VPs." But it raised the next logical coaching question. If decision making had a perfect score for this team, what would that look like? That question generated a very fruitful conversation. "What would be the benefit? What would we have that we don't have now?"

invite other points of view, and demonstrate a commitment to consider alternatives. Once a decision is made, there is a cultural commitment on the team to support one another and stand shoulder to shoulder behind the decision.

High-performing teams also invest in review, which helps them learn what worked and what didn't work about the process, including decisions that were effective and decisions that made a mess.

Conversation Starters:

❑ What is one area where the decision-making process is quite successful? What can you learn from that as a team?

❑ What are different decision-making styles you have seen on teams? What worked about those different styles?

❑ If decision making had a perfect score for this team, what would that look like?

Suggested Team Activity:

❑ Identify an important and timely situation where there is a need for decisions. Describe the current decision-making process. What are the different roles and responsibilities? What's clear? What's murky? What is the team's "standard approach" to situations like this? What would be a totally different approach, and what might the benefit be?

4. Proactive

A proactive team is a team that takes initiative and rises to the challenge. This team embraces change and sees it as vital to the team and the larger organization. The team is nimble and flexible in addressing opportunities for change, responding positively and creatively. Proactive teams are always looking for a better way.

For high-performing teams, the world is a book of blank pages. They don't neglect or disown the pages already written. Those pages of experience are invaluable, but they don't dictate the future. Creativity is the lifeblood of excellent teams. Creating new solutions, inviting out-of-the-box thinking, probing and testing conventional wisdom and old habits—this spirit of change mastery is alive on excellent teams.[23] Just as important, this spirit is curious and often playful, not fearful or panicked.

Proactive teams invite new ideas and differences in points of view. They are willing to probe for a contrary or dissenting voice because they see in it the possibility for deeper understanding and ultimately a better outcome.

You've heard this said: "It's easier to ask for forgiveness than permission." It's often true. On truly proactive teams, there is an environment that supports creativity and action. There is an empowerment core to this team when it comes to change and innovation.

Yes, it can be abused; that drive and initiative needs to find its balance point within the seven factors. Teams that are proactive take responsibility for this attribute. It is a team quality. A commitment to being proactive is not the same as giving team members permission to be soloists or create a team of mavericks. Think of it like an excellent jazz band. There is plenty of opportunity to improvise but not every band member is improvising simultaneously. When one member is taking his or her turn, the rest of the ensemble is holding the foundation, maintaining the tempo and the underlying harmonic structure. The improvisation soars on top of a solid foundation.

Proactive teams are mutually supportive and open to challenge. They're willing to stretch, and they won't settle for the easy answer. They are engaged as a team and hold a higher standard for their team and each other.[24] To be proactive as a team is important because it encourages creativity and innovation, tests old habits, and explores territory beyond the customary horizon. It is an essential attribute for teams operating at the speed of business today. These teams know that the life cycle of great ideas is short and getting shorter. Top-performing teams are often building the airplane while flying it, and frequently changing the design along the way. It can be both exhilarating and scary.

Conversation Starters:

- What's necessary in order for creativity to flourish on teams, or on this team?
- What gets in the way of creativity and innovation on this team?

- ❏ Where has this team expressed its creativity? Be as specific as possible.
- ❏ How does this team respond in the face of imminent change?

Suggested Team Activity:

- ❏ Identify a team process that needs to change. Brainstorm multiple out-of-the-box ways that process could be handled differently. Don't let "that's not realistic" stall the brainstorming. The exercise is for the purposes of stretching outside the comfort zone. Any new action that might result is a bonus.
- ❏ Start with this question: What is one clear and visible way the team could practice being proactive in the next (time frame), month or week? Then gather for a report on the impact.
- ❏ Worth considering: for some teams, improvisation activities (usually with a trained facilitator) can inspire creative agility and the experience of building on each other's contributions.

5. Accountability

Team members hold each other accountable. There is clarity of roles and responsibilities with high follow-through. This is more than a high level of individual accountability. Team members actively support each other to meet team goals by holding each other accountable.[25]

Accountability is another team strength that is shifting from vertical to horizontal as the work of teams adapts to a faster-paced, more distributed world of work. It requires a fundamental shift in mindset from seeing accountability as an individual responsibility to seeing accountability as a team responsibility. When accountability is seen as personal responsibility, the focus and the pressure are on individual results. Accountability becomes a proof test: Did you do what you said you would do? Or didn't you? Individual team members feel the pressure and vulnerability. It can lead to complaining about others, excuses, blaming, and accusations. It's a mindset that drives distance between team members.

The spotlight on the individual performance breeds judgment. How do you measure up? And that can breed comparison between team members that fosters more competition instead of cooperation. It may not be an obvious team effect, but even when the influence is kept under the surface, it can be like a constant inflammation. Team members become wary and self-protective, sometimes self-justified. It is isolating.

In contrast, high-performing teams see accountability as everyone's responsibility; it is a team value for the sake of "our team's performance." Individuals are naturally accountable because the team's results and recognition are at stake. The sense of comparison is shifted from "How am I doing?" to "How are *we* doing?" and "What's needed?"

Team accountability is mutual accountability, and it comes from a place of commitment to the team versus commitment to personal performance. In this coresponsible place, holding each other accountable is not about nagging. It is not looking for "gotcha." We expect team members to follow through on commitments they make. We want reliability in performance. This is about a team standard and, just as much, a commitment to help and support each other.

On some teams the idea of team accountability, where we rigorously hold each other accountable, can feel threatening. This is often the case, ironically, on senior leadership teams. Team members were promoted to those top positions based on their ability to get the job done and be accountable for performance. They are accustomed to viewing their world through a vertical lens. That exclusive focus is often a reason why silos develop. They are not as familiar with accountability on the horizontal plane, engaging across the conference room table. In fact, in some cases there is unspoken collusion along the lines of "You don't mess with my territory and I won't mess with yours. Okay?"

Where an individual focus on accountability makes it personal, and consequently isolating, a team focus on accountability creates a connected and shared sense of purpose. The reason for accountability and the motivation to follow through is for the sake of the team.[26] You can feel an important and significant shift in the energy of the team when there is commitment to the team's performance. It removes an emotional charge that often accompanies individual performance accountability. And when that charge is removed, we are left with three "abilities."

Responsibility: The ability to see what needs to be done and respond, take action. All action on the team is interconnected. If someone is not completing a task, there will be an effect somewhere in the team web. The response on high-performing teams is a conversation, not an accusation, that focuses on "What do you need?" even "How can I help?"[27]

Reliability: A consistent track record for follow-through. The team can truly count on each and every team member. It replaces the energy required to be vigilant and monitor one another with a more relaxed confidence that we are all doing our jobs the best we can.

Accountability: To be accountable is to be held to account, not in judgment, but truly held to account for what happened, whether it was successful or not. In a sense there is a valuable layer of learning that goes with being accountable. Without the emotional charge that goes with judgment, the conversation remains at a level of team consideration. There is a shift from explanation or defensiveness to a report on what happened, which can lead to team learning and better results as a consequence. There is more clarity and more honesty in the environment that is created when teams are team accountable. They have the three abilities working for them.

Conversation Starters:

- ❑ What is the team accountable for? (separate from what individual team members are accountable for)
- ❑ What examples show team members demonstrating team accountability?
- ❑ If this team were a top performer in mutual accountability, what would be different? What does this team need to learn or practice to reach that level?

Suggested Team Activity:

- ❑ One simple exercise is to create or review team agreements for team meetings and have the team report on their performance against those guidelines. Many teams have agreements of this kind but regularly ignore them. By paying attention to this seemingly simple application of accountability, the experience is reinforced and team meetings become more efficient and effective.

❑ Look for a team process where there is lack of clarity because the roles and expectations are vague. Take the time to identify a set of clear agreements about that process and then review the impact; look for what's working and what might need to be done differently. The exercise will improve accountability for the chosen process and will help reinforce the practice for the team.

6. Goals & Strategies

The team has clear, challenging objectives; there is alignment on strategies and priorities. Targets and outcomes are clear and reinforce a strategic vision. The team is highly resilient and not easily defeated in their goals.[28,29,30]

Strategy sets the direction. From that master plan, objectives are set. To achieve those objectives, goals are defined: the "what" and "by when." Strategy answers the question "Why? Why are we heading in this direction?" Fulfilling the team's purpose is a journey. Any successful journey needs a destination and map to get there. Strategy provides the map. And by the way, given the inevitable ups and downs of any team journey, metaphorically speaking, it should be a topographical map for good measure.

Goals create the stepping-stones and define the necessary tactical performance markers. Goals answer the question "How? How will we get there?" and "How are we doing along the way?" This all seems obvious. But the way teams need to operate in today's rapidly changing landscape means this whole process of strategy-objectives-goals needs to be more adaptable.[31]

Everybody knows about SMART goals, although if you ask six people what the acronym stands for, you are likely to get at least six different answers. Here is one typical example.

SMART Goals Are:

Specific – **M**easurable – **A**ction oriented – **R**ealistic – **T**ime sensitive

Yes, of course. All of that makes sense. But SMART goals may not be smart enough for today's teams. In the dance of creating results, there is a need to be solid, sure-footed, and also nimble, or agile if you prefer. The music is constantly changing.

This can be both exhilarating and unsettling. It is necessary to be able to shift and turn, to adapt and retarget—to ready-**fire**-aim—to make adjustments *while* being in action. It points out the increasing need for calm in the midst of the storm. Teams deal with more ambiguity and more change of direction than ever. There is a need to be on track and stay on track, but the track must be somewhat malleable. Too much rigidity will lead to excessive friction created by insisting on a track that is strained and overheated.

This is a tension that high-performing teams are able to navigate. When things change, they have the ability to respond effectively, not panic in the face of new demands. They can adjust course, not bail out.[32]

They know that in addition to being SMART, goals should have excellent **AIM**. They should be:

A = **Adaptable**. As conditions change, high-performing teams are adaptable but still consistent with the mission, strategy, and objectives for the team.

I = **Interconnected**. High-performing teams recognize that action has impact. Changing conditions require changes in goals and tactics, but all of that has impact. Goals are not created in a vacuum. There is a network of connections, an ecology of consequences to take into account.

M = **Motivating**. Not every task or every goal will light the lights of inspired action, but some attention to what makes a goal motivating can shift the perspective from "It's my job" to "This is meaningful, and important." Linking the tactical to the deeper purpose enriches the task and motivates those who perform the work.

Conversation Starters:

❑ What goals on this team are important but hard to measure? What are some creative ways this team could measure those goals?

❑ What are this team's Key Performance Indicators (KPIs)? Obviously, part of the motivation for achieving the goals with those KPIs is the consequence if the team *doesn't* succeed. Look beyond that. What is truly motivating—even inspiring—about achieving the team's KPIs?

❑ What are recent examples where the team needed to be flexible and adaptable on an initiative when the course changed? If it was a successful example of being agile under the circumstances, what made that possible on this team? If it was less than a great success, what would the team do differently next time?

Suggested Team Activity:

❑ Key Performance Indicators are quite common for individual employees and becoming more common for teams. If this team does not have team KPIs, take the time to define them.

❑ One way goals motivate teams is through the expectation of reward or recognition when goals are achieved. Have the team look at specific team goals and look for ways to highlight or create reasons to celebrate as a team.

7. Alignment

There is a sense of common mission and purpose. The team values cooperation, cohesion, and interdependence. Team members are pulling in the same direction.[33]

It's important to frame this discussion about alignment so that we are all on the same page. Aligned, in other words. Our focus as team coaches is on *team* alignment. This is a different focus than where the alignment conversation almost always goes. It usually focuses on organizational alignment: how teams, especially leadership teams, align with the vision, mission, strategy, and goals of the organization.

That vertical alignment is very important, obviously. It is crucial for organizational success and a clear area of responsibility for teams. That objective, and the work of the team to create vertical alignment, could become a topic the team handles in the ongoing coaching sessions. How the team engages with that topic will be material for team coaching. Team dynamics show up in that important conversation. But in addition to the team's need for vertical alignment, there is also a need on the

For context in how important this is, here are a few very revealing data points about alignment on teams.

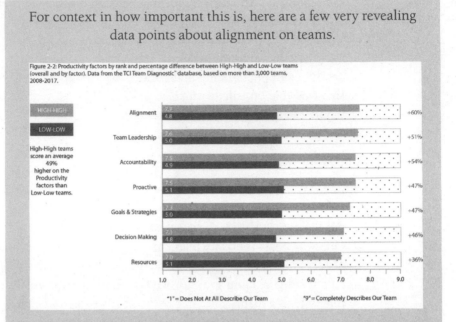

Figure 2-2: Productivity factors by rank and percentage difference between High-High and Low-Low teams (overall and by factor). Data from the TCI Team Diagnostic™ database, based on more than 3,000 teams, 2008–2017.

Of the seven Productivity Team Performance Indicators, the one that scores the highest on High Productivity—High Positivity teams is, you guessed it, alignment. On Low Productivity—Low Positivity teams only decision making scores lower. Also worth noting, of the seven factors, the spread between how High-High teams score alignment versus how Low-Low teams score it is also the largest spread for the seven. High-performing teams simply do alignment significantly better.

horizontal plane for internal team alignment. The horizontal dimension is our primary focus for this Productivity factor.

Experience shows that a high level of alignment is not always easy on teams, especially for cross-functional and leadership teams because of the very strong vertical orientation of everyone around the table. The responsibilities and incentives are mostly set up to favor that orientation. The result is more dedicated attention and commitment to vertical performance and, consequently, competing priorities. These results are all potential barriers to team alignment.

Alignment on teams requires a perspective shift. On aligned teams there is active ownership of team results. This is more than a cooperative attitude or getting along with team members; it is more than compliance with team goals. This is a consistent and sometimes sacrificial commitment to the team. Team alignment includes agreement but is not the same as agreement. Team alignment focuses on two dimensions: team purpose and the destination: "Who we are as a team?" and "Where we are headed?" Team purpose will be relatively stable; the destination or goals to achieve may be more of a moving target as circumstances change.

Alignment is most important on both team purpose and destination, but team members may disagree on how to get there. In fact, lack of agreement at this level of "how" can be healthy, not a sign of misalignment. This is where the natural diversity of teams shows its strength and where great teams engage. Some turbulence in getting aligned on how to fulfill the team's purpose would be normal. On the other hand, a lack of disagreement is not a proof of alignment. Beware of nodding heads and blank smiles; silence does not mean consensus.

Alignment on team purpose answers the question "Why are we a team? What are we here to accomplish?" There is a unique purpose for every team, separate from the team's vertical role in supporting the organization's mission. It is this unique responsibility that informs team purpose. If this team does not fulfill that unique purpose, it will not be accomplished in the organization.

Team alignment is a combination of feeling the stability of common ground and the synchronization of moving pieces. It doesn't necessarily create a smooth ride, but there will be an underlying confidence in the experience. There will be a sense of team identity. "This is who we are." That identity shows up in shared team values and agreement on team priorities that are different from but parallel to the organization's list of values and priorities.

Most misalignment is not the result of Machiavellian intent, it's the result of a lack of conversation that would bring to light the differences that create the misalignment. The basic process for creating team alignment is to illuminate differences and uncover assumptions and unspoken expectations. Team members bring their own unique lens to what alignment means for the team they are on. The process of creating alignment includes uncovering, articulating, and synthesizing these different perspectives.

Conversation Starters:

- ❏ Where has this team seen disconnect or dissonance in alignment? What was the evidence of misalignment? What was the impact?
- ❏ Where is this team both efficient and effective? What is the role of team alignment in that example?
- ❏ What is this team's brand? What are you, or what do you want to be known for?

Suggested Team Activity:

- ❏ Create a unique team purpose statement that completes this sentence: "We are here to…" Keep it short, clear, and compelling. Use action words.
- ❏ Have each team member privately make a list of the team's top 10 priorities and rank them from highest to lowest. Gather the team and compare lists. This will visibly reveal a level of key alignment for this team.
- ❏ Pick an important team issue. Have team members share their assumptions about how this issue is relevant to the team's mission. Explore the different perspectives that result from where team members position the issue relative to other issues. Ask, "Why did you place it there?" Use the answers to look for underlying differences and the opportunity to align.

Summary

Teams know about these seven factors. They know they are core to team performance. Team members can talk easily about what each one means to the team. Unfortunately, many teams are not sufficiently skilled in these important productivity areas, and conversation at any depth about any one of them as it relates to their team is extremely rare.

One of the outcomes of an effective team coaching process is raised awareness of these key contributors to team productivity. From that raised awareness comes clarity about where these factors are strong on the team and where a factor needs work. A team coaching process supports both the articulation of the current state and support for change over time.

CHAPTER 3

7 Keys to Effective Collaboration

Take an informal poll of teams and team leaders. Ask them to vote on which are the more important factors to measure—the seven Productivity or seven Positivity. Count the raised hands and it's likely you will find the tally favors the seven Productivity factors. The Positivity factors are often labeled "soft." Nice to have but not crucial to achieving business results. And yet when team members are asked about the best teams they've been on, they inevitably recall with great enthusiasm the impact of these seven. They stand out as memorable attributes of those best teams.

The growing emphasis on employee engagement is a sign that organizations have come to recognize the value of a positive work environment, one where the working conditions are more life-giving, not life-draining. It makes sense, of course. We are human beings, not mechanical gears in a machine; relationships matter. In fact, in a knowledge-based economy relationship *is* where the work gets done. The mindset is shifting, but still many teams simply don't know how to go about developing a sustainable, supportive culture of that kind.

Trust
Respect
Camaraderie
Communication
Constructive Interaction
Diversity
Optimism

This chapter is a guidebook to the Positivity world, with seven stops on the journey, each one offering an important contribution that has the potential to propel the team forward. Ultimately there is a compelling business case for each one. Teams that are competent in these areas accelerate the collaborative work of the team and make team performance sustainable.

The seven Positivity strengths are drawn from a number of sources, including appreciative inquiry, emotional intelligence, positive psychology, and formal research into team behavior that works. Similar to the Productivity strengths, each of these is unique in its contribution to effective collaboration, and, at the same time, an integral part of the whole, interconnected with the rest. These seven weave together like separate colored threads creating a sustainable team fabric.

1. Trust

It is safe on this team to speak your mind, openly. Team members can count on each other. The team does not operate in a fear-based environment.

Trust is the oxygen in the team culture. Some teams are breathing easily and deeply. Some teams are on respirators. When trust is low there is a wary, often fearful atmosphere. Metaphorically, team endurance is limited; sprints are impossible.

Trust is created in relationships and it is built over time. It is built from promises kept, and it is built from differences resolved, when those involved can walk away feeling heard and honored whatever the outcome. The perceived sense of safety, however, is a prerequisite to the action that allows trust to be built. Without a sense of safety, team members will be reluctant to take the risks necessary to build trust.[34] Team members monitor the safety of the environment before stretching into the sorts of conversation or action that will test and build trust.

The opposite is also true. The fear of reprisal will create a tacit agreement among team members to play nice, not create waves. This often leads to withholding from engagement and doesn't allow trust to be exercised. The consequence is a cautious, vigilant environment. Cliques and covert conversations erode trust.[35]

Let's be clear. The reason trust is important on teams is not only because of its social function. High-trust teams are faster at problem solving, resolve conflicts quicker, brainstorm more freely, are more inclusive, and are less hesitant to contribute. Trust building is good for business. Low-trust teams pay a heavy transactional price that slows them down in a world where speed and agility are necessary for competitive performance.

There are two fundamental ways to build trust on teams. Both work. One is relatively easy but often ignored; the other is more challenging. Let's start with the easy one.

Team members who know each other on a personal level have deeper, more connected relationships. When team members only interact with each other from their functional roles, people are reduced to function. Learning more about one another's personal stories gives team members a human dimension and a higher level of regard that can't be easily ignored. Taking the time occasionally to get to know team members' backgrounds, experience, successes, and even their stories about stumbling, all build trust This is especially valuable on new teams or teams going through reorganization.[36] The very natural process of getting to know team members will happen gradually, and intentionally accelerating that process provides great benefit to team formation. Creating and maintaining a culture of trust is challenging. Finding ways for team members to build closer relationships is one simple and effective way to improve team trust.

The second way to build trust is to engage in disagreement or conflict successfully and survive. Both ways of building trust depend on having a safe environment for taking risks, and that is especially true when the conversation is heated. Friction has the potential to make bonds stronger. Team members who focus on the issue, not the person, cross into new, vulnerable territory in that relationship. Team members push the threshold and expand the available space of trust. Trust is a measure of relationship safety and dependability; disagreement tests the boundaries and resilience of both and in the process, builds stronger trust.

Behaviors of High-Trust Teams

Team members:

1. Talk straight. They are open and honest. They speak from their own experience. They tell the truth as they know it. There is transformative power in transparency.

2. Are willing to be vulnerable. They will take risks for the sake of improved connection and communication.
3. Are dependable. You know and can count on them. There is high value placed on being authentic and true to oneself.
4. Show up—and most importantly, they stay even when things get uncomfortable.
5. Extend trust. Go first.
6. Protect the safety of others. They notice when safety is compromised and speak up.
7. Are aware of their impact.
8. Take steps to recover trust when it is broken.

Lack of trust on teams yields untold harm to the team's performance and to individual team members.[37] "Trust is an issue on our team" is such a common experience, it is nearly universal, and our data confirms it. Some teams find a culture of trust; most teams need to create it. It takes intention and action, and it takes time. You can't walk in on Tuesday morning and say, "Okay, from today on we will be a team that trusts one another."

In a similar way, although team-building events can have powerful impact, they do not build trust. They give teams an experience, so the team can talk about trust and how it shows up on their team. The conversation is a starting point, but the key to trust as a sustainable team strength is seeing it demonstrated as built-in behavior. Trust in action speaks louder than words.

Conversation Starters:

- Look at the eight behaviors of high-trust teams. Have the team pick one that they would say, "We're good at that." Then ask, "Where does it show up? What does it give the team?"
- Have the team pick a second trust behavior where they would say, "We could use some work on that." Ask, "What is the impact? What's one thing you could do as a team to improve that?"
- What will make it safe enough to engage in challenging conversations as a team?
- What are ways you already know that build trust?

Suggested Team Activity:

❑ Look for examples where trust was improved through either getting to know team members better or through disagreement or conflict. Tell the story. What are the lessons learned? Where could they be applied on this team now?

❑ Start team meetings with a simple, individual check-in. It could be business related, as in, one professional highlight from the past week. Or a more personal check-in as in, one skill outside of work that might surprise people.

❑ One low-risk way to build trust on any team is to put an emphasis on dependability. For teams that may not be ready to reveal anything that feels private or personal, or are particularly reluctant to engage in disagreement, becoming a more dependable team builds a reservoir of goodwill and trust.

2. Respect

There is an atmosphere of mutual respect and genuine positive regard. Contempt and hostility are not tolerated. The team encourages and empowers team members to contribute.

Respect is often less visible than trust. Look closely at the choices people make in the ways they treat each other. Listen for how people converse with each other. Notice the words team members use and the accompanying tone of voice. The nature of those conversations and the regard that is shown to one another creates an unspoken field where respect, or lack of respect, lives. Respect shows up in nonverbal ways too. When a respectful tone is set, there is a sense of honoring the other. Respect is gained from appreciation of high standards of quality, integrity, and competence in the work.

Respect is not about deferring to others without reason, although sometimes deferring to another is an example of respect in action. Respect can be demonstrated when a team member defers to someone else with appreciation and acknowledgment of the other's contribution. Showing appreciation is a simple, everyday example of respect and a simple way to build respect on a team.

Respect is about more than good manners and civility, although it's certainly about those two as well.[38] Respect sets a foundation for relationship interaction. That foundation can be solid and supportive and it can be crisscrossed with barriers and traps. In fact, one way to get clear about respect and its impact on teams is to look at the flip side. What do we know about the experience when respect is missing? Disrespect carries with it a feeling of being devalued. Discounted. Not regarded. In some cases disrespect renders individuals completely invisible. And in other cases, too visible; they become separated and excluded from the team. Disrespect can be dismissive or patronizing.

Disrespect also shows up in how people talk to each other, in the tone they use and the words they choose, and it can be demonstrated in clear nonverbal ways as well. We watched in one team meeting as two team members glanced at one another while a team member was giving her presentation. The rolling of the eyes was subtle, but its effect was clearly disrespectful.

Respect is inexorably tied to status and rank. The conditions that qualify for respect on a team are cultural, local, and sometimes unique to the team. Superior status can be the result of education background, title, technical expertise, age, years with the company, gender, race, perceived cultural differences, and the list goes on.

Respect tends to be given where trust is earned through interaction. How and with whom to show respect is deeply cultural. There are wide differences in how cultures express respect and see its importance within that culture. Awareness of these differences is especially important on geographically diverse teams and multicultural teams. By the way, in the United States, that diverse cultural geography could be one team member from the East Coast and another from the West Coast. Respect as it applies to different cultures also applies to business team cultures. Maybe you've seen or been a part of the issues of respect that surface between, for example, sales and manufacturing. "You don't understand our world."

Disrespect deepens the divide. And that quite literally affects the bottom line. Divisiveness can lead to resentment; resentment can lead to revenge. It's not pretty to admit but it happens, and the consequences affect the team's ability to function. You see team members hoarding resources, breakdowns in communication, various slippery forms of passive-aggressive behavior, outright contempt, and gamesmanship that waste time and resources. It becomes a cultural environment that exacts a powerful emotional toll on the team.

Teams involved in merger and acquisition or reorganization are especially susceptible, as the question of rank and status throws the new team into confusion until it sorts itself out. That situation is also an example of the benefit of team coaching; it can dramatically accelerate the process of integrating teams and establishing a new team culture.

In practice, what do we actually mean when we say, "Show respect"? Here are guidelines for team members that can help create a strong and supportive culture of respect.

- Respect sees and values. Show appreciation and give recognition freely.
- To show respect starts with setting aside judgment and being genuinely curious. This provides an opportunity to stretch and learn from being open.
- Look for opportunities to blend rather than confront; assume everyone is doing their best with what they have. Ask, "Where are we aligned? Let's start from there."
- Consider that once in a while, although rarely, it is at least possible that you are wrong. Be open to influence.
- Look with sharp eyes at underlying assumptions, especially your own.

Genuine positive regard is a powerful foundation on which to build a team. It certainly doesn't exclude disagreement, even impassioned disagreement. It is possible to take a strong stand for differences and for seeing things differently and still interact with visible respect.

Conversation Starters:

- ❑ How is respect clear and visible on this team? What is one way this team regularly shows respect? Where is it missing?
- ❑ How is respect different from trust?
- ❑ What are informal ways this team could give recognition to team members as a way of showing respect?
- ❑ What are the status indicators on this team? What is the impact?

Suggested Team Activity:

❑ Create intentional opportunities for team members to practice acknowledgment and appreciation of one another.

❑ It may be easier for some teams to talk about the impact of respect by sharing stories of other teams they have been on, whether there was great respect and the effect it had, or there was disrespect and how that affected the team. Telling such stories about how respect affects team performance makes the concept of respect real in business and behavioral terms.[39,40]

3. Camaraderie

There is a strong sense of belonging to the team. The team celebrates and acknowledges accomplishments. Empathy, playfulness, and humor are present. This is the social aspect of being on a team, where team morale or team spirit resides.

It would be easy to dismiss the value of camaraderie on teams. It's too "soft" or too vague. When we introduce the topic of camaraderie to teams, sometimes—at least with some team members—the reaction is, "I'm here to get the job done, not make friends. That's why they call it work." And yet, looking back again to best team experiences, one theme that consistently appears on the list of qualities on those memorable teams was a sense of belonging, being part of something "bigger than myself." There was an almost tangible team spirit and a feeling of pride and team identity. Fortunately, the field of neuroscience has supplied the data that gives real credence to the power found in "esprit de corps."

It turns out humans are wired to be in relationship and work together. Fundamentally, a felt sense of inclusion in the group creates ease and better blood flow to the problem-solving areas of the brain.[41] Exclusion—just the fear of exclusion, in fact—activates fight-or-flight responses, shunting blood away from productive thought processes.[42] Cognitive ability drops by as much as 70 percent. In simple terms, teams get dumber in those environments where that sense of belonging or inclusion is absent. They get a lot dumber.

Studies also show that high-performing teams have high levels of oxytocin, a chemical the body produces that reinforces social bonding.[43] It is associated with higher levels of empathy, generosity, and trust, which lead to higher levels of cohesion and cooperation.[44] And yes, by the way, oxytocin is also known as "the love molecule"—bonding babies to mothers and mates to each other. You can read all about that at another time. The key for teams is the link between high performance and the "buzz" you feel on great teams. It's real and it helps create mutual respect, a strong sense of team identity, and mutual admiration that leads team members to give 100 percent.

Camaraderie often shows up as informal playfulness and humor. But camaraderie is more than just having fun, more than drinks at the pub. It is also about creating a common sense of purpose and a mindset that "we are in this together." There is a stronger sense of loyalty to the group and more commitment to the team's success than individual success. There is a sense of pride in what *we* achieve together. The bar gets raised. We want to show up playing our "A" game for one another.

This commitment to support shows up in two important ways. One very practical way is more cooperation, the ability to ask for help and the willingness to pitch in. And the other is the emotional support: rooting for one another; consoling one another; sharing stress, celebration, anxiety, or disappointment.

Camaraderie creates a positive energetic field, a climate with more sunny days. It's simply more pleasant to come to work. And even on the stormy days, metaphorically piling sandbags, standing shoulder to shoulder to keep the flood back, is characteristic of bonded teams.

With more emphasis placed on teams as the means to improve organizational performance, it becomes imperative that teams learn to collaborate effectively. And that becomes a powerful business case for camaraderie. There is less blame, criticism, and better problem solving. Teams are more creative and productive. Team members are more engaged. Communication levels are high. There is a deep reserve of goodwill that can be drawn on when times are tough. The experience is rewarding. Team members are more attached and more reluctant to leave, which improves retention of the best talent and creates a competitive advantage for recruiting.

Research shows that friendships at work are a key to employee engagement. Gallup found that close friendships at work boost employee satisfaction by 50 percent.[45] In the midst of everyday work pressure, friendships can create an oasis, a restorative respite. There is time to set the burden down, talk informally about family and personal interests, share personal celebrations and challenges—more of the whole human range of experience. Camaraderie creates the space for that. Camaraderie makes it safe to be known for who we are without masks and builds a more authentic team culture.

Is there such a thing as *too much* camaraderie? Yes. It's that classic case of when a strength becomes a weakness. The overemphasis on relationship can lead to groupthink, where dissenting voices are hushed. Decision making then depends on consensus, and decisions are often revisited. Disagreement is strenuously avoided or becomes an underlying drama on the team that drains energy and time in side conversations and group processing. The team strains to make sure everyone is heard and included and that no one's feelings are hurt. Taking care of relationships is valued over taking care of business.[46,47]

But camaraderie is not only about being friends with each other or even, for that matter, expecting everyone will like each other. That would be nice, but it's not necessary. Camaraderie is fundamentally about belonging and identifying with the team. It can be created entirely in a work context: getting to know and appreciate the challenges and rewards team members experience in their different roles. There is awareness of different styles and different backgrounds, and the ways those differences make the team stronger.[48,49] Camaraderie can be built over a challenging issue the team addresses together. Some of the best team-bonding stories are about what

> We worked with a team of regional VPs in a financial services organization who knew each other from years of working in the same organization and rising through the ranks more or less together. They especially appreciated the in-person team coaching sessions as a way to reconnect and wondered how they could build on that outside of the coaching. They decided to have "happy hour" on Friday afternoons just to check in, share stories, and connect, with no agenda but with an agreement that it was okay to bring work knots for the group to help untie from their experience.

the team had to overcome. Chances are you have a story like that from your own experience.

Remote, virtual, geographically dispersed teams have a special challenge. Camaraderie is still very important and possible, but it takes extra effort. When team members relate primarily through technology, the relationship experience tends to be functional, efficient, and often impersonal. Still, there are dozens of ways to create opportunities to build stronger relationships.[50,51]

Conversation Starters:

- For teams in a common location, what are examples of special events or experiences that built stronger team bonds? What was the value of that experience?
- For virtual teams, what are five things you could do in a conference call to create closer connection?
- What are some informal, everyday examples of camaraderie at work?
- When have you felt this team's "team spirit"?
- How are new team members integrated into the team?

Suggested Team Activity:

- Have the team list a number of especially challenging situations the team has faced. Look for examples of cooperation, mutual support, and asking for help. What was the role of camaraderie in those situations? What was the lasting impact?
- More teams gather for purposeful volunteer efforts that also build camaraderie and a sense of meaningful, shared contribution. Teams work together to clean urban parks, or volunteer to handle a water stop at a fund-raising walk or run. What is a cause or activity this team could support?

4. Communication

Clear and efficient communication is valued. Team members make listening well a priority. Effective communication processes satisfy the need for clarity, speed, and content. Teams practice direct communication over approaches such as politicizing, gossiping, or stonewalling.

Staying connected and "up to speed" in the fast-lane world of business is challenging and becoming more challenging. The burden to produce results *and* accelerate every aspect of working together puts tremendous pressure on every interaction and every effort to keep the communication wheels spinning. Under that kind of pressure, exasperated team members ask, "Who's got time for this?" They navigate around the debris left in the trail of communication handled on the fly. This is a world where the desire for clarity and stability meets the reality of ambiguity and the speed of change.[52]

Most teams say they want better communication but often confuse "better" with "more," and nobody needs more. There's no way to hold back the endless avalanche of email, text messages, conference calls, and meetings, virtual and physical. No. More is not better. The goal is clear: useful and *efficient* communication.

Ask any team, "Is effective communication important to team performance?" The answer will be, "Yes—obviously." But to really appreciate how essential good communication is for teams, reflect for a moment on the opposite. You may have been on a team or two where communication was amiss and a mess. Instead of clarity, there were side conversations; communication that is covert. Instead of being an open and inclusive group, there were cliques. Useful communication was hard to find and often clouded by rumor and gossip.[53] Pressure creates stress; stress generates fear; and in that foggy environment communication slithers sideways and becomes obscured, delayed, and misinterpreted. As poor communication floats through the system, it attracts more toxicity.

The price of poor communication on teams is staggering: mistakes, misunderstanding, frustration, damaged customer relationships, blame, and defensiveness. These crippling conditions create potholes on the road to team effectiveness.[54]

Efficient Communication

The key word from the definition of team communication we proposed is "efficient." In practical terms, that means communication that has these four qualities:

Timely. At the speed of business these days, timeliness is essential. There is little value in communication that lands too late to be useful. Similarly, communication that arrives too early or without current context creates confusion, risks misunderstanding, and raises more questions than it answers.

Relevant. There is a chronic source of frustration on teams that goes by the initials WAIRT. Why am I reading this? Is there an action step for me in this? Is this simply background information? What is the context, the expectation? The rationale for communicating broadly, in order to be thorough, is often well-intentioned. Not always. Sometimes it's the result of being lazy on the part of the communicator, or simply an act of covering one's rear. Communication that is not relevant is the opposite of efficient.

Sufficient. As we've said, a team's desire for better communication is not a desire for **more**. It should pass the "just enough" test. Sufficient is also about being cognizant of how the communication will be received. This includes the choice of the most efficient delivery medium. Sometimes a lengthy email is the right choice; sometimes a quick text is sufficient.

Responsible. Consider the purpose for this communication and anticipate its impact. In fact, in many cases, starting with an awareness of the impact will inform the content and form of the communication. Any significant change in process or people deserves context and special attention. By anticipating the questions that a proposed communication will raise, the sender will be in a better position to craft the message. Imagine the impact of simply receiving an email that says "All-team meeting in conference room B at 3:00 today." That would certainly raise questions, and adrenaline levels.

Responsible and efficient communication is also about the ability to be direct and respectful.[55] Teams say, "We want open, honest conversation" but typically fall short of that standard. Instead, conversations are often careful, sometimes purposely vague rather than direct. Team members spend wasted time sifting through the tea leaves to find what they think must be the real message, or they focus their attention on calculating who is and is not their ally. High-performing teams have learned to avoid communication by rumor or gossip.

Finally, it's important to remember that responsible communication is more than what happens in the sending. It's not communication until the loop is closed, the message received and understood. Just *sending* a message is not communicating. It's uttering. One of the most important skills for team effectiveness is the skill of listening. More than just hearing, it is truly listening with curiosity, openly, for understanding, for meaning, and for connection.

Why Communication Is Important to Teams

The business case is obvious:

- Improved productivity
- More efficient decision making and problem solving
- Better work relationships
- Less stress and conflict
- Smoother sailing and fewer storms to navigate through[56]

Communication carries the team on the team's journey, and it is central to every aspect of team performance. Communication is essential to creating and maintaining trust.[57] Respect is communicated—as is lack of respect. Communication lets people know what the goals are and creates alignment. Communication is the vehicle for follow-up that ensures team accountability. Because it is so essential to the performance of the team, it is sometimes taken for granted, even overlooked. We've been communicating our whole lives, but that doesn't mean we're skilled at it. The more conscious a team is about both the "what" and the "how" of communication, the more effective that team will be.

Communication that is timely, relevant, sufficient, and responsible is a moving target that needs to be customized for effectiveness for every team. To do it well requires vigilance and the ability of teams to adjust and adapt to changing circumstances.

Conversation Starters:

- ❏ What are current ground rules for communication on this team? What are the unspoken assumptions?
- ❏ If communication on this team were ideal, what would need to change? What new behaviors would the team see?
- ❏ For this team to become high-performing, what specific agreements or protocols around team communication are needed moving forward?

Suggested Team Activity:

- ❏ Give examples of indirect communication habits on teams. Assume for a moment that there's a reason for the sideways communication. What's that reason? What would be a different way to get that outcome?
- ❏ The other half of communicating is listening. On a scale of 1 to 10, how good is this team at listening? What would raise that score? What would the benefit be?
- ❏ Pick one area where there are persistent communication issues on this team. It could be a lack of communication in an important area. It could be an area where the delivery is inefficient or not timely. Find the pain point, identify the root source, and brainstorm alternative ways communication could be handled.

5. Constructive Interaction

There is a clear commitment to constructive interaction between team members. The team avoids criticizing, defensiveness, and finger pointing. The team gives and receives feedback well. Conflict is seen as an opportunity for discovery, growth, and creativity.

Just so we are clear: This factor in the team-effectiveness model, Constructive Interaction, is about more than just handling conflict on teams. It is truly about creating conditions for constructive interaction between team members. At its most fundamental, it is the consistent attention teams put on making any interaction—including the difficult conversations—respectful, open, and purposeful, and in the end, mutually constructive.

One clear example would be the ability to regularly give and receive quality feedback. It is an important team skill, although by observing teams over the years it seems clear that most teams aren't very committed to feedback, even if they agree it's important. The most common reason given for this deficiency, in spite of its value, is time. In a rush and under pressure at work, it is easy to skip this opportunity, usually because it is awkward or uncomfortable, and it's uncomfortable because there may not be a clear and respectful protocol. Even if there is one, teams don't practice feedback regularly.

As a consequence, feedback is saved until a "more opportune time," and the emotional charge grows in the dark. It's no surprise then, when we hear that simple phrase, "I've got some feedback for you," it comes with a short fuse. Usually by that time an exercise in constructive interaction has turned into an exercise where the goal is constructive conflict.

The important question is not how to set up team conditions to avoid, quash, or sanitize conflict. The question is how to effectively manage the power and inherent energy, passion, commitment, and courage that is possible in conflict. With that in mind, make sure your tray table is in the upright and locked position and your seat belt is fastened low and tight across your lap. We're about to head into turbulence: conflict on teams. The truth is, if your destination is "high-performing team," you can't get there from here without encountering a rough ride from time to time. The business climate we live in every day gives us much more stormy weather than sunny and clear. Take a glance at your world of work. What's the weather like for your business today?

Unfortunately, too many teams are so turbulence-averse, they waste time and energy trying to fly around it. That tactic is understandable on one level. We've all experienced the downside of conflict. Entering the storm feels risky; things could get out of control. We all have memories, scars, and bruises of situations where conflict was destructive.

Intellectually, we may know that serious debate, differences of opinion, even arguments are all normal in groups and teams. The *fear* is that the disagreement will escalate or become personal, there will be confrontation, everything will derail, and the net result will be irreparable damage to the team's ability to work together. We're doomed.

So people hold back to keep the peace. They maneuver around hot issues as if the floor were covered with egg shells. When that happens, teams pay dearly for their "peace at any price." They miss the gold that is possible from getting messy.[58] Dissent, disagreement, and conflict on teams are inevitable and useful.[59] Conflict arises when people care about the outcome. We *want* teams where the members care. Indifference is death.

We believe that the hallmark of exceptional teams is that they have learned how to extract the energy in conflict without having the bomb go off. *Constructive interaction* represents a team competence: the ability to take full advantage of the interaction that occurs in challenging conversations or discussions in a way that is *constructive* for the team. Teams that learn how to do this explore more options, make better decisions, and are more innovative. Teams with the ability to stand in the fire are made stronger, tempered.

There are fundamentally two types of conflict.

1. **Functional conflict:** Disagreement involving tasks, issues, ideas, principles, or process; this is sometimes referred to as cognitive conflict.[60,61]
2. **Relationship conflict:** Conflict about people or values; arguing over who's right, focused on winning. This is sometimes referred to as affective or dysfunctional conflict. It focuses on the players and can quickly escalate into attacks, blaming, incendiary comments—exactly what teams fear most about conflict.[62,63]

With functional conflict, it is clear that a challenging conversation is for the benefit of the team. With

> **Functional conflict example:** There is consensus on the team that the current time line for the project's completion is unrealistic and general agreement about the reasons why. There is strong disagreement about how to get the project back on schedule. Different team members have strong opinions about solutions and sequence.
> **Relationship conflict example:** The same fundamental scenario, but in this case the team is stuck at blaming one another for the current mess, recycling old issues from other delayed projects, name-calling, claiming rank or expertise, arguing over who has the right answer.

relationship conflict, it is for personal interests and often focused on nonteam issues.

The atmosphere of the conversation is a clear indicator for which of those two is in play. In both cases there can be very strong passion, heat, and conviction, but with functional conflict it feels more open, more inviting; there is more room at the table and a sense that the struggle has a team goal. The team is headed somewhere even if the ride is bumpy. By the way, that doesn't mean it will be pleasant. It is conflict, after all, and likely to be uncomfortable at the very least.

With relationship conflict it is **ex**clusive, not **in**clusive; it feels closed, tight, bruised, and embattled; it feels dangerous and potentially destructive. It doesn't feel like we're headed anywhere useful.[64,65]

A Process for Handling Conflict

Here are steps that create a repeatable process for working with conflict when it appears.

Step 1   Start early. Before it became a fire, it was an ember. It may have been a minor irritation that was the result of a simple misunderstanding, differing expectations, or misaligned assumptions. You've probably been in that position before: irritated, frustrated with a colleague but feeling too busy to address it at the time. That irritation is a signal to check for the underlying cause. If the irritation persists, it often becomes an inflammation and a harboring complaint. The antidote for a complaint is often a request. What is the request that would address this situation? If team members allow the early signals to fester, they naturally build momentum. Of course, not all conflict on teams follows a gradual heating cycle.

Step 2   Be willing. Take the initiative. Be committed. Then stay, even when it is uncomfortable. This may be the most important of the six steps. For team members, taking initiative is a personal statement of commitment to constructive interaction; it is also a visible signal to a team member or the team that the agreement to engage, constructively, is being honored.

Step 3 Look for areas of alignment. Consider the dissenting or contrary view (or views if there are more in the discussion). Even if only the tiniest fraction were true or useful, what would that be? Find common ground, even if there's barely enough room for both of you to stand. Then take a stand for that.

Step 4 Listen for different points of view. Stand in the other's shoes—maybe not literally, but team members might change seats at the table and try speaking on behalf of that other point of view. What is there to learn? Practice empathy.

Step 5 Listen for understanding. Practice active listening.[66] Summarize what has been said. This will naturally slow down the pace of exchange, and it has a tendency to take some of the heat or charge off the communication. It also builds empathy.

Step 6 Search for solutions or actions. Be generous and inclusive. Explore for ideas outside the usual or familiar. This will help expand the universe of possibilities.

In the course of the conversation, team members should:

- Aim to listen as much as they speak.
- Ask questions as often as they state their position. Ask open-ended, curious questions and ask for clarity.
- Acknowledge and appreciate one another from time to time along the way.

Worth noting: how teams handle conflict will look quite different in different cultures. There will be deeply held protocol for conflict that everyone takes for granted; it's assumed everyone knows how to behave. As coach, it's important to know the local ground rules. Working with conflict can be particularly challenging on cross-cultural teams with multiple cultural norms.[67] That makes it especially important to uncover those underlying operating assumptions and have a conversation as a team: "What guidelines do we want to create for our team?"

We worked with a team that was especially amiable. They had been together as a team for several years. They could see the value in a willingness to engage in debate and disagreement—it just didn't happen on that team, or so they claimed. Still wanting to take advantage of the potential within conflict, they decided to create a role for "Devil's Advocate" during team meetings. It was a rotating role so no one team member was stuck with the label. This creative adaptation provided the missing voice for concern and doubt, and it forced the team to be more rigorous in their positions and rationale. Because the role was endorsed by the team, it was clear the contrarian was working on behalf of the team, not against the team or any individual team member. It also enlivened the team conversation.[68]

Benefits of Constructive Interaction

Conflict can't always be resolved but it can be managed. That's the primary value of a team-conflict process. Even when trust between team members is shaky, teams can trust the process. The result of a thoughtful approach to conflict on teams is worth the turbulence. Thorny problems are solved; resilience, trust, and alignment are built; team members learn they can fully participate; and they can bring their ideas, passion, and conviction to the team.

Conflict is inevitable. The question is, how can teams take maximum advantage of it? And how can teams make excellence in managing conflict a team value, something everyone on the team is proud of?

Conversation Starters:

- What are the unspoken agreements around conflict when it shows up on this team?
- What are the forbidden topics?
- Pick a situation where the team or team members handled a difficult disagreement effectively. What contributed to that success? What tips from that experience can be applied to other similar situations?

Suggested Team Activity:

- For teams about to begin a conversation about creating new behavioral norms, a great place to start with a team is a discussion around two questions: What is your perspective on conflict? What are your assumptions about conflict?
- An area where teams can practice Constructive Interaction is in giving and receiving feedback. Take time to create norms and agreements about that exchange process and establish a structure and accountability for practice.
- Teams that have learned to distinguish between healthy, functional disagreement and toxic relationship conflict can benefit from the creation of a code word or gesture that sends a signal to team members, "We may have crossed that boundary." The team agrees that the code word or gesture signals to the team to de-escalate conflict and return to a safer, more productive conversation. A team of English football club fans chose "yellow card" as their team code word. Another team simply made the "time-out" gesture their structure.

6. Diversity

The team is open-minded and values differences in ideas, backgrounds, perspectives, personalities, approaches, and lifestyles. Diversity is considered vital.

One of the core strengths of teams is the value that diversity brings to a team's overall performance. When teams value and empower diversity, they maximize the team's potential by bringing out the unique contributions of every team member.[69,70] There are a number of clear, proven advantages to diversity on teams, including a broader range of experience and expertise; creative thinking from multiple perspectives; a richer mix of ideas and possible solutions. Diversity, well managed, can absolutely deliver results to the bottom line.[71] The research is very clear about that.

But simply assembling a diverse team is no guarantee that the team will benefit. There has been a great deal of attention paid to the *fact* of diversity and less on how to make it a team competence. Like Communication, or Trust, or being Proactive, some teams are simply better than others. To develop that competence, we need a deeper understanding of diversity and what makes it work on teams. We need to expand the conversation.

Organizations tend to think of diversity in visible terms: gender, race, nationality, age, and physical ability. It's an important focus and comes complete with its own set of challenges. But at the team level those are just the visible tip of the diversity iceberg. Under the surface lies a vast variety of ways team members are different.

- Education
- Experience
- Background
- Values
- Role (Formal and informal role; how team members inhabit those roles. No two leaders, or engineers, or designers are identical.)
- Style of communication
- Style of decision making
- Different ways of processing information and handling conflict
- And much more

Mostly we are not aware of these invisible differences until they show up in interaction, sometimes surprisingly. With all that diversity, most of it hidden from view, how do you get anything done in collaboration?

To understand diversity is to understand that there are two compelling forces at work. One is the drive to belong, to be with "people like me." It is a safe environment; it feels comfortable. However, too much emphasis on belonging leads to pressures to conform, to comply, to hide or camouflage differences. We might see team members smiling and nodding and simply going along with what everyone seems to think. Overemphasis on belonging becomes assimilation.[72]

The second force at work is the drive to be seen as unique and "valued for who I am." Too much emphasis on uniqueness has its own risks. It can lead to conflict, isolation, and not pulling together as a team.

The key to making diversity work is the ability to create a social balance of both the drive to belong and the drive to be unique. This is more than simply appreciating differences. The goal is to create an inclusive container where all voices are not only welcome, but invited, encouraged, and empowered to share. The dreamer and the pragmatist; the one who makes quick decisions and the one who ponders; the one who wants everything in order and the one who thrives in uncertainty. And not just accept it, as in, "Oh, well. If we must." Not just acquiesce but actively recognize, invite, encourage, acknowledge diversity. To value diversity is to appreciate the uniqueness of each contributor and to see it as vital to the combined strength of the team.

"Diversity" is the description of a state. Inclusion is diversity in action. It's how great teams make diversity work. The result is a culture of inclusion where team members feel they belong *because* they are included, even with all their differences.[73] When inclusion is the key to belonging, *both* aspects are honored: belonging and uniqueness. When that happens, teams are able to unlock the potential that lives in the team. Variety really is the spice of life on work teams.

In the end a great team is less like a smoothie and more like a great salad.

Conversation Starters:

- ❑ Where do you see diversity valued on this team? Give examples. With each example, describe the different contributions. Be as specific as possible.
- ❑ Using the diagram in the book as a continuum, from Assimilation to Isolation, where does this team line up?
- ❑ What are some of the invisible diversity forces at work on this team? Look at decision making as an area for discussion about diverse styles.

Suggested Team Activity:

- ❑ Encourage the team to listen for the voices on the fringe. They don't have to accommodate every voice by giving it voting or veto rights, but the simple act of listening and letting those voices know they have been heard and attended to is important.
- ❑ Some teams consciously ask for the unpopular voices in meetings along the lines of, "What is not being said, or asked? What is the voice no one has spoken for?" Asking the questions reinforces taking a stand for inclusion, and you might be surprised by the results.

❑ Play this game. "If _____ were here, he/she would say…"
Then fill in the blank with someone everyone knows who would
have a distinct opinion or point of view. That could be a real person
in the organization—for example, the CEO or the head of R&D. Or
it could be anyone at all, real or fictional. If Napoleon were here…If
Snow White were here….

7. Optimism

*The team has an inspiring shared vision. They are forward looking
and appreciative of one another. There are low levels of cynicism, pes-
simism, helplessness, hopelessness, or dwelling in the past.*

Of the seven Positivity competencies, Optimism may be the one
most challenging to support and defend. You run the risk of being cast
with fuzzy thinkers or the touchy-feely crowd. You risk being labeled a
Pollyanna, out of touch with reality. There are people who will say optimism sounds like propping up with clichés instead of getting down to
business. You can almost hear them: "Spare me the cheerleading, the
vapid smile, and cheery tone. I'm wrestling with real issues. I don't need
camp songs." But optimism isn't about avoiding reality or pretending
everything is okay. It's not about whistling a happy tune when things are
hard. It's actually about the strength to go into the dark, believing in the
team's ability to handle whatever comes their way.[74]

The leverage point for optimism comes down to a simple, powerful truth: We create more of what we believe. We look for evidence that
confirms our beliefs. This is as true for teams as it is for individuals.
That voice in your head that says, "This is doomed," has a whole history
of examples to throw on the table as proof. If that's what you believe,
chances are that's what you will create. The voice that says, "We've bat-
tled bigger challenges than this and come through," has the voice of a
champion. Teams have those voices too. Think about teams you've been
on, and you will know this rings true.

One of the four guiding principles for our work with teams is this
declaration: "The team has within it the means to excel." You might say it
is an expression of optimism and you'd be right, but it is more than that.
It is a stance we take. For coaches or team leaders, if you *don't* believe

that, you are likely to look for evidence that the team is not capable.

Optimism is a mindset. It's not just about being positive; it's more than balloons and ice cream. It contains a backbone of confidence and commitment.[75] It doesn't depend on sunny days. Optimism can thrive on stormy days; in fact, it's on days like that when optimism can be the difference between persevering and giving up.

Optimism is forward leaning and future looking. Optimism scans the horizon for possibilities. Optimistic teams are resilient, proactive, and creative. They believe, "We can find a way."

Optimism is both a sign of certain conditions on teams and an underlying "field" of energy. Optimism builds from success on a team, often in the face of struggle or challenges shared and overcome. Teams that succeed become more optimistic about their ability to weather the next storm. It is not a guarantee of success, but it is an attitude that is more likely to foster success.

> The rank order for the seven Positivity factors is also revealing. (figure 3-1) Here is the order from highest score to lowest for High Productivity—High Positivity teams and the same for Low—Low teams. What stands out are the three areas where High Productivity—High Positivity teams excel: Constructive Interaction, Trust, and Optimism. High-performing teams have the ability to engage in disagreement, maintain high levels of trust, and believe in the inherent strengths of the team.

That conclusion about optimism is not just another optimistic view. Studies show that when people have a positive mindset, they are more productive and more engaged.[76] Optimistic teams tend to press on in the face of challenges, believing they have the ability to succeed. Optimistic teams experience less conflict and more alignment. Attitude, morale, culture—whatever you call it—when it is positive it delivers business results.

The good news: Optimism can be learned by simply choosing—and then living—the choice. Teams that are truly optimistic believe in their ability to succeed because the belief is more than wishful thinking; it is anchored in results produced. Belief is a fine thing and essential, but it's insufficient. Action, even success in small steps, reinforces optimism and commitment. Beliefs are self-fulfilling prophecies, so the advice is

Figure 3-1: Positivity factors by rank and percentage difference between High-High and Low-Low teams (overall and by factor). Data from the TCI Team Diagnostic™ database, based on more than 3,000 teams, 2008-2017.

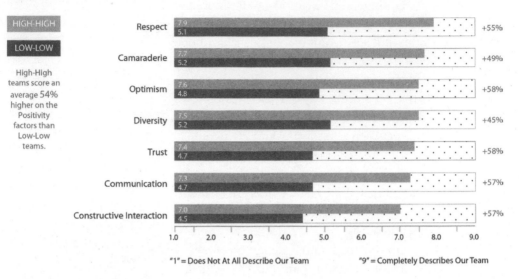

to choose wisely. Teams that believe their situation is an inescapable experience of hardship, failure, and turmoil will inevitably breed more of the same. Teams that believe they have the capacity, ingenuity, and resilience to succeed will breed more of that too.

Conversation Starters:

- What are the business benefits that accrue to optimistic teams? Note that this question might reveal as much about a team's belief about optimism as it does about the team's perception of the possible benefits.
- What would enable this team to be more optimistic? What would you see and hear on this team?
- What is this team's belief about the influence of a positive team attitude? What is the impact of that belief?

Suggested Team Activity:

- Pick several recent team situations that were particularly challenging. A good place to look is situations that were the result of unexpected changes in circumstances beyond the team's control. As the team began to address the situation, what was the level of optimism on the team? How did it change over time? This could also be an exercise to explore similar events from previous teams team members have been on.

Summary

These seven Positivity Team Performance Indicators are all unique and at the same time interdependent. Improvement in any one area naturally affects other areas. For example, better communication builds trust; developing a team culture of can-do confidence and optimism reduces conflict; valuing diversity and inclusion fosters more respect.

The seven are indicators that reveal the current state of the team. They are also areas where the team can build competence. When teams focus on developing strength in these seven, they take action, then learn from the action they take. Over time, teams build the muscle for strong, engaged interaction, and that leads to improved business results.

CHAPTER 4

The Foundations for Team Coaching

The team-effectiveness model gives us a target for great teams: a blended combination of both High Productivity and High Positivity qualities. This chapter lays the groundwork for the foundations on which the team coaching is built. We will look at what distinguishes team coaching from other group processes, look at defining "team," and clarify the roles of the various participants in a team coaching process. The chapter concludes with what we believe are the core, guiding principles that form an essential framework for effective team coaching.

Distinctions for Group Process Work

Team building. Group facilitation. Group coaching. Team coaching. These four forms of group process share common ground, and each one stands on its own with a unique purpose and method. Whole books and training courses have been created to define and teach each of these. Clearly the short description here is a condensed overview in order to see the overlap and describe the distinctions between them.

Team Building

Team building typically refers to a single-session event. The purpose is to create learning from an experiential activity.[77] Team members participate in the exercise, then a follow-up conversation harvests the team members' learning from the experience. Team-building activities take many forms, some more physically challenging for participants. From the perspective of team learning and development, the best team-building sessions are designed with focus on a particular aspect of team dynamics. In other words, there is a clear learning objective for the experience.

For example, the goal of the team building might be to build stronger muscles of trust, experience the value of clear plans and goals, create an opportunity to notice what happens when roles and responsibilities or leadership are vague, or experience the benefits of mutual support and collaboration.

Many team leaders came up through the ranks participating in team-building activities and off-site or away-day sessions for team development. As leaders of their own teams, it is understandable that when they see the need for a more cohesive and effective team, they look to options based on their own experience. That's the familiar choice.

Although the experiences may be engaging, even powerful, when team members get back to work, too often the experience and the learning quickly fade under the pressure and speed of everyday life.[78] Without a process to integrate the learning, people are left with good stories to tell but little in the way of substantive change in how the team interacts. If nothing changed after the event, team members are likely to grumble that it was a waste of precious time when everyone is under grinding pressure to get results.

Group Facilitation

Traditional group facilitation is a special methodology designed to help the team work through a specific issue in order to come to a resolution point. The role of the facilitator is to be a neutral agent on behalf of the process. Facilitators have a special skill set for encouraging member participation and for moving a process forward, getting a process unstuck, and leading to an agreed-upon result. Facilitation of a group process typically has a specific, one-time objective.

Even if the process takes more than one session, it is a single issue with a clear destination for the facilitation, and the group's attention is on achieving that resolution. A skilled facilitator actively encourages full participation and manages the flow of the conversation.

There is a secondary benefit as well. As teams go through the facilitation experience, they become more aware of how the team collaborates on achieving a common goal. For example, they might discover how team members listen, or how the team handles challenging conversation, but this learning is ancillary to the facilitation objective.

Group Coaching

The simple distinction between "group coaching" and "team coaching" refers to how participants are involved in the process. Group coaching is essentially individuals receiving one-on-one coaching but in a group setting. Within the group there is a common interest in achieving personal goals; there may even be a common coaching focus such as leadership development, but there is no interdependence within the group. Group members do not have a team affiliation. Group coaching is an efficient way to provide individuals with a coaching experience in an environment that is mutually supportive.

Group coaching sessions typically take place on a consistent, agreed-upon schedule. Each group member has personal goals for the coaching. In some cases, group coaching may include peer coaching as well, where group members pair up for additional one-on-one coaching with each other.[79]

Team Coaching

The goal of team coaching is improved team performance.[80] Along the way issues will be addressed, problems solved, goals achieved, and there will be an emphasis on what the team is learning. The focus of the work of team coaching is team dynamics—to help the team be more skilled, more efficient, and more resourceful in their work.

A team coaching process takes place over a prearranged period and may include team-building activities and training on relevant skills for team improvement. Team coaching sessions might also include group facilitation around specific issues the team needs help resolving.

Team coaching is also an ideal way to take advantage of the impact from experiential work. Well-designed and implemented team-building events can have a powerful impact on teams and team members. These activities access learning at the emotional and somatic levels, areas that are rarely engaged in the usual training classroom or everyday team conversation. The key to integrating the experience into new team behavior is the domain of team coaching, and that's what makes team building with team coaching complementary. Team coaching provides the ongoing structure that will draw out the learning and provide ways for teams to practice the lessons learned.

The Overlap

All four group processes use similar skills, for example: listening, awareness of group dynamics, leading a process and still being flexible, keeping the goal in mind, creating safety, challenging and championing. One of the key differences is where the person responsible for the group process has his or her attention.

1. In team building, the attention is on an experience and what the team or individuals learn from the experience.
2. Facilitation uses group-process skills to help the team reach an appropriate and useful decision or bring an issue to clear resolution.
3. For group coaching the process identifies personal goals and provides the support structure for individuals to achieve their goals.
4. Team coaching is a methodology designed to improve the way the team interacts in order to improve business results.

Defining Team

You may recall the comparison of team pictures we mentioned earlier: a scrapbook of photos from decades ago compared to team photos of today. Back then, the top-down, hierarchical model was the accepted norm and sufficient for the pace and process of work. Yes, teams went through development stages. They still do. But Bruce Tuckman's rhyming model was introduced in 1965, more than 50 years ago, when there was a reasonable expectation that teams would be together for years. Hence, *Forming, Storming, Norming, and Performing* was a more or less predictable sequence. Today, teams go through the same four stages, but at the speed of teams these days, those four are just as likely to be simultaneous as sequential.

That old photo shows an intact team because that was the only model. Describing it as "intact" would have been unnecessary. It was a standard team. Look around, scan the literature landscape for teams today and you will find information about cross-functional, virtual, agile, matrix, networked, and distributed teams, to name a few. Innovation came to team structure out of necessity, given the shifting world of supply chain, globalization, technology, and a relentless demand for improved results and a faster pace.

Every aspect of what we might traditionally think of as a reference source for a team definition has changed or adapted, on every level. Team meetings used to take place in the conference room down the hall and lasted an hour. Today, you might see 15-minute stand-up team meetings, or a collection of global teammates connected for a weekly meeting across 12 time zones, participating on different devices: laptop, desktop, and phone. The grand halls of business are now wi-fi connections. Welcome to the new world of teams.

We started this section with a goal to provide a definition of the word "team." The truth is, the word is barely sufficient to describe the multiple forms and adaptations in everyday use in organizations. Teams continue to adapt to shifting strategic directions, restructuring faster to meet market and organizational changes, and their team membership, including team leader, is in constant cycling.

Team Size

Our data shows that, overall, the average size of a work team is just under 10. Senior leadership teams tend to be smaller, six to eight on average. Project teams are larger, usually around 14, but they include team members whose roles weave in and out during the course of the project. The fact is, there isn't clear consensus about team size, let alone optimum team size, if you search the team literature or ask teams. We're simply not going to agree on a definition of team, and taking a stand for any particular definition seems like a pointless exercise. The key to working with teams is more about understanding the process and less about naming the form.

Here are a couple of examples that illustrate that idea. In a conversation to discover the need and possible fit for team coaching, the team leader said that one challenge was the size of the team. "How large?" we asked. The reply was, "120." "Really??" It was a shocking number even after years of surprises. However, we did not try to correct the team leader in his understanding. Instead we got curious about the challenge. It was clear that this team leader was using the organization's nomenclature for team definition, so we embarked on learning the local language instead of insisting on our own. Clearly, in this organization nobody blinks when there is a reference to a "team" of 120 people.

In our experience, when team size gets above 12 or 15, we start looking for nested teams—teams within the "team." With much larger teams, we customarily refer to them as "meta-teams" as a way to distinguish the scale of the work. Even meta-teams can demonstrate the essential qualities of team identity, common mission, interdependence, and coresponsibility for results. They can also benefit from an assessment based on the 14 Team Performance Indicators of Productivity and Positivity. Obviously, compared to the relative intimacy of a leadership team of eight, team coaching work with a meta-team will be vastly different in terms of logistics and interaction.

A second example is a team form we have come to call a "cross-boundary" team. It describes a situation where the team is generally split into two camps representing different organizations, or it could be different sectors of one organization. One of the underlying challenges for these cross-boundary teams is that they may have—in fact often have—competing priorities, and the fundamental differences often result in behavior that is lose-lose rather than win-win.

A classic example comes from advertising, where there is an account/creative representation on the agency side, and from the client's side, the product and marketing representatives. They clearly have a common mission and they are interdependent, but often the cultural differences and separate priorities undermine the ability of the whole team to collaborate effectively. It's another example of paying more attention to the process and understanding the presenting conditions and less attention on defining the form.

Is This a Work Group? Or a Team?

What we come down to, after we accept the kaleidoscope of team forms, are guidelines for teams rather than a rigid definition. For the purposes of a fit with team coaching, we also want to find clear ways to distinguish between the dynamics of *teams* compared to the dynamics of a *work group*.

Instead of "either one or the other," it is actually more accurate to see groups and teams on a continuum, with work groups at one end and teams at the other, with no judgment implied that one is better than the other. The ultimate question will be "Is the form suitable to the goals and demands placed on it?" The commission for the individual members depends more on the task to be accomplished than any arbitrary definition.

The primary distinguishing characteristic, starting from the goal to be achieved, is this: does reaching the goal require interdependence among members, or can the results be successfully achieved with members operating independently? With work groups, the output comes in the form of individual results, combined with others. With a team, the output is the result of a combined team effort in addition to the individual team member's efforts.

For example, if a work group is given the task to write a book, it's as if each member writes a separate chapter. The result is a collection of the efforts of individual contributors. An advisory group would be one example where a work group makes sense.

Work output for a team would look more like the performance of an orchestra. There are different sections to the orchestra but together they form one entity, making music. Each section contributes a unique component to the whole; different sections will be featured at different times; there is alignment, a shared identity and common purpose in the flow. Project teams stand out as excellent examples for the team definition because they have identity, clear shared mission, and critical interdependence in order to complete the project.

Here are several other ways to distinguish between the two.

Goal Setting. In work groups, attention is primarily on individual goals; that's the level of responsibility. For teams there are individual goals, but there is also a sense of common mission and identity with the collective outcome based on achieving team goals.

Accountability. In work groups, accountability tends to be individual; on teams, in addition to individual accountability, there is an awareness of mutual responsibility for team goals. Some organizations have begun defining team KPIs in addition to individual performance measures.

Meeting Purpose. With work groups the purpose of most group meetings is to report on individual progress and adjust the output commitment and deadlines as necessary. With teams there will be information sharing, discussion, collaboration; there may be decisions to make as a team or team problems to address; there may be disagreements about team goals or the process to achieve them.

Oversight/Leadership. For work groups, the flow of the work is vertical, between the leader/manager and individual members. Interaction on a horizontal plane is minimal and transactional. With teams the flow of the work is horizontal and vertical. Effective relationship norms are important for team effectiveness.

Just as important as a clear understanding of the differences would be answers to the questions of "fit": "Which form would be best in a specific situation? What would be the benefit of working as a work group versus a team?"

Many senior leadership teams operate as cross-functional work groups. Each member of the "team" operates very independently, with an almost exclusive focus on the member's individual area of vertical responsibility and the team that person leads. Stronger interdependence may not be absolutely required, but the benefit may also be overlooked. Working more collaboratively has the potential to accelerate performance through shared best practices and the diversity of skills, perspective, and insight that make teams strong.

Note that on some senior leadership teams there is sometimes an unspoken, "hands off" agreement between team members. They are protective of their territory and the status or rank that goes with the position. They want to avoid interference, and collaborating can look like a loss of control or independence in their operating style.

In the end there is no master template that will give the "right" answer about which form is best. As we said, there is a natural continuum, and a team is best suited somewhere along that line.

Who Is on the Team?

An effective team-development initiative works best when every essential member of the team participates. That seems obvious. What's less clear is who should be included. After years working with teams, it is continuously surprising how often it happens that there are people not included on the list of team members who believe they should be, and people included on the team list for whom it comes as a surprise.

Determining who should participate in the team-development process takes more than simply drawing a circle around names on a horizontal section of the org chart.

Suggested questions to help determine who should be included:

- In order for the team to fulfill its mission, who needs to be included in the learning and development process?
- If the team were facing an important turning point, what skills would be required and who represents those skills?
- Where are the essential communication points in order for the team to operate optimally—not just to accomplish the project at hand or resolve one issue, but to sustain effective operation and improve performance over time?

In one case, working through these guidelines with a senior management team, it became clear that one person missing from the list was the team's administrative assistant. That person sat at the hub of team communication and had invaluable insight into the everyday stresses of the team. The admin provided an important perspective and practical experience that was otherwise lacking.

Clarifying Roles

Roles, responsibilities, and relationships form the infrastructure for team coaching, and because team coaching may be a new undertaking for teams, clarity about those roles is especially important, and the earlier in the process the better. This is an opportunity to design an effective working relationship based on shared understanding, honest exploration, and commitment.

Role of the Coach

The coach's role defines a particular way of working with the team that is different from the working relationships the team may be more familiar with.

Individual coaching is now widely known in organizations. There may be a variety of opinions about the value, but the form itself is familiar. Team coaching shares many of the same fundamental attributes: the agenda, action, accountability, and results all belong to the team. The experience for those receiving the coaching will be quite different when we compare individual coaching, which is a private, one-on-one dialogue, to team coaching, which is a vulnerable, public conversation between team members.

In a coaching model, the role of the coach is primarily focused on inquiry/asking versus advocacy/telling. It shows up in how the coach asks probing questions, observes the team, and invites reflection. Because team members are more familiar with the consultant model— the analyzer, evaluator, problem solver—it's possible the team will assume the team coach's role is similar—that the coach's job is to interview the team, analyze the issues, and propose or direct a solution to the issues uncovered.

Similarly, without any other team coaching experience, some teams and team leaders may also have in mind sports coaching when they think about coaching teams. But there are essential differences. The sports coach is actively managing the team—making decisions about team direction, deciding who plays and who doesn't—and has an important teaching function. This potential for misunderstanding a team coach's role in a business setting is the reason for checking assumptions and clarifying expectations as early as possible.

It is useful for the team to understand that the team coach's attention will be primarily on the team dynamics—how the team interacts with one another. This is where efficiency and strength are developed. Worth noting: coaching is a change process, and systems, like teams, are naturally resistant to change. Team resistance is normal, and there will be times when the coach, as change agent, will not be very popular. An important role for the team coach is to create and help maintain a safe environment in which team members can engage in meaningful, sometimes risky or challenging conversation.

In team coaching, it is the team and not the team sponsor who is the coachee. The team coach is advocate and champion for the team as a whole, not any single person on the team, even the team leader. During the time frame of a team coaching engagement, team membership may change, with new team members joining or some leaving. Even a team leader may change, but the commitment on the coach's part remains the effective development of the team.

In simplest terms, team coaching provides the structure, support, and empowerment for teams to engage in crucial conversations that lead to new, more effective behavior and improved business results. The coach is a catalyst who has an important contribution to that process. The coach's primary role is to be a learning and process facilitator, holding the team accountable for team results.

Role for the Team

In a coaching model, the core of the work takes place in the conversation between team members, guided and supported by the coach. The primary role of the team is to show up, literally and figuratively, and engage whole-heartedly in the team conversation. In a coaching methodology, the team is responsible for setting the agenda, discussing options, making decisions about action steps, and taking the action steps they commit to take.

One of the benefits of a coaching approach is the emphasis on the team being responsible for their own results. When the team takes initiative for choices and change there is inherent buy-in to both the team's process and the team's results. The team is both more resourceful and more accountable.

Role for the Team Leader

Because our approach to team coaching is a systems-based approach, we recognize that the team leader has a special role based on function, and that a team leader is also an integral part of the system. The team leader has leadership direction and final decision-making responsibility; the team leader is also a member of the team. The consequence of these two inherent roles for the team leader is an awareness that there is a necessary balancing act in the relationship of team, team coach, and team leader. On one hand, it needs to be clear that the agenda for change is owned by the team and not just a command from the team leader. On the other hand, there is clearly authority and rank that is inescapable, especially in open-team conversations. Sensitivity to this balance is everyone's responsibility: the team leader, the coach, and the team members.

The Organization's Role

The organization has an obvious stake in the outcome of this team coaching project. There is a significant investment in the team, and the organization reasonably expects a business return on that investment. There is also an expectation that a successful team coaching project will have a more viral effect as the success touches other stakeholder relationships and the learning ripples out into the organization.

Where it gets sticky: the organization's desire for a report on the process and outcomes needs to be balanced with the team's need for confidentiality so that team members will be as open and honest as possible. Coaching, whether individual or team, will always be much more effective when it is protected under the cover of confidentiality. It is our belief that any reporting to those in the organization not on the team should be first approved by the team. If team members are concerned about repercussions, they will hold back and the potential benefits of the process will be minimized.

Four Guiding Principles

Effective team coaching is built on a set of beliefs. Before the work begins with a team, these beliefs create a mindset. They reflect assumptions and expectations for the work with the team. These four guiding principles form a solid foundation on which the coaching is built.

Principle No. 1: Teams Exist to Produce Results

You might say, "Of course." Teams have a mission, a purpose for being. The organization is counting on this team for certain essential outcomes. That mission, and the attendant results, exists regardless of the people who fill the roles on the team. Whatever changes or adjustments are made on the team, whatever action the team takes or does not take, in the end, it is for the sake of the mission of the team. Teams that pay more attention to individuals or team member relationships than they do to the mission can lose sight of the reason the team exists.

Within the team coaching process there will be many times when the focus will be on individual performers, or pairs, or small groups of individuals, but always for the sake of the results of the team. By the way, this emphasis on results does not mean "results at any cost," especially not human cost because that would undermine the sustainability of the team and ultimately sabotage the ability of the team to fulfill its unique mission. On the best teams, there is clear awareness of and commitment to the compelling mission of the team.[81]

Principle No. 2: The Team Is a Living System

Adding the word "living" here is important. In contrast, consider the automobile engine. It's also a system with many interdependent parts. Too often, the traditional view of teams is based on a mechanical model where faulty parts are identified and repaired or replaced so that the engine will run smoothly again. We even have a phrase for it in English, "working like a well-oiled machine." Except a team is a human system, and human systems are naturally dynamic. They grow and change; they adapt to changing conditions. They create friction and that friction is energy for the team when it is used well.

Teams are inherently messy and chaotic, and they need to be. They have values, a history, a present, and a future. Ask any new team member about the personality of the team they have joined and within a week or two they will have a clear sense of the pulse and personality of the team.[82]

For human systems and teams, "high-performing and sustainable" do not sync with "well-oiled machine." It's too mechanical and rigid. Too often the well-oiled team becomes more committed to a smooth ride than they are to achieving results.

As a living system a team also has survival instincts, and that can be both good news and not-so-good news. Fortunately, this urge to survive can sustain a team during challenging times. Unfortunately, the same urge for self-preservation in a dysfunctional system perpetuates the unhealthy conditions. The system creates conditions for success and conditions that lead to expulsion or quarantine. You know this about the team you are on whether anyone ever speaks about it or not. There is a way that "things are done around here" that forms the ground rules for success on this team. Obey the rules or you might find yourself on the outside looking in, permanently. In contrast, healthy human systems are always evolving, giving birth to new ideas, new projects, new vision. They are inclusive and life-giving.

Principle No. 3: Team Members Want to Be on High-Performing Teams

This needs a broader context for it to make sense. Given Abraham Maslow's compelling observations about the hierarchical order of wants and needs, it is clear that individuals want, more than anything, survival, and then personal safety, and then fulfillment and success.[83] People do not necessarily have "team member" as a lifelong ambition. Even within organizations, an individual's number one priority is Number One—the need to survive and put bread on the table. So where we start with this principle is the *fact* of being on a team.

The impact of globalization, accelerated by digital connection, means team members today are much less likely to meet face to face; likewise, personal interaction has been replaced with functional email, texting, and instant messaging. The social role of the water cooler is a relic of a past age. This one-dimensional drive for productivity and efficiency at the expense of human connection runs against our human wiring. The sense of being part of a purposeful community is withering under pressure. But being in a community, or tribe, or team is as natural to humans as breathing or laughing together. We are shaped and conditioned by millions of years of working in collaboration for a common purpose, whether it was elk for dinner, raising barns in the countryside, or bringing new products to market.

Given the natural human drive to be in a community, it makes perfect sense that individuals would prefer to be on successful, high-performing teams. It fulfills a natural desire for inclusion, security, and the means to make a contribution. That desire also provides an underlying motivation for the work of team coaching: the drive to be among the best. Much of the work we do as team coaches is to remove the barriers and create the supportive conditions so that the individuals can fulfill this very human drive and teams can excel.

Principle No. 4: The Team Has Within It the Means to Excel

This is a rather bold statement. In fact, it is more of an operating stance than a declaration of absolute fact. To be clear about the impact of why we take this stance, start by making the alternative assumption: assume that teams do NOT have the means to excel.

With that as an operating perspective, we are constantly noticing the lack, the weakness, the evidence that the team is not able to perform, and we use that evidence to focus on fixing the perceived problem. "See? There it is again." The team operates under a cloud of expectation that it will never excel. With that frame of mind, the team is likely to create the conditions that fulfill the expectation.

On the other hand, if we start from a declaration that the team is creative enough, resourceful enough, and capable enough to excel, we create a positive, encouraging atmosphere and the expectation of success.[84] Challenges along the way become opportunities for creative response rather than evidence that the team is once again failing.

This is a bold stance—that the team has the means to excel and the creative capacity to find its way. And yet, when the team takes on this mantle of belief and empowerment, it sees itself in a different way. Natural human creativity is encouraged and rewarded. Teams take initiative. When teams take hold of this belief, they are more nimble in response to changing conditions and more resilient in the face of challenges. Teams learn how to more effectively collaborate, and that learning sustains the team well beyond this initial coaching engagement.

Summary

Team coaching is still a relatively new service offering; it is new territory for organizations to explore. There is a desire to understand both the process and the potential benefit. It is new territory for practitioners too. The generalized assumption underlying the topic of team development is "What's the big deal?" A team is a team. We've all been on teams. Team development should be a reasonably easy and natural process of skills training, or team member bonding, or better interpersonal relationships. Those are all potentially part of a team's journey of development, but the pathway is not as clear or as simple as that assumption implies.

Our experience during the past 10 years has been an ongoing story of clarifying, building better understanding, and working with teams to uncover assumptions and expectations that are hidden barriers to progress. This chapter provides the solid foundation on which team coaching is built. In the next chapter we describe the team coaching process that supports teams as they move from where they are to where they want to be.

For Team Coaches

- ❏ Imagine you are meeting with a team leader who is curious about "this thing called team coaching." He asks you, "What is *my* role in this process?" How do you describe the role of team leader in a team coaching process? What concerns might you anticipate from the team leader? How would you respond?
- ❏ On the continuum of work group and team, think about specific examples from your own experience or generate a few from your imagination. If it's an imaginary team, give the scenario a membership, an outcome, and a leadership or management function to oversee or lead the results. What do you notice about the distinctions that help shift the placement on that continuum between work group and team?
- ❏ Reflect on the description of the role of the coach. What additional notes would you add? What are important qualities for an effective team coach?

For Team Leaders

- ❑ Who is on your team? Look beyond the group email list. Who are the essential individuals necessary for your team to fulfill its mission? For those who aren't on the standard roster, what is their essential contribution?

- ❑ Looking at team membership, it's customary to consider the mix of personalities and skills—what people bring to the team effort. Another important perspective would be the importance of individuals for the team's learning agenda. How are the members of the team contributors to ongoing learning? Also, look for people who are not normally considered members of the team who would be excellent inclusions for what they can contribute to the team's learning. They might be stakeholders.

- ❑ If you lead a team larger than about 12, what are the particular challenges for you as the team leader? What are the special challenges from the team member point of view?

- ❑ Where would you place the team you are leading on the work-group-to-team continuum? Is the team currently in a place that you would say, "This is the best fit for the work we are responsible for?" How has the team shifted on that continuum? What caused the shift? What was the impact?

CHAPTER 5

Now Replicate That Model—Team Coaching in Action

Fine. We know *what* makes great teams great. Great teams excel in the 14 factors that form a powerful blend of Productivity and Positivity strengths. The question now is, *how* do we transfer what we know into what teams do?

Those great teams that we remember stand out in our memories for many reasons: for the feeling team members had when working together, for the camaraderie, for the accomplishment, for the striving together, for the fun (usually), and for the connection that sometimes lasts years after the team experience. To say those teams are extraordinary reflects well on the team, and it is a simple fact. They are very rare.[85,86] Too rare. Most teams are underperforming, not living up to their potential. Organizations are rightly concerned about this gap between how teams perform and what is possible.

Also troubling from an organization's point of view: all of those great teams were created by accident, which, as we noted before, is not a viable long-term business strategy. Organizations are searching the landscape for a reliable and consistent way to improve any and every team's performance.

What we're proposing here is a repeatable process that can deliver team performance improvement in both Productivity and Positivity, and a process that can support teams throughout the organization. Intervening to bring one troubled team back up to fully functioning, or a team here and there, that's triage, and that is not a visionary business strategy, either. If 90 percent of all teams are not achieving their potential, there is an organization-wide need for a systematic process that will benefit any team.

The initiative we're describing is a change process. In order for teams to improve how they work together, team members need to learn and practice new behaviors with one another. That's why a coaching model that includes both support and accountability is a natural fit. In coaching we understand that change—significant and sustainable change—takes place over time. A one-time event like a team-building day or a "better communications" workshop can create awareness and insight, but the report we hear from organizations over and over is that those options don't stick. Without continuing support, people soon fall back into the old ways.

Learning new behavior simply takes time.[87] We know this from personal life experience of changing habits or learning new skills. It takes time. Sad but true, because it would be great if there were a pill for that. There isn't.

Key Differences between Individual and Team Coaching

Before we go into specifics about the process, it's important to understand the context in which the work happens. One way to do that is to compare the more familiar individual coaching experience with what happens in a team coaching environment. We will see that, in addition to the fundamental attributes they have in common, there are significant differences between the two that impact how coach and coachee interact.

Coaching Is Coaching. Yes, and . . .

Coaching is now a familiar tool for personal and professional development. With the rising interest in team coaching, a natural question arises: "How is team coaching different, and what does that mean in terms of effective delivery?" In fact, individual and team coaching share a great deal of common ground. Fundamental coaching competencies and skills will be familiar for those making a transition to coaching teams. That glossary of individual coaching skills still applies, but there will be variations and adjustments to make for teams because of the shift from one-on-one to one-on-many. You will learn more about the specifics of team coaching competencies and skills in chapters 6 through 10, the content of which is based on more than 20 years of coaching both individuals and teams.

Different at the Start

One of the fundamental differences between individual and team coaching is where the coachee is at the beginning. For individuals, there is a high level of commitment from the start, even if it falters later. There's a change the coachee wants to make or a goal a coachee wants to achieve, so the coachee has engaged a coach to help make that happen. The value of coaching is apparent and it's personal.

In contrast, when working with a team there is likely to be quite a mix of attitudes and reactions to the prospect of team coaching. There may be some enthusiastic team members eager to start. There will be some who are indifferent; some who are skeptical; some who are passively or even actively resistant; some who are in the mode of, "Let's wait and see how this unfolds." There may be questions about the reasons for the team coaching; some team members may be suspicious of the motives. There are likely to be questions about the process. With some teams, there may be an underlying feeling of being judged, which triggers defensiveness.

The team coach starts with a team that's often all over the map. There may be some level of compliance, but not likely wholehearted commitment from the team as a whole. We know that trust and relationship connection are key to effective coaching. With teams, that will take time and attention. The threshold that marks the shift from "mixed" to "more aligned and engaged" may be elusive at the start of the work with teams, but the process of coaching over time builds that connection.

Coaching Focus

The coaching focus is also different. With individuals, the focus is on a future vision, something the coachee wants to accomplish. The coachee is looking for stepping-stones to reach that goal, and it's personal.

For teams, there is a stronger focus on the current state of critical, time-sensitive issues that affect team performance. The context of the coaching has a different, present-tense, "this is business" energy to it.

The Coaching Environment

In order to be effective in our work, part of our role as coaches is to create an environment that supports change: a safe environment for individuals or for team members to become vulnerable in ways that promote engagement and deeper conversation. With individual coachees, there is a single relationship to consider. There is simplicity and clarity in the design of the coaching alliance.

In the work with teams there will be relationships on multiple levels. There is the obvious relationship between the coach and the team, and with it, the need to set expectations, uncover assumptions, and clarify roles. The coaching environment also includes the relationships between team members. In order to create a safe environment for doing the work with the team, there needs to be safety within the team to have that courageous conversation. On a practical level this means having team agreements that support that safe environment with practices that keep those agreements fresh and relevant.

There is also a special relationship between the coach and the team leader. Very often it's the team leader who initiates the inquiry for team coaching and provides the initial background. As team coach, there is an accountability relationship to the team leader and by extension, to the organization, and this relationship is different from the relationship with the team as a whole. Intentional design of these multiple relationships is crucial to team coaching success.

The Structure of the Conversation

With individuals, coachees speak to the coach directly, whether it's a virtual or an in-person session. In a systems-based approach to working with teams, coaches are certainly tuned in to individual voices, but coaches listening for the voice of the system hear that team voice only indirectly, through the voices of individual team members and through the coach's ability to listen below the surface of the conversation.

The team has its focus on the issue at hand and the different positions team members have on that issue. As the team engages in that conversation, coaches observe and listen to how the team interacts, looking for the dynamics that show up as repeating patterns that impact team performance.

To be clear, listening for the voice of the team is **not** the same as working toward homogenous consensus. Sometimes the metaphorical music the team is creating is made up of chaotic, clashing notes. The job of the team coach is not to make the music more harmonious; that would be the team's job if that is important to the team. The coach's job is to highlight the diversity of tones that make up this unique team harmony. In the work with teams, the goal is to reveal all of the voices, even the unpopular and marginalized voices. Coaches encourage the different voices and highlight that diversity. For a coach, this is an opportunity to be curious on behalf of the team: what's it like on this team when you have two really strong and apparently contrary ways of addressing this issue?

Where the Impact Lies

With individuals, the conversation is a private, confidential, one-on-one dialogue. It's simple and efficient. A coaching question elicits an answer. One question equals one response.

With teams, the conversation is public, and that can be edgy and vulnerable. That's why there is so much emphasis on creating and integrating agreements around team conversation; it helps ensure the psychological safety necessary for truly open, honest, and productive team conversation.

With teams, there is an important and essential shift in emphasis from dialogue to discussion. The coach's question is designed to initiate a team conversation. The ultimate value is in creating engaged, productive conversation among team members because that's where the work of the team happens. Coaches need to be alert to times when the team is talking mostly to the coach, explaining, or venting, rather than talking to each other. It could be time to redirect the flow, and it can be as simple as saying, "Tell your team members what you want them to know."

Worth noting: sometimes it's easier and more comfortable for team members to have a conversation with the coach than it is to have a possibly more challenging conversation with other team members.

Complex and Constantly Changing

Another key difference between individual coaching and team coaching is the sheer complexity of everything going on. With a team of say 10 members, there will be 10 different points of view, 10 different agendas, different personalities, different expectations, different priorities and styles of communication.

It might look something like this: The coach has an ear tuned to the content of the issue under discussion by the team—an important but chronic issue the team seems unable to resolve. At the same time, the coach is aware of where they are in the agenda for the session: the session is running about 20 minutes behind schedule. The coach is tracking the action items the team is accountable for and simultaneously aware of a stagnant or resistant energy in the room and the now noticeable side conversation between two team members. In team coaching, the coach's attention is constantly pulled in many directions at once. Coaches need to choose when and how to interact in the process instantly because the moment for that impulse is already passing. In this one short paragraph we've identified a number of things the coach might do in the moment and there are certainly a dozen other possibilities as well. There is no recipe card that will have the answer ready. The good news is, whatever the coach chooses, there will be instant feedback about how that worked and information about continuing on that path or taking a different path.

Team coaches are always dancing in the moment. That's the nature of coaching, whether it's individuals or teams. With teams, we're dancing to the team's music, with often multiple, sometimes conflicting tunes, and the music is constantly changing. That's the nature of the work with teams and why working with teams is a dance that requires exceptional agility.

The Process Overview

A successful team coaching program will have these three phases:

Phase One: Discovery and Assessment
Identify the current state of the team through discovery and assessment; engage the team in setting priorities, action planning, and accountability.

Phase Two: Ongoing Coaching

A schedule of team coaching sessions focused on acquiring more effective team practices. Ongoing coaching provides the structure to support change and learning in order to achieve team goals for improved team results.

Phase 3: Completion and Next Steps

At the end of this initial team coaching journey, the team looks back to review the learning, measure results, and celebrate where the team is today; the team then looks to the future and plans next steps.

CAVEAT: The recommended process described here has a proven track record for improving team performance. We know it works. We also know everything about the process needs to be customized for the team situation. These are guidelines; there will certainly be exceptions and variations in a hundred different ways. This is not cookie-cutter coaching. There are lanes for this road, but coach and team will travel as they will, and an off-road experience is an alternative.

Phase One: Discovery and Assessment

Discovery

The team coaching process starts with a discovery conversation to understand the team's situation and explore the potential fit for team coaching. This is typically a meeting between the coach and team leader, or sometimes a representative from HR. It is a conversation to determine whether there is alignment between the team's need and what a team coaching process can deliver. If there is a good fit, the discovery process leads to a proposal for a team coaching project, or memo of understanding that sets out the purpose, process, and expected outcomes. The discovery process lays the groundwork, so it is very important at this early stage to make sure there is shared understanding about the process and the expected outcomes. The impact and value of team coaching will be measured against this early understanding.

An alternative discovery process would include individual interviews with team members or a group interview with the whole team.

This would be more inclusive and provide a wider net for understanding the current situation and issues. It would also give the coach direct observation of the team dynamics in action. In our experience this interview option is more often included at the assessment stage after a team coaching project has been given a budget green light to proceed.

Discovery involves gathering basic information about the makeup of the team and the current team circumstances behind the inquiry for team coaching. But there is more to discovery than just information gathering. Discovery often includes education about how the process works, including clarity about the roles for team coach, the team, the team leader, and how the organization's interests will be served.

Another important aspect of this discovery conversation is an emphasis on uncovering assumptions and expectations. This is especially important if the team leader or sponsor has no previous experience with a team coaching process, and it is very useful even with those who have some experience; it helps to learn what was most effective and least effective in the earlier project.

There are two fundamental goals for discovery: one, find the need, and two, check for the fit with team coaching.

- **Find the need**

  According to our data, there are at least several thousand potential reasons for engaging in a team-development project. Here are some typical examples:

- Merger/acquisition/reorganization. A need to accelerate the process of integrating team members so that the team can be more effective quickly.
- Underperforming. A need to identify team issues, create a plan for improvement, set specific targets and monitor progress.[88]
- Mission critical. Project teams are typical examples. Time and money—often very large amounts of money—are at stake. Healthcare teams also qualify; teamwork is regularly and literally a life-or-death issue.[89] All senior management teams fall into this mission-critical category.
- A newly formed team is a candidate for team coaching as a way to create a baseline picture of assumptions and create a culture committed to performance excellence from the start.

It's obviously important that the team coach have a clear understanding of the team situation. It's also important to emphasize that in this interview the team coach is more than a note-taking journalist. The coach's job is to probe and be curious, wondering, for example, "Is this a team issue? Or a personnel issue? Or is this a team issue disguised as a personnel issue?" A complete discovery process looks beyond circumstances to understand the underlying pressures and challenges for the team.

As complete and forthright as this conversation might be, it will be an incomplete picture because the rest of the team is typically not included in the discussion. Although it is the basis for the initial project agreement, it is just one person's point of view—the team leader. As valuable as that insight is, there will be inevitable bias based on the team leader's experience in the role and the team leader's expectations for team performance—particularly this team's performance. Discovery establishes a starting point. The assessment stage will be more inclusive, taking the conversation much deeper and providing more clarity.

- **Check for the fit**

There are two simple questions that address the question of fit for this work: Why team coaching? Why now?

The first question gets at the reasons there is a need, at least as seen through the eyes of the team leader. The question also begins an explanation by the team leader that will reveal the team leader's assumptions and expectations about what team coaching can deliver. This creates an opportunity to clarify and create viable expectations for process and outcomes.

There is a third purpose for discovery that is an accompanying result of the process. The team coach naturally creates a relationship with the team leader or sponsor simply by having this early conversation. The team leader exposes some level of vulnerability in the discovery process, sharing information about issues facing the team. This relationship between team coach and team leader will affect the ongoing process because the team will be watching how the coach and the team leader relate to one another.

Assessment

Once there is agreement upon a compelling need and a good fit, the next step involves assessing where the team is today—information that clarifies the team's strengths and areas for improvement. This leads eventually to an action plan for team development. The goal of coaching is to help the team move from where they are to where they want to be: to move from Point A to Point B. The obvious question then is "Where is Point A? Where do we start?" There are a variety of ways to create this "starting line."[90,91]

One common approach is to conduct individual interviews with team members, or for the sake of efficiency, conduct one group interview with the whole team. The private, one-on-one interviews are likely to be more candid simply because they are private instead of public. Because of the personal connection inherent in the team coach's conversation with individual team members, the interview process builds a level of relationship and trust at a very early stage, and this can be a strong foundation on which to build the sometimes challenging work of coaching the team.

There are disadvantages to individual interviews too. They are time consuming and sometimes turn into a release valve for team members to vent and complain. They can test a coach's ability to stay neutral and curious simply because of the personalities involved. The interview process also can have the effect of putting the responsibility on the coach to interpret the interview responses and decide on a direction for the team.

An alternative to interviews is an anonymous team assessment instrument that captures the input from all team members and provides a view that paints a portrait of the team, showing where the team says they are strong and where there is opportunity for learning and development. Full disclosure: the company that the authors cofounded, Team Coaching International, was formed to support this team-assessment process in order to conveniently and quickly create that whole team picture so the work of team coaching can get underway.

The online instrument, the TCI Team Diagnostic, is based on the team-effectiveness model described in this book. The items that team members score are all written from the collective, team point of view. For example, "On our team we have clear goals." Or, "On our team we tend to avoid conflict." The outcome of the assessment is a clear graphic picture of the team's view of its relative strength in each of the 14 team effectiveness measures. More information about the assessment tools can be found in the section "TCI Four Integrated Assessment Tools." By the way, many coaches who use an assessment instrument like the TCI Team Diagnostic also do interviews as a way to personally connect with the team. They find it creates a relationship basis for work with the team; the coach becomes a known quantity before the work begins.

Getting Started

The launch of a team coaching process is a crucial opportunity to create a solid foundation for the ongoing work with the team.[92] A best practice is to hold an initial meeting with the team to provide context for the project, clarify roles, and set expectations. This gathering gives the team leader an opportunity to position the importance of the team coaching initiative, specifically for this team, and underscore the team leader's endorsement. With a virtual team this might be done in a one-hour or 90-minute introductory session. When the team can meet in person, a couple of hours might be enough, or it could be part of a half-day or full-day agenda.

In an ideal world this session will happen before the team meets to look at and discuss assessment results; in fact it often takes place before the assessment process. We also recognize that this "ideal world" scenario may not always be possible. Under time and commitment pressure, the team coach's only interaction with the team and introduction to the process might have to happen via email, an option that is far from ideal. A team coaching engagement is a significant investment on the part of the team and the organization. Because this initial introduction to the process is such a valuable step to ensure the success of the work, we are very strong advocates for committing the time and budget to do it well, making the most of the investment.

Design the Working Relationships

The agenda for the first team session in the coaching process will depend on what was covered in the introductory meeting with the team. An agenda might include resetting the important context for this team. A short refresher on expectations for the different roles might also be included.

This process will include creating alignment on the relationship between coach and team, clarity about the role of team leader in the process, and possibly a discussion with the team about how the process and team progress are reported to leadership in the organization, if reporting is expected. Most of all, this step will set the guidelines for the interaction between team members. We often say the measure of success for this work is in the quality and courage of the conversation team members have with one another. That's where the real work happens.

Reveal Assessment Results

We are now ready to begin the process that defines the baseline for the team: here is where the team is today, at Point A. No surprise, when the team is invited to give a candid evaluation of how effectively they work together, there is often a natural tendency for teams to focus on what's *not* working and skip what *is* working. It's also normal for teams to stay quiet while they monitor the safety level for speaking up, or they wait for the team leader to speak first.

Obviously, it is important to uncover those improvement areas the team identifies. Just as important is the value to the team of being clear about what *is* working, and not just for the celebratory effect. Those areas where the team is strong can be leverage points to support areas of development where the team is not as strong. For example, a team might score low or have complaints around communication but score high or generally agree that the team is strong when it comes to accountability. Combining those two pieces of information results in an opportunity to establish goals and practices designed to improve team protocol around communication and then rely on the team's natural strength for holding one another accountable to improve that key area.

There are basically two outcomes from this process of unfolding assessment results. One goal is an engaged, open, honest, and generative conversation between team members about the dynamics that impact the team's ability to achieve results. This is not a generalized discussion of, for example, "the importance of trust on teams." As much as possible it is a conversation that looks at specific situations and team behavior to point out where, specifically, the team sees trust working, where it is missing and why, or the conditions that consistently undermine trust.

The second outcome from this team discussion on assessment

results, is awareness of the patterns in how the team interacts. In fact, how the team manages *this* conversation mirrors how the team manages any other conversation. Team dynamics are out in the open and observable. This is valuable insight for the coach, and it is valuable for the team because as the team becomes aware of their habitual ways of interacting, they can begin to make choices about what they want to change.

In the course of engaging in the assessment conversation, there will be a natural momentum that moves from noticing standard operating patterns and their impact on team performance, to a desire to take action to do something about those areas that need work. The primary goal is a better understanding of the team's dynamics and how those dynamics affect specific areas or issues that are important to the team. A team that wants to improve its decision making makes that commitment not because they crave a higher score or recognition, but because poor decision making is a problem that is hobbling team performance. This becomes an opportunity for teams to get specific about where there are breakdowns in decision making and why.

Leads to an Action Plan

Coaching naturally progresses from an expansive exploration of possibilities to defining goals and action steps.[93,94] Simply raising awareness of team dynamics, especially as those dynamics impact important team priorities, is valuable but insufficient. As a coaching model, we expect to move from talking to doing.

The action plan sets out the agenda for change. Think of this as a map for the team's journey. That road ahead is actually a two-lane road. In one lane is the work *of* the team—the business results for which the team is responsible. The second lane is the work *on* the team—the team dynamics. As the team starts its journey, teams are clarifying the strengths this team brings to the process. The assessment stage puts a pin in the map for the team to see "We are here based on our bearings from these 14 landmarks." Now it is time to look down the road and determine where they want to be in the future and create a plan to reach that destination.

There is great value in hearing team members describe the ground conditions as they speak directly to one another about their experiences.

This is the heart of coaching: rich, candid, conversation that engages the team. It is a process that can be messy. It can also be cathartic as team members finally get to share, in a safe environment, the pent-up opinions, needs, and desires that have been unspoken or shared in cliques or private conversations. Coach and team are creating an environment where it is safe to speak up, where team members feel seen *and* heard. It's an environment that will serve the team throughout the coaching process.

Phase Two: Ongoing Team Coaching

Provide the structure to support change and learning in order to achieve team goals for improved results. Hold the team accountable.

On the team's journey to effective results, this is where good ideas and intentions turn into real-life, everyday action everyone can see. The ongoing team coaching sessions provide the support structure for change. These sessions keep the team on track toward its goals and engaged in the process.

The structure and frequency of these ongoing sessions vary according to the needs and availability of the team. Most teams opt for monthly sessions of two or three hours over a period of anywhere from four to eight months. Fewer than four months doesn't give the team enough time to integrate new behavior. Some teams will want longer sessions and more time between sessions; many coaches also favor longer sessions, but experience shows that with less frequent sessions, momentum is lost, practices forgotten, and the "busyness" of everyday life takes precedence. Commitment to a consistent schedule is key to maintaining momentum for team development.

In-person sessions are much preferred, but if that's not possible because the team is geographically dispersed, then videoconferencing is the next best option. Successful virtual team coaching sessions will definitely require additional training for team members.[95] A true team coaching session in a virtual format needs a shift in mindset. This is a very different experience with a different, deeper intent compared to the typical conference call. There is a level of being present and engaged in a team coaching session that sets a higher standard than the experience most of us are familiar with, where minimum attention is sufficient to get by.

Team Session Emphasis: Action and Learning

In order for these ongoing sessions to have value for the team, and therefore to maintain or build stronger engagement, it is vital that sessions are clearly relevant to the team's everyday experience. The work in these sessions should lead to improvement that makes a visible difference to team members in ways that deliver improved business results and a more collaborative, sustainable environment.

The effort to practice new skills and behaviors is only valued by the team if that effort leads to results that matter. If improved communication is a team goal, there needs to be a clear, compelling reason. The central question is, what will a focus on this area (in this example, communication) give the team that will make a difference? In order to achieve that improvement, team members will need to interact with one another in new ways. The momentum needed to continue on this course comes from experiencing new results and consciously focusing on what the team is learning from the process. Not every new initiative will work; learning what doesn't work for the team is just as important. Edison found thousands of ways to not make a light bulb. Both taking action and learning from the action taken are essential to building new strengths as a team.

One of the best ways to combine these two parallel purposes of action and learning is to have the team engage in discussion that focuses on an important and current team issue. As team coach, your role is to track the interaction of the team and to reflect or play back what you observe about the team interaction. This will help the team see with fresh eyes how members interact. This will raise awareness about what works and what gets in the way. It will support the process of learning new behavior. For the team, this is an ideal situation where team members do work that is important, timely, and relevant, and they practice new ways of working together. This is not role-playing some aspect of team interaction; it's the real thing in the crucible of producing results.

ACTION and LEARNING Coaching Session Example:

The team: Senior leadership team. Financial services organization. IT operations support.

The issue: When problems arise on the floor, managers and supervisors escalate the problem solving up the ladder to members of the leadership team. The leadership team needs to empower (and train where necessary) the people closest to the problems.

The challenge: This pattern of delegating up is part of the organizational culture.

The process: The team gathered for their monthly team coaching session. The agenda included time for the team to discuss this important issue with the coach observing. The team coach's role was to monitor the team's process and interaction. The coach was able to intervene from time to time to highlight patterns and roles. At the end, the coach led a debrief conversation with the team about what they noticed and what they learned that they could bring into everyday team interaction.

Key turning point: This is a team that spoke up easily and didn't always agree. Team members felt they had permission to take strong positions. However, the team coach noticed that whenever the topic got close to a point where a decision or action step was called for, the team showed a tendency to defer to the team leader. It was a living example of what was happening in the rest of their organization; the issue the team wanted to address was actually being modeled at the top. This raised a question for the team: "Other than simply habit, what keeps team members from taking initiative for leadership? Simply restating an opinion, or remaining quiet appear to be the two common responses on this team. What else could this team do?"

Tracking Progress

You've heard this before in one variation or another: "What gets measured gets improved." Setting clear goals and creating action plans to achieve those goals is key to getting to the journey's end successfully. It's also useful to check the map from time to time to ensure coach and team are still on course. What that means in practical terms is the creation of a way to measure progress. In our approach to team improvement, that improvement will be measured on two parallel tracks: business results and improved team dynamics.

The fundamental question is "How will you measure success?" One team track will focus on business outcomes and metrics. For some teams, that will be easy; the tracking measures, the team KPIs, are already in place. For other teams, establishing specific and measurable metrics will be a new exercise. They will engage in a conversation focused on "What is our contribution to organizational results, and how do we measure that?"

At the same time, it is just as important for the team to track improvement in areas that lead to better collaboration and a more sustainable environment for the work of the team. This progress in team dynamics can be measured in many ways. A team might track a new practice. For example, after a team meeting, team members might score the team's decision-making process on a scale of 1 to 10. Average the scores for all team members, and if it isn't a consensus 10, the team coach would ask, "What would make team decision making a 10?"

As with any good map, tracking the journey will also give the team information about when it's time to change course. The original action plan sets out a direction and plan, but as the team proceeds on its journey of ongoing coaching, it may become clear that there is a new, sharper focus on the intended outcome, and that will require a route adjustment. Part of the value of tracking is the conversation it brings to the table. Questions come up as the discussion looks at measurement results: "What is our measuring telling us? What are we learning? Are we measuring the right things?"

Phase Three: Completion and Next Steps

At the end of this initial team coaching journey, the team looks back to review the learning and measure results, celebrates where the team is today, and then looks forward to plan next steps.

Capture the Learning

The team has arrived at its destination, usually some months after the initial team session. This completion step is an important conclusion to the process, just as important as a well-prepared and effective launch.

The value in the "look back" is in the rich harvest of learning.[96] What does the team know now that can help the team as it moves forward?

Measure Results

We are strong believers in following up here with a new assessment based as closely as possible on the format and experience of the initial assessment. This is a highly effective way to clearly measure team progress over time. Even if some of the performance measures slip, there is great value in the conversation about why that happened. The results give the coach and team another opportunity to mine the experience for deeper learning. Measurement also adds to the completion process by drawing a new baseline. This is the new starting line for team development.

Next Steps

A successful team coaching engagement requires commitment over many months and a willingness to address sometimes thorny issues, especially issues about team dynamics. It can be quite challenging. The reward is a more effective and collaborative team. Yes, there are exceptions. From time to time we see team results that reveal minimal or poor outcomes. But the vast majority of teams make this completion step with pride of accomplishment. Before getting into new action planning it is worthwhile to pause here to acknowledge the effort and celebrate the learning, the progress, and the team's clearer identity.

Now it's time to build on the experience and learning by setting new goals. Moving forward may include additional team coaching, or it may simply be a form of self-coaching by the team. One of the goals for this process from the team coach's point of view is to transfer to the team awareness and skills that improve the team's competence in working together effectively. The goal is *not* long-term dependence on the coach. Next steps might also include some form of regular check-in with the team coach to maintain momentum with the team or to address issues that arise. Some teams do an annual team-performance review as a form of performance management at the team level.

If the team has not already invited stakeholder feedback, requesting that feedback in preparation for completion and planning next steps is especially timely. That feedback provides additional input in designing a next course of action.

Completion gives the team the opportunity to reflect on the whole process, what the team has learned, and how that supports the team moving forward. Time for reflection and completion conversation also helps the team identify effective practices and, by the way, ineffective practices, and it helps sharpen the team's identity and common purpose. The team knows what to repack for the next journey and what can be left behind. This is the time to draw a new team map. "Where do we go from here?" and "How will the team hold itself accountable?"

Team Coaching Process Case Study

Industry: Medical/pharmaceutical

Team: Management team of 10

Situation: Reorganization within the company resulted in two teams merging into one. Existing history of poor internal communication and distrust between merging teams. A pressing need to accelerate integration, leave old issues behind, and create a fresh identity to improve performance.

Process: TCI Team Diagnostic assessment deployed. Baseline results revealed. Action plan created. Seven-month program with four monthly team coaching sessions. Some transition of team membership. Follow-up assessment to reveal progress and plan next steps.

Results:

Productivity Highlights
  Alignment +62 percent
  Proactive +49 percent
  Accountability +34 percent

Positivity Highlights
  Trust +73 percent
  Optimism +59 percent
  Constructive Interaction +55 percent

(figure 5-1) Obviously, not all teams achieve results as dramatic as these, but this is what is possible.

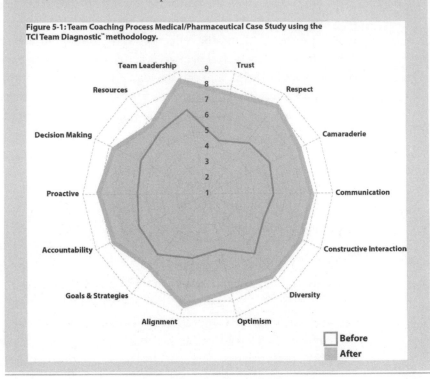

Figure 5-1: Team Coaching Process Medical/Pharmaceutical Case Study using the TCI Team Diagnostic™ methodology.

Summary

We started this chapter with a question: "How do we transfer what best teams do well to all teams?" The answer involves behavioral change, learning, and practice. The ideal support for that process is the team coaching model. That support structure for teams emphasizes meeting goals and achieving results in business terms; it also includes improving the team's capacity to work effectively together. Building team strength and ability not only helps ensure that teams meet the initial outcomes, it creates teams that are more agile, creative, and self-sufficient.

We outlined a three-phase coaching process for teams. It's a process that is well established, proven in the real world of teams, and a process that consistently delivers results for teams of all kinds.

For Team Coaches

- ❑ Whether preparing to coach individuals or teams, in your experience what are the most important questions to answer at the discovery stage?
- ❑ What are the red flags for you that a team is not a good fit for team coaching?
- ❑ If you are already coaching or working with teams, what has been your biggest challenge in shifting to teams? If your experience is primarily one-on-one, what do you anticipate will be the major challenges?

For Team Leaders

- ❑ A coaching model is essentially about action steps and learning, in order to integrate change over time. How might you design your version of a team-development model to work with your own team? What would you say is most important to pay attention to in that structure?
- ❑ What are ways you could measure team development over time? Qualitatively or quantitatively?
- ❑ Based on what you already know about your team, what are three or four things this team needs to learn in order to improve team performance and collaboration?

PART 2

Five Essential Competencies for Effective Work with Teams

Coaching a team is enormously gratifying work. It can also be enormously chaotic, turbulent, emotional, frustrating, and volatile. Team coaching shares similarities with individual, one-on-one coaching, and yet it is very different, with a unique set of challenges. Facing a team of 10, there is simply a lot more going on, and it's occurring on multiple levels, with mixed priorities, personalities, and styles of expression. To be effective with the team requires a special set of competencies and team coaching skills, an awareness of the complex relationships, and the ability to act with confidence in the midst of constantly shifting dynamics.

Years of experience working with teams and training team coaches have helped us distill the essential abilities needed to work effectively with teams. The result of this experience and exploration is presented in part 2. These five chapters cover the five team coaching competencies and associated team coaching skills. We have included stories and examples, exercises, and sample coaching dialogue, all to help clarify and bring to life this essential core material.

These five competencies are present at all times. The art of team coaching is in the choices you make as you observe and interact with the team. Each of the five shines a particular light on what is happening in the team coaching. Each of the competencies provides a unique way of exercising your awareness.

You can think of these five competencies as a pentasphere of shining lights that illuminates the living system that is the team. They are all equally important. They are not a sequence; they are simultaneous. The job of the team coach is to have access to all of these and then choose in an instant what to attend to. They are the keys to team coaching mastery.

CHAPTER 6

Start Here: The Team Is a Living System

Essential Team Coaching Competency No. 1

The Ability to Be System Aware

Human beings are social animals. We gather in community; we have an urge to belong and the biological wiring to detect the signals that make it possible to know the necessary behavior for belonging in that community. It's our nature. Teams are a microcosm of that instinct and naturally form collective rules for how to survive in the system. Those rules are not written down; they are not in the employee handbook. New team members learn the rules by observing and by touching the hot wire or being rewarded with a pat on the back. This awareness is crucial for team coaches because the system is always in charge and always in play.

Based on the model we've described, imagine you're a new team member, about to join a team that you know is High Productivity but Low Positivity. Without any more information than that, you would know how to fit in. You would know the cultural expectations, the underlying reward system, and how to behave to get ahead.

Team members learn a certain way of communicating or not communicating. Teams develop strong patterns and repeatable ways of interacting. Underneath what we see and hear on the surface is the operating system for this team. As coaches, being aware that we are working with a living system helps shift our attention from individuals and one-on-one relationships to the team as a whole. Understanding the ways the system influences team behavior gives us a clearer picture of the team's operating code and a way to identify the pressures that impact team performance.

This awareness of the team as a living system—with personality, strengths and weaknesses, protective rules of behavior—is crucial to effective work with teams.[97,98] We observe the way the team interacts and then look deeper to the undercurrents that influence how the team interacts. As we have said, the team is a living system. Like all living systems, it behaves in its best interest for its own survival. Whether it is highly functional or mostly dysfunctional is immaterial. Survival of the existing system is life imperative number one.

Team Insight

A masterful team coach is like a cultural team anthropologist with unquenchable curiosity and no judgment, simply sifting through the artifacts of team life, looking to understand the culture of the team. What is valued here? What are the taboos? What happens with this team when it is under attack by real or imagined forces?

Team coaches learn the local language and discover the local deities, rituals, and traditions that are honored by the team. Becoming really competent at seeing the system at work takes experience using that particular lens, but the team is revealing itself in every moment. We like to say, "The way a team does anything is the way a team does everything." You can learn a lot about a team simply by watching how they enter the room for their first team coaching session.

Here's a suggestion: As you watch the team interact in conversation, instead of tracking the content of the conversation, pay attention instead to *how* the team is speaking to one another. Listen for the voice of the team and ask yourself, "What is that voice trying to tell me? What does the team want me to know?" It may be telling you, "Finally. A comfortable conversation; one we've had many times." Or, "Oh, my. That's a topic we don't dare talk about." Or, "This is getting awkward and could become contentious; usually someone will make a joke and break the tension. Then we change topics."

The team is not aware of its own system-ness, the team dynamics. That's the water they swim in every day, so no wonder they don't notice. That's not where individual team members have their attention. They have their attention on their own point of view on the topic at hand. They have their attention on presenting their position, maybe trying to persuade others to that position. They are not tuned in to the currents and tides flowing under the surface that steer the conversation taking place.

Much of our job as team coaches involves pointing the team's attention to these undercurrents. Over time the team becomes more aware, more conscious of how they interact with one another. It is no longer unconscious, default behavior. And by making the invisible become visible, you help the team see itself in new, brighter light. With that awareness, teams are able to make better choices.

Human communities, and this includes teams and groups of all kinds, are adaptive systems, which means they change by receiving and then incorporating feedback. They do so reluctantly because from the system's perspective, change is risky, in fact potentially dangerous to the life of the system. Homeostasis is a powerful adhesive holding the team together. Everyone knows the rules of survival. Even if those rules result in painful or dysfunctional patterns, they are the rules of survival on this team. The pressure is on to abide by those rules.

As team coaches, we are change agents. It's our job to support the team through change steps so the team will perform more effectively, and life on the team will be better. Sometimes we are not very popular. There is a reward for this change, a better individual and team experience. But some days it can seem very distant. There are times when our job as team coaches is to remind teams of the payoff, or help the team envision that new place so that the engine of motivation to face the change continues to propel the team forward.

Team Beliefs Matter

Part of the system experience comes through in what teams believe is possible and what is not possible. Those beliefs, deeply held, impact choices the team is accustomed to making. That's true whether the belief empowers and supports the team, or whether it is a belief that undermines and limits the team. For example, with a focus on team optimism, you can see how a team's beliefs about what is possible actually affects the results the team achieves.[99] On high-performing teams there is a sense that "We can do it!" And so they do, more often than not.

The opposite is also true. Some teams are hobbled by limiting beliefs. No one on the team is saying so out loud, but there is a sense within the team that there are insurmountable barriers that must simply be accepted. It's like a voice whispering in the background, "Yeah, but this will never work." Those underlying beliefs provide a constant justification for the way the team operates. These disempowering team beliefs have a structure that sounds something like this: "We don't have [fill in the blank]." "Ever since [name the event or experience], it's been impossible to [fill in the blank]."

As a team coach, you often hear it in the team conversation; they reach a certain point and can't go further, like driving down the road and coming to a dead end. The same dead end, again. "Looks like we will need to work with purchasing to get an exception. That will be a waste of time." Or, "Scheduling shorter meetings. Great idea. We tried that. It doesn't work." Notice in this last example, a conclusion has been drawn; it's not an observation about a single experiment in the past. That previous experience has now been generalized into a team belief. Sometimes, like this example, there is a small bit of truth in the original story. It could be a particular time when the team hit an obstacle or tried a new way of working together and things didn't work out so smoothly. But over time that small bit can be woven into a firm, unquestionable team belief, and that belief sabotages team performance.

In the same way that individuals continue to create more of what they believe is true, teams look for evidence to confirm their team view, and they disregard evidence that doesn't fit that paradigm. Every individual, every team has a personal cosmology that explains how the world works. Identifying and exposing those beliefs gives teams the light of day to evaluate how the team wants to plan and act.

Notice What the Team Values

Teams coalesce around values just as they do around beliefs. The actions team members take are influenced by team values.[100] When teams value punctuality and accountability, those teams are on time and they follow through. If there are team members who don't abide by the unspoken team values, there will be consequences.

Team values are an expression of the team's identity.[101] "Who we are" as a team shows up in the values, and so does "Who we are not." If you look deeper into how a team chooses, you will hear some version of "That's how we do things around here" or "This is how we treat each other." Looking underneath, you begin to see "Oh, this is a value for this team." For example, after observing the team for awhile you might conclude, "Getting into action" is clearly a value for this team.

Some values are not especially helpful. A team value of "smooth sailing" or "don't rock the boat" could easily keep the peace but not allow the free flow of open conversation and potential constructive interaction the team needs.

There are many ways to help teams clarify those unique team values—separate from the usual list of corporate values. One way is to invite the team to recall a particularly successful recent accomplishment. It might be a project completed or a decision made, perhaps under especially challenging circumstances. Then have the team look for the values that supported the team, the uncompromising stand the team took to achieve that result. Woven into the experience will be examples of team values.

Another option is to look at the opposite: a situation that the team would really rather forget. Somewhere in the breakdown—not in the circumstances but in the ways the team responded—they will likely find examples of where their values went missing. The outcome from that experience won't change, but the insight gained about the importance of living their own values can fortify a team when they face new challenges.

Here's a way of distinguishing between values and beliefs. Where team values are integral to the system's way of operating, a team belief is conditional; it's part of a mindset or mental model. They both influence

> Example of a team belief: A competitor introduces a shiny new product and this activates the team to respond by pushing for development of their own answer. There's an underlying belief that "we're always playing catch-up."
>
> Example of a team value: A competitor introduces a shiny new product and the team meets to consider their response. The conversation is open, inclusive, courageous. There is a team value at play— "we value listening to all of the team voices; disagreement is a healthy sign of creativity."

behavior, and it's in team behavior where they become visible. A belief would focus more externally on the circumstance and how the team chooses to respond; a value would be an internal system code of behavior.

The System Lives in a Time Continuum

As a living system, the team has a past—or at least a formation point in time—a current state, and an anticipated future. Because it is a human system, those time dimensions have influence.

Teams have a history; they have a journey they have been on. Over the course of that earlier lifetime, they had experiences that shaped team attitudes and beliefs, which in turn form expectations for today. A grand victory as a team in the past can boost the confidence in the team today. That grand victory becomes part of the team's identity and an important part of the team's narrative. It's a story they tell new team members. New team members learn about those victories and take on the mantle passed down by those who came before.

The past can also harbor ghosts that affect the team. The scandal or ineptitude surrounding a former manager or team member can haunt the current team, and the team might not even be aware of that impact. It's like a shadow falling on the team. It can be the other way around too. A particularly inspiring team member or charismatic leader can haunt the team months or even years after leaving. The team laments, "If only Georgina or Lens were still here."

Historical events or time periods within the organization can also influence the current team, dragging it down from performing well. Turn the clock back to the financial crisis of 2009; remember the mood within the organization. You didn't have to be a team in financial services to feel the gloom and helplessness. With layoffs seemingly opening trap doors in the floor every week, no job felt safe. This was a shared experience on a global scale, influencing every team in every organization.

Teams have a present "state" that the team, as a system, wants to protect and preserve. The underlying beliefs are the truth: this is the way the world works around here. The unspoken message is, adjust or adapt because "this is reality." Teams don't often question those beliefs because to do so would be to question the natural order.

These underlying beliefs about the team and the team's circumstances help shape the team's perspective, whether that perspective is optimistic or pessimistic, whether the team feels empowered or powerless. "Who we are" reflects the mindset of the team and the team's identity. It has tremendous influence on the morale of the team, and how the team approaches everyday action and decision making.[102] This cultural mindset influences how the team deals with success and failure, how the team responds to change and uncertainty.

Teams also have a sense of the future ahead of them. Teams have expectations and operate with those expectations. You can feel it in the attitude of the team; it's in the air, in the posture, in the tone of the informal conversation.

For Coaches: A New Mindset and Perspective

For some team coaches, seeing the team as a system may require looking with new eyes. In a way, it's like this: you can't see the wind, but you can see the effect of the wind in the movement of the leaves in the trees. Seeing the system may require shifting from attention on people or individual relationships to attention on the whole—recognizing that the essence of the team is in the spaces *between* the people. It is an entity without form that is more than the parts. There is a "voice of the team" speaking, separate from the individuals.

For team members and team leaders, this is also a mindset shift. A team is still both: the individual team members and the collective system. Seeing the individuals is familiar. When team members can also identify with the team and who "we" are together, what's at stake is at the team level, not just the personal level.

Whether team coach or team member, this is a practice of seeing with new eyes. It takes a soft focus of the whole, versus the laser focus on the individuals, like the illustrations you see that ask you to find three tall ships hidden in the drawing. At first it seems impossible, and then suddenly you can make them out from the complexity. Then it seems obvious and you wonder why you couldn't see them before.

One way to practice that soft focus is to watch the team interact and listen to the flow of conversation. Pay less attention to tracking the content of the conversation and more to the dynamics at play in the conversation. Imagine you do not speak the language. What are the patterns you see? How do team members interact? What is the underlying tone of the conversation?[103] Where is it getting warmer? Where is it growing colder? What is this team's natural tempo?

Seeing the system is a first step in really understanding our role as team coaches. When we can see the team as a living system, we create a new relationship, which is more than a combination of many individual relationships. As team coaches, this system—the team—is our coachee. We are there to support this team through a growth and development process. To be coach for a team starts with an understanding and appreciation for this systemic entity and our relationship to it. The questions we ask reflect that: Where is the team today? What does this team want? Where is this team strong?

The team is a living system with a life of its own. It is powerful. In fact, the system is stronger and more resilient than any one individual team member. You may have seen this firsthand: a strong, bright, eager new leader joins a team with great plans and ambitions. Three things can happen. One, the team smiles and nods and nothing changes. Two, the team drags its feet, has objections or questions; there is often a great deal of off-line processing required. It can feel like pushing smoke. The third is actual change.

If you work as an executive coach, you know this from the conversations you've had with your coachees. The coaching conversations frequently focus on the leader's relationship with the team. The team leader may have great vision and energy for taking the team in a new direction, but the system is saying "no."

Team Coaching Skills

System Aware

In part 2, each chapter provides context for one of the five team coaching competencies, then introduces team coaching skills associated with that competency. In many cases you will also find sample dialogue to illustrate use of the skill and exercises you can use with a team that link to that skill. Note that some skills could just as easily be included under more than one competency; there is not a binding link. The familiar glossary of coaching skills generally applies to teams as well. We have selected certain skills especially relevant to team coaching or common skills with a particular orientation for working with teams.

Curious Coaching Questions

Simple open-ended questions that invite exploration and reflection.

Sometimes referred to as "powerful questions," curious coaching questions send teams in a wider search rather than to a specific destination. At their best they are provocative, guiding respondents into uncharted territory. There is often a momentary pause as team members consider the question.

Part of the skill in using curious questions with teams is acquiring the patience to wait, rather than jumping in to fill the silence or assuming the question wasn't clear. The hesitation in the response from the team could be the strength of the question asked and the need for a little time for reflection. It might also be team members sorting out the impact of speaking up in the group. Curious questions are expansive. You can feel a broad landscape of possibilities.

The opposite of open-ended, curious questions is questions that have definitive answers. Closed-ended questions typically result in simple "yes" or "no" answers. These questions often start with "Is?" "Does?" "Do?" "Can?" or "Will?" For example, "Is that the only way?" "Can you implement that change?" The answers come quickly. Instead of a range of responses from different perspectives, with closed-ended questions there is finality, a sense of completion, discussion closed.

The best powerful questions tend to be short. For example, "What do you want?" and "What else?" Longer, more complex questions force the team to spend energy understanding the intent of the inquiry. That need to understand shifts the thought process from a mode of reflection to a mode of analysis, and you can feel the difference in energy—from a feeling of opening up to one of closing down. Here's a simple guideline: most curious questions start with "What." For example, "What's important about that?" "Six months from now, what would you like to celebrate?" "What if it were easy?" "What would you create?"

"How" questions tend to invite tactics, problem solving, action planning—very useful outcomes, but be aware of that shift in direction. Be sure that it is the right time to move into action, that the exploration is complete. There certainly is an appropriate time for analytical thinking, for getting down to the details, for getting specific answers to planning and process questions. Most teams, team leaders, and team coaches are well practiced in that form of question and response. This realm of curious coaching questions may not be as familiar.

Every question sends coachees somewhere to find an answer. Curious coaching questions send teams on a deeper, more reflective discovery mission. Questions of this kind are at the very heart of coaching.

Summarize

To recap the conversation in order to help get everyone on the same page.

Keep this skill handy. It's one you can draw on over and over, and there are times when it will save you when you're lost—and when the team is lost too, or losing their way. It's simple, really. This is the skill of summarizing what you have heard. It's meant to be a check-in so that everyone is operating from the same location on the map, including you.

Summarize from the perspective of the team's conversation. This is not a "he said—then she said" summary; it's not about recapping the individual positions. It's a review of the team's conversational steps and perhaps wanderings. It is a quick review of the topic being discussed, the themes presented, as in "this is what we've heard so far," and then checking with the team for alignment.

This is a lifesaver skill for the coach when the sometimes bubbling overflow of individual team opinions and positions creates confusion about where we are in the moment. It also comes in handy when a coach's attention is diverted to something happening in the team dynamics, or the coach is triggered by something that happened and momentarily loses connection. When you summarize, you create a breathing space for yourself, a chance to collect your thoughts, and an opportunity to unhook yourself from an emotional snag. You also give the team a chance to respond to your summary and contribute to a course correction if needed.

The team appreciates the summary because summarizing demonstrates the coach is listening and wants the conversation to be productive, even at the risk of appearing lost or confused.[104] In the process you build trust with the team just by checking in to make sure you are tracking and the team is having the conversation they need.

Sample Dialogue

Coach: (multiple opinions without a clear direction to the conversation)

Just so I'm sure I'm following this, let me summarize what I've heard so far. You can correct me if I'm off track. You started this topic when team decision making came up in the conversation. Based on what happened with two vendors, it seems that the selection process and plan were not clear. There was an observation about how decisions are made on teams, a question about individual roles in making decisions, a couple of people who basically think this is normal, why get in a twist, and at least one on the team who thinks this is a crucial "weakness" and needs to be fixed. My air traffic control screen is starting to get overwhelmed. Maybe I'm the only one, but from the looks on your faces I'd say others are a little lost in the subject too. Does that sound about right?

Team Member 1: Ultimately, it's Paul's call.

Team Member 2: But I don't think we're at "ultimately" yet. I think I have something to contribute, but I'm not sure what's expected of me. I think the coach is right about the confusion.

Team Member 3: We don't have a standard process.

Team Leader: It's not *always* confusing. Sometimes it's clear. Smooth sailing, and sometimes, yeah, I get the feeling it's disjointed, and in the rush to get things done maybe we're not clear about our roles in the decision on the table.

Team Member 2: Right. Am I being asked for an opinion? Or do I have a vote?

Coach: (to the team) So, let's use this vendor-selection process as an example. What is the current process, and what's working about it? We'll also look at what's *not* working.

Acknowledgment

Reveals a quality of the team, a value or a personality trait.

Acknowledgment articulates a strength of the team that the team may not even be aware of. It is different from praise or compliments. A compliment focuses on behavior, as in being punctual or following through on an action plan. An acknowledgment gives the team a sense of "this is who we are." The team feels seen in ways they don't usually talk about. For example, "This is a team that cares about getting to the root of the issue, fearlessly." Or "This is a team that knows how to work hard *and* have fun." An acknowledgment often elicits a sense of pride; team members sit up straighter. As coach, when you give an acknowledgment that truly, authentically resonates with the team, you can feel it land.

It's not wrong to compliment a team for an accomplishment, especially an important breakthrough or achievement. Just be aware that a compliment might come across as the coach's judgment or evaluation, as if the team's accomplishment were pleasing to the coach or even motivated to please the coach. An acknowledgment is all about seeing the team and recognizing a strength that is part of the team's identity.

An easy way to start an acknowledgment is to start with, "I see a team that..." Then look for a personality trait or a value: "...a team that cares about quality." "...a team that knows how to disagree and not make it personal." "...a team that believes in itself."

Spin & Fade

The skill of knowing when to intervene and when to watch silently and observantly.

You may have seen a juggler do this trick. The juggler puts a plate on a tall wooden stick and gives the plate a spin. The plate spins smoothly. After a while, what starts to happen? The plate slows down and begins to wobble. The audience can see that if nothing happens, the plate is going to fall and crash to pieces. But just in the nick of time, the juggler steps in and gives the plate a spin and off it goes again, spinning gracefully.

Metaphorically, that is the job of the team coach. As long as the team is having a productive, rich, engaged conversation, it would just be wrong to interrupt. As coaches, we are not being paid by the number of questions we ask or how smart the questions are. When the team is on a roll, let 'em keep on rollin'. And when that plate starts to wobble, step in and give the conversational plate a spin.

That "spin" can be most anything. It could be a question for the team, it could be a summary of what you've heard the team say, an acknowledgment of how the team engages in the conversation, or a simple observation about how the team interacts. The art of spin & fade is to watch the energy and flow of the conversation. Give the plate a spin when you, and probably others, can feel the wobble.

Exercise: Practice the Skill of "Summarizing"

To summarize is to play back the flow of a conversation. The summary brings people back onto the same page; it is a check-in with the team and a restart of the conversation, often at a deeper level as a result of the summary intervention.

Summarizing is a useful tool you can practice in nearly any meeting or coaching session. Just be sure that you pick a natural moment when summarizing feels like it's called for and would be appreciated. Otherwise, it is likely to sound artificial and contrived. A brief summary reestablishes alignment and moves the conversation forward.

Recommendation: at your next team meeting or coaching session, look for several opportunities to summarize and make note of the impact.

Exercise: Exposing Team Beliefs

What a team believes has enormous potential impact on team results. Those beliefs are built into the code, so they are only visible in behavior and attitude when someone shines a light on them. This simple exercise is designed to give the team the flashlight.

Team members should have paper and pen or some other way of taking notes. On a flip chart page or projected slide is the title, "We believe" and under it this fractional sentence:

If we _____ then surely _____ will happen. Guaranteed.

Divide the team into pairs or triads or some combination.

Give These Instructions:

Use this general form of "If A," then "B." Modify the wording as needed. Positively worded versions and negatively worded versions are both welcome. For example, "On our team, if we work hard then surely we will be highly rewarded." Or, "If we work hard it will go completely unnoticed, the results will not be appreciated, and the bar will be raised." Work in your small groups. Get creative but speak the truth. You'll have 10 minutes for this. When we get back together, we'll share.

Amidst the humor and irreverence there will be pearls of great truth as well.

Exercise: Mining for Values

Values show up in the choices people make and not necessarily in the words they profess. To uncover team values, lay aside a vocabulary list and focus instead on team situations.

This can be done with the whole team or in small groups first, depending on the size of the team.

1. Think about three or four team situations that were especially successful. Good decisions were made. Effective action was taken. There was a strong feeling of team pride, as in, "We're that kind of team."
2. Find three or four of the opposite kind. The wheels were coming off the team wagon. Frustration. Disappointment.
3. Start with the team breakdown situations. What was missing there? What value or values were absent?
4. Then look at the successful situations. What was showing up in those interactions? What team values were visible in the choices that were made?

Focus on what value is revealed versus analyzing what process worked or didn't work. Use this as a starting point: "Clearly, we are a team that values…"

Sometimes the team may need to pass through more than one layer to get to the very heart of a value. The team might start with, "We care about the details." The coach might say, "That's an expression of a value. What's beneath that?" The next layer might reveal a more specific value focused on customer service and give the team value the name "service first." Or the team value might be more about quality performance, with a name for the value something like "We get it right."

Notice that a team value can be more than a single word. It may take a few words to express the essence of a value that is unique to that team. It will be more personal, in a team way, than generic words from a list. When the team finds the right expression, it resonates and the team can feel it. "Yes, that's it."

Exercise: Tracking the Journey Activity

This is an activity you can start in the first team coaching session and build on in future sessions. You can also use it as a one-time activity. The project involves a large roll of white paper that can be pinned or taped to a wall. The team gives instructions to the person doing the drawing—it could be the coach or team member. The road is drawn first. The team describes the shape and course of that roadway from when the work began up to today. The team suggests landmarks passed along the way, road signs, detours, bridges crossed, and so on, building a picture of the journey to date. This is a picture that can be used to summarize the process and highlight learning and achievement. It's a picture that can be updated at each session and can be used at the last of the ongoing sessions to capture the learning from the journey.

The journey is typically drawn to the present moment. However, it can also be used to imagine the future, create a vision for the road ahead and the destination. Another variation on this exercise is to have each team member draw their own picture of the journey as they see it today. Each team member is given a flip chart page and pens. When everyone has had a chance to draw a picture, the pages are displayed in gallery fashion, and team members are given an opportunity to speak about the picture they drew.

CHAPTER 7

Now Tune In

Essential Team Coaching Competency No. 2

The Ability to Be Tuned In—Listening Recalibrated

The team is a system. That's true. But it's not monolithic. It's actually throwing out signals, simultaneously, on multiple channels. Like listening to an old-fashioned radio, the ability to tune in is the practice of scanning the bandwidth, turning the dial, then selecting a channel to explore. This chapter is about seeing and hearing on different levels. Tuning in is about scanning the band, finding the different stations, fine-tuning to get the strongest signal, and then making note or taking action.

To be effectively "tuned in" requires excellent listening skills, to be sure. But there is more to this competency. We may be tuned in to one thing at a time, but we're receiving on many channels. It's like having multiple receptors; each receptor provides a particular stream of information. There is a receptor for the words of the conversation the team is having; a receptor for the tone of that conversation and the emotional impact that's generated; receptors for what's not being said, for the assumptions people make, and still more. In the midst of this, the coach's job is to make choices up and down the band and then tune in to a particular channel to listen more. And it must happen instantly and continuously.

One of the first places we scan for deeper listening is the discussion the team is having in the moment. This is the "conversation band." The loudest and clearest channel on this band is the *content channel*.

This is naturally where the team has its attention, and for good reason. The team has a business issue to address or a decision to make, and the players responsible for making that happen are engaged in that discussion right now. The team coach can play an important role at this level by facilitating the conversation, ensuring clarity where there might be confusion, encouraging participation, and maintaining an environment conducive to forward progress. This is a familiar channel, one we've paid attention to all our lives. It has a clear purpose: to sort out the issue and options and take action.

Questions. For What Purpose?

This nod to the importance of helping the team work through an issue by facilitating a problem-solving conversation comes with a caveat: Be clear about the purpose behind the questions you ask. Be aware of the tendency to ask questions as a way for you to gather information so you can be better equipped to solve the problem.

It's a natural temptation. We want to be helpful. We might believe that our value to the team is in speeding up the problem-solving process. So we listen to the team's conversation with an ear for our own analysis. We might even be carrying a judgment about this team's need for our help. In the meantime our attention is on our own internal process—not on the team. Gathering information to understand the situation so the coach can be better equipped to solve the problem is actually not the coach's job. If the coach's goal is a better understanding of the problem and the team's dynamics—fine. But actually solving the problem is the team's job. The coach's job is to help the team become more effective in their collaboration. And that means having attention "over there" on the team instead of on the coach's personal thoughts and opinions.

To tune in on the team includes listening not only on the surface but under the surface. This is listening that is open and curious, expansive; it's the opposite of listening focused on driving hard to get to a solution. There will be time for action planning; that's a well-practiced process. But moving too fast to get into action too early misses the opportunity to go deeper, explore new territory, create new awareness and understanding.

The frequencies below the surface, below the content level, may be fainter. They might be harder to hear or harder to pull out from the background noise. For the team coach, mastery comes from practice and in helping the team to have its attention there. That's where the greatest rewards are.

Weather Changes

The weather changes constantly. So be prepared for weather changes.

Every conversation creates an accompanying mood. It's like an energy field. Two dear friends meet for lunch and the conversation creates delight, or excitement, or deep caring, depending on the tone. You can feel it if you're observant and sitting at a nearby table, even without eavesdropping on the words. Humans are equipped with a limbic antenna for this. It's there to sense potential danger, and it works just as well on a thousand other emotional settings. Reading this energy field is something humans have been practicing for millions of years.

That energy field is both a consequence of the conversation and a key influence on the conversation itself. A heated debate can escalate into a fiery exchange, and it can be quickly extinguished by a funny remark. By tuning in to this energy and how it is changing, we tap into information that every team member senses but isn't usually conscious of. Putting words on that energy or its impact helps the team to go deeper, to look at patterns in the team dynamics or what that moment means to the team.

For example, imagine working with a financial services management team, following their team discussion. They are celebrating a successful quarter, congratulating one another. They're especially happy about the excellent sales numbers for a new investment product. It's a "balloons and confetti" atmosphere. You can practically hear the champagne corks popping. And then someone brings up the fact that a key client, after 15 years, is changing firms. The air just left the room.

The team might want to dive right into strategizing how to get that client back, or what to do to make sure this client or that client doesn't follow. That would be natural, and of course it will be important for the team to look at what happened and how it might be prevented in the future. But this ability to *tune in* to the mood shift that occurred provides an opening for the team to explore what this loss means. What's important to this team? What does this team value? What can they learn from this experience?

One minute the conversation in front of you has the gentle quality of a walk on a sandy, tropical beach. Sunny. Warm. A pleasant breeze. The air, fragrant. Then something happens in the conversation, and suddenly you're in the midst of a prairie storm with rumbling thunder approaching from the distance. You've no doubt been in that situation. And probably, like an experienced meteorologist, you could forecast the coming storm based on your awareness of what was happening in the conversation.

Not every shift needs to be noted and discussed, but from time to time, drawing attention to the energy field and the way it changes will help the team become more aware of what is being created in the moment and how they can explore the impact.

When the coach senses it would be worthwhile to highlight a shift in the energy field, the coach shares that observation without any attachment to being "right." When trying to describe something as intangible as an energy field, all words are an approximation, a way to invite response: "Yes, it's like that." Or, "No, it's more like this. . . ."

In fact, it often makes sense to start with a short disclaimer, as in, "I may have the wrong words for this, but this is what I'm sensing." The coach can also ask the team to describe that shift in the energy field. "Something just happened. What was that?" This trains the team to pay attention to the environment they create and the impact it has on the team conversation.

Listen with Curiosity

Tuning in is also a practice of being patient and then responding, instead of instantly reacting. It's a way to hold off on interpretation. Here's a simple example. As a team coach, imagine that you're listening to the team. They're discussing their progress on improving a key business metric. The discussion is a bit bumpy, maybe a little heated. A couple of the team members seem to be holding back, maybe disengaged, and then, unexpectedly, someone throws a wrench in the blender. The team is likely to focus on the person who threw the wrench, or the position that person was taking.

For you as coach, it's an opportunity to be curious. What was the intention behind throwing the wrench? What was missing or so important that this person's response was so strong and disruptive? Is this a pattern for this team? It's easy to get caught up in the team's instant reaction. For the team coach, it is a moment to look underneath at the motivation. Assume some level of positive intent. What was this person trying to accomplish, in spite of the method?

Listen for Assumptions and Expectations

At the individual level, all assumptions come from a belief that "other people see the world the same way I do." Given a certain set of circumstances, like meeting a deadline for a project, all reasonable people (modeled after me) would approach the project and time line in the same way. Which also means that if you and I are working together on this project, I have a set of expectations for you based on what I assume is the right and proper way to complete this project. When it turns out you are a human being with different expectations, there is a strong possibility for confusion, disagreement, and all the attendant emotional consequences that go with that.

A great deal of conflict on teams is the unintended impact from a clash of unarticulated assumptions and expectations. These are invisible trip wires for team members. With unclear expectations and unarticulated assumptions, it is very difficult to create alignment.[105] It is also nearly impossible to hold team members accountable if they have different understandings of the assignment and different but undiscussed expectations for how to proceed together. No wonder things tend to go awry.

For teams, part of the challenge when the mess happens is that team members tend to go to explanation or defense as a first reaction, often focused on "who's right" rather than "where did we miss?" It can quickly devolve into "You said . . ." "I said . . ."—a cycle that is not especially helpful and can make the individual positions even more entrenched. For you as team coach, one ear in the tune-in process is an ear for unexpressed assumptions and misaligned expectations.

The Listen-to-Speak Ratio

Another important channel for the coach to monitor is the one that focuses on the tendency of the team when it comes to how much the team listens to each other compared to how much the team speaks "at" one another. Obviously different team members will have different styles. Some may naturally speak more than listen. Different team topics will lend themselves naturally to one more than the other.

The aim here is to get a sense of the team's usual balance. As coaches, we're looking for the ratio of asking and telling, sometimes referred to as advocacy and inquiry. To be an advocate is to take a position, make a proposal, or state an opinion. An inquiry is a question, and in the best use, it is a genuinely curious question into the rationale for a position or for understanding different perspectives and conclusions. This is not an interrogation; inquiry is not a series of leading questions intended to build a case for a point of view. That would be advocacy disguised as inquiry. True inquiry is open and inviting.[106,107]

Team members are mostly trained in organizations to be advocates, solve problems, and take a stance. That behavior is encouraged and rewarded. Unfortunately, when there are multiple points of view or conflicting proposals, most people turn up the volume on their advocacy. Positions become more inflexible, questions turn into cross-examination, fortress walls come up. The balance gets completely tilted toward advocacy, and then the potential for learning, alignment, and common ground shrinks. What we know is that on high-performing teams there is a much better balance. In fact, for the most part, the ratios favor listening and asking over speaking and telling.

This topic of balance can benefit from some personal reflection for those in the coach's chair as well, as an opportunity to tune in to your own tendencies. The goal in this work is engaged, productive conversation within the team. Look at your own intervention pattern. As coach, how much are you listening and asking versus speaking and telling?

There is no definitive proportion to aim for as a team coach. Each team situation and each conversation will dictate different levels of your participation. The art of the work is in finding the optimum balance. You can adjust the balance by tuning in to the impact you are having. Notice: Is the level of intervention and the style of it helping the team to stay on track? Is it time to be more directive, or time to retreat so the team must expand into the conversational space?

Encourage Team Engagement

For coaches, if you notice most of the communication is flowing between you and the team instead of between team members, it may be a sign: it's time to have the team focus on talking to each other. As we mentioned in chapter 5, be aware that sometimes team members would much rather talk to you than to one another. Talking to the coach is a safer conversation and usually much more comfortable than engaging in a tough, maybe intense conversation within the team.

It's also true that sometimes teams feel compelled to explain why things are the way they are; they can be defensive. They might see the team coaching as a sign that the team is in trouble, not performing up to standard. The team can feel judged. A little of this ventilation is normal, but at some point it is no longer a contribution to the discussion. When too much of the conversation is happening between the team and coach, it's time to reset the dynamic and have the team talking to each other.

Notice the Harbingers for Change

As coaches we are agents of change. We know that teams as systems often resist change for lots of understandable reasons. The coaching process asks team members to behave in new ways. The process requires practice; it upsets the familiar, predictable patterns. Team members complain, "I don't have time for this." In the face of the discomfort and resistance, coaches listen closely for signs of movement or readiness, knowing that sometimes teams need small steps forward in order to build momentum before real change happens. This "wanting for a change" is a frequency to tune in to. There is an urge or yearning showing up. It's a reference, often subtle and fleeting, that speaks to an underlying desire for something different, a different team experience.

It's like a bubble below the surface. It might be in a comment a team member makes, along the lines of, "Maybe I'm the only one, but there has to be a better way." It might be in the body language of a team member or in a risk one of the team members takes. Tune your coach's monitor to this frequency, where you look for signals, even faint signals that the team is moving in the direction of change. It's a bubble, rising, and it may not hold together when it reaches the surface. The team might not be ready to change but there is something stirring. By noticing the bubble and naming it, the coach raises awareness on behalf of the system's own desire for change.

The urge or yearning can take many forms. It might be a desire to get into action or a desire to pause and celebrate or appreciate; it might be an urge to get messy and tackle the difficult issues. There is momentum in the urge that leads the team in a certain direction. Your curiosity as a coach is, "What is the direction?" and "How will that support the team?"

Listen for the Hidden Channels

There are conversational stations that are easy to hear on the team radio band. There are also any number of channels that are inaudible until you go tuning for them. Teams have developed their unique ways of having team conversations. The ground rules are deeply imbedded. Everyone knows how to behave and knows where the boundaries are. It's familiar and well practiced. When you tune in, you might look for the unfamiliar frequency, as in, "This is the conversation you always have. What's the conversation you *don't* have?"

A sample of looking for other hidden frequencies:

- Here's what's being said. What's not being said?
- Here's the conversation topic that is comfortable and familiar. What's the topic that is taboo?
- You've done a thorough job of identifying the weaknesses in the plan. That seems typical for this team. Looking at the same situation, what are the strengths?
- I notice that this team is very careful about sharing opinions, especially opinions or ideas that may be unpopular or risky. What would happen if you allowed the conversation to be messy?

Look beyond the Conversation

The conversation itself is clearly one significant frequency band for tuning in to the team. Another very different but equally important band is the physical environment; in fact, all things physical, including body language and the embodied experience the team is having.

Remember, the goal is productive, engaged conversation. The physical space and the layout within that space will affect the quality of the conversation. Some years ago, we worked with a management team in a manufacturing company. Our first session with the team was scheduled in January at the client's facility: a training room in the factory where the heat had been turned off over the weekend. Everyone was so cold it was a distraction, and that was multiplied around midday when one of the manufacturing lines on the floor below started up with a rhythmic pounding that shook the building. Clearly, less than ideal conditions for team conversation.

Even the traditional conference room setup, or the boardroom with an elegant table bolted to the floor, creates its own challenges. Tables tend to become protective shields, creating not only physical distance but conversational barriers. When team members take their familiar seats at the boardroom table, that action reinforces individual rank and position rather than a sense of one team.

The setup of the physical space matters. It can support conversation or be a barrier. It's why we highly recommend a half circle of chairs without tables when facilitating an important team conversation, with a prohibition on phones, tablets, and laptops. The open space invites the sort of vulnerability that can lead to deeper conversation.

Body language is another very strong source for signals. Notice the team member with his arms crossed leaning back in his chair. What's that about? Or observe the team member who keeps checking her watch and tapping her foot. Even where people choose to sit is a signal. Here's an example: Two teams were merging into one as the result of a reorganization. Team coaching was initiated to help with the integration of these two teams. The newly combined team was showing clear signs of stress; a competitive, adversarial, uncollaborative tone was ruling the day.

In the first session they arranged to sit with their former teammates, with a gap between the two former teams. It didn't take a genius to tune into the team frequency. The morning session included a lot of "we" and "they," reinforcing the separation. After lunch, the coaches invited team members to change chairs and sit next to someone new. The issue didn't go away, but the tone of the conversation was more inclusive.

Tuning In Mastery

We tend to put our attention on what shows up on the surface. It's present and visible; we can talk about it easily. But like the tip of the iceberg, it represents only a small portion of what is going on with the team. The tides and currents under the surface have a powerful effect on the team and what shows up on the surface in the team's conversation. The source of what shows up above often starts here, below the surface. This tuning-in competence gives team coaches a lens to see below the surface.

This ability to listen through the noise and hear the faint signals—to hear more deeply and bring that to the team's awareness—provides valuable information that can support the team's process.

Team Coaching Skills

Tuned In

Clarifying

Where there is confusion, uncertainty, or apparent misunderstanding in the team's conversation, this is the skill of finding clarity.

It's natural enough to experience confusion in a one-on-one conversation. With a team conversation, the potential for confusion and misunderstanding is vastly multiplied. It's actually amazing to hear a team, mired in a thick mess, continue to repeat the same words, sometimes with more volume, expecting to find mutual understanding. In fact, one of the most persistent obstacles to effective team discussion is simple misunderstanding. People engage and continue to engage in a conversation based on what they think is meant or what they assume they know.

As a listening skill, clarifying helps bring those assumptions to light so they can be inspected and resolved. Clarifying also builds stronger communication because it shows respect for better understanding.[108,109]

The skill is used by the coach for the purpose of creating clarity for the team and, by the way, clarity for the coach as well. The coach might also notice team members in a fog and encourage them to ask for clarity. This model is taking responsibility for the communication.

Phrases that begin the process of clarifying:

"This is what I heard you say."

"I'm hearing three different topics or maybe they're three perspectives on the same topic. Let me pull the threads apart."

"There seems to be confusion. Let me see if I can clarify what's been said."

This is a skill that makes the exception to the rule about preferring open-ended questions. For simple understanding, it is often appropriate to ask a closed-ended, yes-or-no question. For example, "Did you mean…?" "Are you saying…?" or "It sounds like we just shifted topics. Is that right?"

Active Listening

Focused listening and playing back what you hear and see to make sure you are hearing what was intended.

In a team conversation, people can become very passionate about their position on an issue and in the process, stop listening. Instead, they simply fire back their point of view, reload, and fire that same round again. Active listening breaks the pattern and provides a simple means for mutual understanding, and in the process it shifts the tone from launching missiles to dialogue.[110]

In active listening, the "listening" part is about being fully present. Locked in. This is listening on many levels: to the words, of course, but also to the tone of the conversation, the shifting energy, body language, and what's being said or not said between the lines. The "active" part is sharing what the coach hears and sees. The goal is to share a picture of both the content and the experience as accurately as possible. Where clarifying focuses primarily on the content of the conversation—what's being said—active listening is more inclusive.[111]

"Let me play back what I'm hearing." This phrase has the effect of a pause button followed by a short rewind. The playback includes both content and context, the ebb and flow. It includes observations about impact, the energy or emotional field that was created, and what may have been noticed about body language. This is a report, not an interpretation, so in general it is best practice to use the team's words as much as possible.

Like clarifying, active listening is a skill the team coach can use both for the team's benefit and the coach's benefit. It's a skill that team members can use with one another as well.

Polarities

Listening intentionally for the reverse so that "both sides of the coin" are revealed.

This is an awareness of opposites or contrasts, or a way of seeing both ends of a continuum. Here's the most common example. As you listen to the team, you are obviously aware of what is being said. The skill of finding polarities is to become curious about what is **not** being said. And not just at the content level. What is the conversation the team might be avoiding? Where are the boundaries—the places where the team stops? What are the taboo topics? What's the conversation you're not having?

Polarities often take the form of questions. For example: "What's showing up?" It could be a topic that keeps recurring. It might be a team habit of defending or rationalizing. It might be an energy or emotion. Its polarity would be the question, "What's *not* showing up?" Mind you, not that it *should* show up. It just isn't. For example, in the course of a conversation where the team describes recurring problems with a key supplier, you might reasonably expect to hear frustration or at least a desire to figure out how to settle the issue. If you don't, it might make you curious.

Other examples of polarities:

Where do you see alignment?	Where do you see misalignment?
What unites this team?	When do they split or fragment?
Where do you see resistance?	Where do you see flow?

Name the Energy Field

To give a name or description to the atmosphere created by the conversation or by the mood of the team.

Something invisible is being created in every moment. It's an energy field that is the result of what's happening with the team, even in silence, and most frequently it's the result of the dynamics of the team's conversation. It's like the currents that flow under the surface of the water. They can't be seen, but they can pull the team off course. For the most part, team members are focused on the content of the discussion and their personal position on the topic.

In the midst of this is an energy field. Team members can sense it but might not be conscious of it. That energy field can be sharp and edgy or smooth as silk. It can be emotional as in sad, or it can be delightful. When you point to it or ask the team to describe it, you bring awareness to the surface. This awareness gives the team valuable information about how the team interacts.[112]

The tone of the conversation has an impact. Here are a couple of simple examples. Notice how many different ways there are to ask, "What were you thinking?" or "When did you realize the plan was not working?" In each case, the words are carried on an emotional plane. Those different ways of asking send different submessages along with the words. You could write the script notes for yourself. "He asked, casually." Or "He asked, with obvious venom." The way the message is wrapped, the context that holds the words—that whole package is what gets delivered. Once that tone is generated, the next person to speak is speaking into that energy and emotional field. That's one reason arguments can escalate quickly. One hot comment ignites another incendiary response.[113,114]

One of the easiest ways to introduce this awareness to teams is by using weather as an analogy. Imagine this scenario. The team is about to address a troublesome issue that is getting worse. Market share is slipping in spite of the action the team has taken. Even before the conversation has started, you can sense the undercurrent. This, then, will be the emotional atmosphere in which the conversation takes place.

Sample Dialogue

> **Coach:** Before you launch into your review of the situation, what's the weather here right now?
>
> Team members describe gathering storm clouds, thunder in the distance, rising wind, find shelter.
>
> **Coach:** What is there about this issue that creates that foreboding forecast?

This opens a conversation about the impact of the issue on the team. Now, imagine that the conclusion of this discussion ends with great ideas generated, the possibility of a new product to bring to market, and resources identified to support the effort.

Coach: What's the weather right now?

[After a number of responses] What created the change in the weather?

Metaphor/Image

Uses the power of imagery to capture the essence of an experience or discussion.

Using metaphor has other applications beyond comparing weather to the energy field. Sometimes a metaphor captures a whole experience or line of thought for a team. The team can also use imagery to describe the team itself or qualities of the team in certain situations.[115,116]

Sample Dialogue

Coach: You're about to make this presentation to the board. What's a metaphor for this?

Team Member 1: Homeless. Begging for money for a meal.

Team Member 2: I'd say we're like the teenager bringing Dad's car home with a big dent in the trunk.

Team Member 3: . . . and we're about to ask for money.

Coach: What's the image you'd *like* to hold for this meeting?

Exercise: Active Listening

Active listening is a practice of focused attention. When engaged listening is absent, communication weakens and relationships are affected, and that can undermine the team's ability to collaborate.

A simple exercise with a team.

Divide team members into pairs. If there is an odd number, one person joins a pair as an observer.

Team members choose to be A or B.

Instructions for Bs: find a topic you are very enthusiastic about. You'll be talking about the topic for about two minutes.

Instructions for As: You can take the As out of the room and give verbal instructions or gather the As in one corner of the room and give them a prepared handout. Instructions are: Listen to your partner. When a personal thought occurs to you, raise your right hand. It could be anything. You notice the color of their shirt, the temperature in the room, what you might have for dinner tonight. If it is a judgment, raise your left hand.

After about two minutes stop the exercise. Have the two team members talk between themselves for a couple of minutes first to burn off the energy of the exercise, then debrief the team as a whole.

What was that like?

What was the impact on the presenters (Bs)? On the listeners (As)?

Where do you notice this level of listening on your team?

Exercise: Collecting Clues for the Undercurrent Rising

This is an exercise primarily for the coach's own awareness practice, but of course it could be perfectly appropriate for the coach to share those observations with the team. The goal is to identify clues that indicate a desire for change. The nature of those clues will depend entirely on the team. The clues may take the form of comments or they might be nonverbal signals.

Coaches tune in, looking for clues that indicate a possible urge or yearning for change. These signs are harbingers for the possibility of change. By highlighting a signal, it is possible to make it visible enough for the team to grab hold of.

Instructions: Practice by consciously planning to tune in for these signals in a particular team coaching session. Set a time frame for this practice; as little as five minutes would heighten your awareness. After the session or at a break, make notes about clues you identified and the nature of those clues.

CHAPTER 8

Be an Observationist

Essential Team Coaching Competency No. 3

The Ability to Be a Reflective Observer—The Exquisite Mirror

We invented a term for this competency. It's the ability to be an *observationist*. That is, an observer with a job to do. Just being a good observer is not enough. You need to do something with what you see and hear. Adding the word "reflective" gives this competency two additional dimensions.

To be reflective is to consider. In this case the team coach and the team are in a place of reflection, looking thoughtfully. The subject of that reflection will be the team, team dynamics, and awareness of old habits—the topics that lead to new levels of insight and ultimately to the changes that support the team's development. "Reflective" is also the special role of the team coach, who reflects back to the team observations and questions for the team's thoughtful reflection. As team coaches, we have the job of holding up a mirror for the team so they can see more clearly who they are and how they interact.[117,118]

The Team Operating System

Turn on a device, whether it's a computer, a tablet, or a smartphone, and what we see is the application running. What is not visible is the operating system (OS), but it's the operating system that controls what is visible. In our role as observationist, we notice the effects of the operating

135

system on team behavior. The team's attention is on the application (app) itself. Our work with the team is designed to help the team look at the code that runs the operating system that delivers the app that we all see on the surface.

The key to being an effective observationist is noting behavior and the effect of the behavior, knowing that it is part of that unconscious code. In order for the team to become more effective in their work together they first need to recognize the current state of the system: how they operate. Your role as an observationist is to share what you see and hear and invite the team to look in those places too. "This is how things are done around here." As they become aware, they ask, "Is that way of interacting working for us, or not working for us?" By sharing your observations and training the team in that reflective skill, you provide a way for the system to receive information, and the team is able to make new choices.

Team Rules

One of the first places to look for operating system clues is to look for team rules. Systems create rules of behavior, and they create rules quickly. It's a survival instinct. Those rules, sometimes called behavioral norms, define aspects of team dynamics, team participation, and team performance. They are unspoken but everyone knows the rules. New team members learn them by observation and by subtle reward and punishment. These rules maintain order and relationship safety, which is why they are so resilient over time. You can start to see these rules just by watching the team.[119]

Here's an everyday example: probably nine out of 10 teams have a rule that says, "Meetings start late." You know it's a team rule because everyone obeys it. Are meetings that always start late the best use of people's time and attention? No, of course not. The rules don't need to make sense or benefit the team. A rule's a rule. Imagine you're a new team member. Your first team meeting is scheduled for Tuesday morning at 10:00 a.m. What time do you likely show up for your first meeting? If it is scheduled for 10:00, you're probably there at 10:00 or even a little before. You wait. Alone. In silence. At 10 minutes past, people arrive and the meeting gets underway. What time do you show up for the second team meeting? Right.

Another familiar example: the new team leader. Team members know there are going to be new rules or changes to the old rules. A great deal of the energy in the leadership transition is spent by team members trying to figure out the new rule book without a book.

Here's a real-life example. On a team we worked with, the former team leader operated like a helicopter parent, hovering over the team. She was a micromanager who had been in that management position for 10 years. Anything of concern was escalated up to the team leader. Then the new leader arrived. In this case, someone who believed in empowering team members, who encouraged initiative and was willing to live with the consequences. That created a whole set of new rules to assimilate, and you can imagine the accompanying disruption and resistance.

Predictable System Patterns

In a similar way, teams develop patterns for how they deal with recurring team situations. They have a process for that; you might say, "There's an app for that." It's a default process. It's like a small piece of operating system code that, when triggered, when the process is called for, the team response is a programmed cascade of action. These patterns are wired in. They are unconscious but just as persistent and predictable as team rules. They keep the world spinning in its proper orbit. Working with the team over time, you begin to see those patterns repeating.

One of the most obvious and most important places to look for patterns is decision making. There will definitely be a pattern for that: a pattern for how input is given and received; how contrary ideas or positions are treated; the pace of the decision-making process; where authority is located; and how, or even if, there is accountability assigned. Other areas where norms are set and strong are the team's consistent and unwritten protocols for communication in the team.[120]

The team is showing up in every moment with all its quirks and patterns. There's no way to turn that operating system off. So if the coach notices a behavior that looks like a pattern in a coaching session, make a note; watch to see if it repeats. For example: you might notice how the team decides about something quite mundane, like where to go for lunch. It's almost certain that the process for this lunchtime decision is duplicated in other decisions back at work. Or a team that tolerates interrupting each other in the coaching session—that pattern will surely be in place during regular team meetings. By being an observationist, you can learn volumes from what you observe even in your very first meeting with the team, beginning with whether the meeting starts on time.

Make the Invisible Visible

Watch a team at work as they address an important team issue. Ask yourself, "Where is the team's attention?" The attention is almost always on the issue, and more specifically each team member's attention is on the position they have staked out on the issue. A team member's attention is on the content of the conversation, not the flow or the way the team is interacting with one another, not on how the team listens, and not on the underlying tone that is being created by the conversation. And yet under the surface of the content is where the code resides that controls what gets talked about, who speaks, and who doesn't.

What is happening below the surface may be invisible to the team, but it has visible effects. By making the invisible visible, teams learn how they interact. They see the impact, and when they do it leads to more transparency; decision making accelerates; disagreement is less threatening; trust is built; communication improves.[121]

The Elephant in the Room

There are certain topics that some teams will not discuss. In this case the issue is not exactly invisible; everyone is aware of it, but no one is willing to bring it up for a team conversation. Oh, there may be side conversations between certain people, or a spontaneous but hushed conversation around the coffeemaker, but to actually bring that topic out into the open, to put it out there right on the conference room table? That's not going to happen. That very sensitive topic may not be invisible, but it has an invisibility cloak over it.

This is a topic that is too prickly or potentially too explosive. Careers could be hurt. At least, that's the belief. It may be a belief founded on past experience on that team or on other teams, but the belief now has roots in this team. And so the team wastes enormous energy walking around the subject-that-must-not-be-named.

And yet these topics, when they are openly discussed, provide a rich opportunity for learning. Teams that learn to step up and take on the tough issues learn a new measure of team strength and build trust, respect, and new skills. The environment the coach creates can be the safe practice area where teams learn to handle the tricky issues, especially those that feel dangerous.[122] By tracking the team's conversation, including the underlying tone, or sometimes body language, coaches can often get a glimpse of that elephant in the room. Maybe for the coach it's a vague sense, a disturbance in the air, or like a shadow passing the window. Under the surface there may be a feeling that there is a conversation that's being avoided; it's a conversation that has become a closed loop in the team's OS code, so the team goes around and around the topic, never finding an exit.

Publicly declaring that there is an elephant in the room may be just the intervention the team needs to break the cycle of silence. Also, by the way, there are times when the team has been waiting for the right moment, and when the coach shines a light on the avoidance, it becomes just the nudge the team needs in order to open up.

The Team Lens and Filters

Teams have ways of seeing their world and the opportunities or obstacles in it. That perspective is a lens and a filter. Only certain images get through the filter. With that lens the team sees what it expects to see, whether that is good news or not. How they view the situation through the lens of that perspective influences how the team acts.[123]

Here's an example: a country-level leadership team learned that reporting responsibilities were changing, and a new position was being created at the global headquarters. They would now be reporting to this new position in a new reporting structure. The team's reaction was uniform. "This is a really bad idea. We're doomed. More complexity. They never listen to us." And so on. Some of the concerns were legitimate, for sure, but these concerns were embedded in and amplified by a perspective of "this will never work." You can imagine the affect that would have on the team's interaction with this new key stakeholder.

The good news: it is possible for teams to change perspectives. It's a simple process that starts with an observation: this team is in a perspective and it doesn't seem to be a very helpful or resourceful one. The current perspective is identified, named, and discussed. The conversation revolves around the question "What will be the effect on the team or the relationship with stakeholders if the team continues to hold this perspective?" Eventually the team will explore alternative ways of looking at the same circumstances and choose a more resourceful way of looking at the issue.

Agility to Zoom In to Individual and Zoom Out to Team

We know that a team is more than a collection of individual parts. That's true, especially from a systems point of view. It is also true that a team is made up of individual parts—human parts. Individual members of the team want to be heard, recognized, and respected as individuals. Yes, team coaches need to be system aware. Team coaches also need the agility to shift focus from the wide-angle, landscape view, to the individual, portrait view. This focus shifting is ultimately for the benefit of the team, but in the moment it is personal. Seeing the individual within the system is essential observation competence.[124]

Team Roles

One example of that shift from the system to the individual is the recognition of informal roles for individual team members.[125] One place to focus your observationist lens is on the presence and impact of these informal roles on the team. Different from the functional role on the team—like sales manager or learning and development department head—informal roles sometimes come with the personality of the team member and are sometimes created because the team, as a system, needs that role filled. For example, a team with aggressive, combative team members may need a role of peacemaker. It's not a title on the organization chart; if the role emerges, it will be the result of someone responding to the system's calling for peace.

Informal roles come in all sorts of characters: the devil's advocate who is always taking a contrary point of view; the eternal optimist; the skeptic and the authority; the dreamer and the practical one; the one who obsesses about the details. There may be a role for a joker or a scapegoat.

The roles become part of the code, like team rules and patterns. If team members aren't clear about their informal role, they can check with their team members.[126,127] The team often has observations about one another's informal roles.

The goal is not to eliminate informal roles; they are normal for groups and teams. Shining a light on this aspect of the team creates better awareness of how individuals respond automatically out of their role.

Identify Voices

A team is not one monochromatic, homogeneous voice. It is a harmony of many voices that is sometimes sonorous and sometimes the equivalent of clanging metal garbage can lids. For example, imagine this scenario: In the midst of a team conversation a voice speaks up, takes a strong stand, and shares a point of view. "We need to take action. We can't afford to wait." You have just heard a voice for action. That voice lives on this team. It's a voice of the system.

There may be a different voice for "Let's be patient. We need more information." Now you have a voice for slowing down. That's a voice of the system too. This is not a competition to see who wins the volley. Both voices live on this team. Some voices will be more popular than others, but all of the voices contribute to the team's experience, even the unpopular voices. As a team coach, one of the things we are observing is the contribution of these different voices and, in addition, when they join in the chorus and when they stay quiet. This quest to include representatives from all of the various contributing voices is important because an inclusive mixture is the most accurate picture of the team.

Find Allies

Some team members will be very strongly tied to the voice they speak for. The wire between impulse and speaking is short because what they are speaking for is so important to them personally. At first it may appear that they are a lone voice speaking on behalf of that position, but that may not be true. There may be others who care too, just not as strongly. For others, that position may not evoke the same personal passion, or they may be less willing to take the risk of voicing a contrary position. Speaking up for something that others don't appear to endorse can be isolating. It's much easier to go along with the apparent consensus on the team. To speak up under those conditions takes courage.

It's worth checking, as a team coach, to see if others on the team would align with that view. Maybe they have felt the pressure to go with the majority; maybe they haven't considered an alternative to the loudest or most popular voices; maybe, until this moment, they didn't realize they were willing to stand side by side with this alternative position.[128] Finding allies has two benefits. One, it supports—even validates—the voice of whoever had the courage to speak first. Two, it shifts the impact of that voice from a single individual's position to a position that more than one team member shares. It shifts from a personal stand to a strong voice in the team.

Highlight Diversity

When you observe that there is more than one voice on this team, you are pointing to and highlighting diversity within the team. That's one of the seven Positivity strengths described earlier. "On this team there is a strong voice for 'get into action,' and a strong voice for 'be patient. We need more information.' What's it like on this team to have those two strong but opposing points of view?"

Sometimes these different points of view need to be resolved. The conflict handicaps the team. Without abandoning the importance and value of diversity on the team, it may be important to find alignment. In the Venn diagram of this team issue, what is the common ground? But resolving the tension is not a goal in itself. The fact that there is tension is an everyday reality for the team. Does that tension somehow serve the team? Or does it undermine the team's ability to function well? How can this team learn to work together, acknowledging the substantive differences but at the same time holding on to the team's mission?

Some voices speak with great skill, and some voices get under the team's skin. There are times when team members react more to the messenger than to the message. Part of the team coach's role will be to pull that apart, so the team can listen to the message. There will be some subjects where there is abundant alignment; there will be some subjects where there will be great diversity of opinion. The goal is not consensus;

the goal is understanding, looking for potential alignment even if there is disagreement. There are no "right" voices or "wrong" voices. No one has the whole truth; everyone has a piece of it. The collective voices have the truth for this team.

Create Team Observationists

The more aware the team is of their own dynamics—the patterns they follow without question, the tendencies they show when the conversation gets challenging, how they reward and punish in their system—the more equipped the team will be to update the operating system. All of this runs below the surface of the usual team conversation, and it has enormous impact on the team's ability to perform. The team coach provides a valuable service as an observationist, drawing the team's attention to the dynamics that affect the interaction and conversation of the team. But the ultimate goal is to make the team capable of this insight too and not dependent on the coach. Part of our role as team coach is to transfer the know-how to the team.[129]

Team Coaching Skills

Reflective Observer

Mirror

To reflect back to the team your observations and curiosity about how the team interacts.

A shiny glass mirror is a powerful instrument of feedback. No doubt we have all had personal moments when we look in a mirror, see what we see, and in that moment get a clear message from the reflection. A message of delight, sometimes, but more often, an awareness that something has to change. The shirt. My weight. My life. The feedback in the mirror leads to action. What we hadn't noticed—or maybe what we were avoiding so we wouldn't notice—is right there in front of us in the mirror, and we can't pretend we don't see it. Awareness is the beginning of change.

As a team coaching skill, "to mirror" is to reflect back to the team the behavior and dynamics the coach observes.[130] The skill is most effective when it is as neutral as possible, unattached, as close to simple observation as you can make it. Mirroring comes from a curious place: "Isn't that interesting?" That curiosity leads to exploration with the team, moving from observation to consideration: "How is that working for you? What's the payoff? What's the downside?"

The basic question for the team is, do these patterns help or hinder the team conversation, how decisions are made, or how the team performs? When you hold up the mirror for the team, it gives the team an opportunity to see the unconscious ways they interact. When they are aware, they get to choose whether to continue or try something new.

What We Often See in the Mirror

Patterns. Teams develop patterns of behavior; all systems do. It's more efficient to have a repeatable pattern than to always be inventing new ways of operating. Look for the recurring patterns in how the team interacts. For example, what is the pattern in decision making? Does the team openly discuss options and come to a conclusion as a team? Or is the pattern more like cautious conversation, watching the team leader's reactions and then deferring the decision to the team leader?

Places to look for patterns: What does this team practice? Do well? Overdo? Under stress, what's the default? How does this team depressurize?

Team rules. We introduced this topic in the previous chapter. Team rules describe the unspoken "way things are done around here." Providing a mirror for those apparent team rules is another example of the skill. Examples:

- The two senior analysts on this team control the agenda, no matter what the memo says.
- All agreements made in team meetings are conditional. Team members can make exceptions for themselves and their teams unilaterally.
- Budget and forecast deadlines are fluid.
- When production numbers do not meet targets, blame purchasing and "the usual breakdowns in the supply chain."

Team roles. These are the informal roles team members have on the team.[131] They are well established over time. For example: the "director" who is always calling for action. The "philosopher" who paints the big picture. The "mechanic" who wants to fix the problem. The list goes on. There are times when these roles are a valuable contribution to the dynamics of the team by maximizing the benefit of team diversity. On the other hand, taken too far the roles can become an obstacle to discussion and action.

Sample Dialogue: Identifying a Pattern

Coach: May I share an observation? I notice there is freedom on this team to speak your opinions and share your experience. I also notice that at some point it starts to circle around again and keep going in a loop. It starts to lose momentum, and twice I've seen the team change the topic at that point. It's like you chewed the tasty part, then you want to go on to something else but no action was taken. No decision made. Do you notice that pattern?

Team Member: I think we do enjoy the dialogue. I do . . .

Team Member 2: . . . and we don't want to buckle down and do the hard part. It's not as much fun. We want to keep everything at the brainstorming, creative level. Considering possibilities.

Team Member 3: Yeah, but we *do* make decisions; it's not like we don't.

Team Member 2: Yeah—eventually.

The team laughs.

Coach: You see the pattern. Is it getting you the results you want?

Perspective/reframe

To notice and explore the impact of a team perspective; then look for a more resourceful option.

The world is rosy when we look at it through rose-colored glasses. We see what we expect to see and ignore what doesn't fit that rosy hue. We look for evidence that confirms everything is fine. That's true for teams as well. The perspective the team is in affects what the team sees;

the perspective also affects the attitude, the range of potential action steps, and ultimately the team's performance, positively or negatively. Perspectives work both ways.[132]

Here's an example. Two companies are merging, and the decision has been made to merge the two leadership teams into one. Both leadership teams are in the same perspective: "We can't work with those people. They don't understand our business." If that's the perspective they are in, what both teams will focus on is every example of misunderstanding. "See? I told you so." The team is acting out of a perspective but not conscious of it, and not conscious that the perspective is contributing to the problem.

The first step is for the team to become aware that they are *in* a perspective.[133] The fact that there is a reorganization and two teams are merging, that's just a fact. The subject is neutral; how the team looks at it is not. There's a mood or attitude that goes with a perspective that shows up as an energy field. Expectations of the outcome conform to what is possible in that perspective.

The second step is to look for other perspectives in order to find one that is more resourceful. This is definitely *not* about pretending that there are no challenges and that all is well and the sun will come up tomorrow. It *is* about recognizing there are ways of looking at the same set of circumstances without all the charged or limiting beliefs.[134]

Normalize

To affirm that the team's response to its current circumstances is a normal, human response to the situation.

The experience the team is having is normal for this team. They may not like it, but given the circumstances in which this team is operating, it would be normal to see the sorts of dynamics that are showing up on the team. "Normal" doesn't mean approval. If the response by the team to their circumstances is undermining the team's effectiveness, it needs to change. To "normalize" is to reassure the team that the response is understandable given the situation.

Imagine this situation, working with a senior leadership team. The company is an acquisition target and has been for more than a year. Two suitors are vying for the purchase. The team has low opinions of both potential buyers. There seems to be no light at the end of the tunnel. The team, meanwhile, is impatient, frustrated, and starting to take out their discontent on one another. In this team meeting they have started to complain again, and this time it includes team members blaming each other.

[Sample Dialogue]

Coach: This is team behavior I haven't seen before. Bickering. Complaining. Finger-pointing. It doesn't reflect what I have seen in the past, *and* it is certainly understandable given the weight and uncertainty of this pending acquisition. As a team you've endured months of waiting, with no resolution. It would be normal to feel frustrated and on edge. What's that like? What's the impact?

Highlight Diversity

Reinforce the team's awareness and acceptance of diversity.

Diversity is one of the seven Positivity Team Performance Indicators for good reason. It recognizes the value of different opinions, personalities, ways of communicating, and styles of working together.[135] This diversity gives teams access to more ideas, options, and possibilities. It also brings the potential for disagreement and conflict. That's why on many teams there is pressure to conform. There may be an underlying team rule that says, "For the sake of keeping the peace, don't make waves." On high-performing teams diversity is highly valued, encouraged, and empowered. For you as coach, this is the skill of highlighting the diversity by shining a light on it.

Ways to Highlight Team Diversity

Identify the voices. Individual team members respond to the team's process or the topic under discussion in unique ways. The way they respond is an expression of their individual experience. When they speak up, they are speaking on behalf of a stand they are taking, or they're expressing an opinion or emotion. From a systems point of view, they are a "voice of the system."

For example, imagine a team meeting where a new program idea is proposed and received with great enthusiasm and support—except in one corner. One team member is skeptical and explains why. This is a team with multiple voices for enthusiasm; there is also at least one voice on the team for "skepticism." One note in the chorus is skeptical.

The "voice" that the team member is speaking for is not always clear at first. Clarifying that voice involves looking underneath what first showed up on the surface. The team member who expresses a strong opinion that "we need to find a new supplier" is making more than a suggestion about a practical matter. That team member is speaking on behalf of something like "thinking outside the box." Look for a value or priority being expressed along with the practical. The emotional content is often a clue that this is a "voice" speaking.

Look for allies. Very often team members hesitate to speak up when they believe that what they have to say is contrary or unpopular, especially if they believe they are alone in that point of view. A coach can encourage team members to speak up by looking for possible allies. "Who else feels that way?" Finding allies reinforces the awareness that there are multiple voices on the team. To be a Reflective Observer at this point is to reveal what is true on this team: on this subject there are different points of view. The immediate goal is not to resolve the differences or engage in a conversation about who has the "right" way to look at the situation. The coach might simply observe, "It seems the team is at a crossroads when it comes to the proposed expansion. I hear a voice for 'We're ready' and I hear a voice for 'Caution. We aren't ready.' What's it like on this team with these two contrasting voices?"

Caveat. Before jumping to an invitation for allies, make sure that the person who spoke initially feels heard for their personal position. That team member wants to be recognized as a person with a particular point of view.[136] They are not a disconnected "voice of the system." This is especially important if that person is taking a risk to go against the flow. Make sure they feel listened to and their experience acknowledged.

Exercise: Practice the Skill of "Mirroring"

An easy and practical way to practice the skill of mirroring is with a team you are on. Look for an opportunity to share an observation about typical team behavior you see. Start with a simple sentence stem like, "Here's what I'm noticing…" To reinforce the idea that it is an observation, not a judgment, you might add a disclaimer to that sentence stem so it stays neutral. "Here's what I'm noticing—I could be totally wrong about this, but there does seem to be a tendency when we meet to push the harder topics to the end where we have less time, and the discussion often gets postponed. It's happening today. Does anyone else see that?"

Exercise: Practice Identifying Voices

Identifying voices is something you can practice in any team meeting, of course. It's also something you can practice watching a movie or television. As you listen to the dialogue, listen for the position that person is taking that is more than just the words. You can't get it wrong; you're playing solo, and there won't be any feedback. The practice is in listening more deeply for the motivation behind the lines being spoken. Be aware of the emotional content; look for a value that is being expressed. Ask yourself, "What is this person committed to or campaigning for?"

CHAPTER 9

Mindful Agility

Essential Team Coaching Competency No. 4

The Ability to Be Actively Present—Dance to the Music

This competency is about the dance between coach and team, dancing to the team's music and helping the team learn new steps so their unique team dance is more effective. The process requires that the coach be very present, aware, locked in the moment 100 percent. And it is more. The music doesn't stop while you check your feet or check where the team is in the moment. The dance goes on.

Being present is not a passive act. The coach is not a spectator to what's happening. There is a constant dynamic tension between being open and receiving, being present in *this* moment and at the same time seeing the opening and pathway ahead and moving forward. Being present and being active are both necessary conditions for effective team coaching.

In this team coaching competency, the coach operates under the guidance of one core question: "Where are we right now in the process relative to where we want to be—and what must be done to get us there?" To be actively present means to be flexible and adaptable to whatever happens. Coaches often get hung up trying to be one step ahead and have the next brilliant question ready. Planning ahead is useful; just don't be too attached to that plan. There's a risk of being caught off guard when the music changes. The coach may have planned for a waltz when hip-hop showed up instead.

When the music changes, that's the coach's cue. Sometimes the coach seamlessly blends with the new music. Sometimes the coach joins in and redirects the conversation. Sometimes follow. Sometimes lead. The choice will be made in the moment. That's the art of being actively present.

Optimize the Development Cycle

The outcome we are headed for is team development: improve the team's ability to deliver results and the team's ability to collaborate more effectively. In our model that means improving the balance and competence in both Productivity and Positivity.

There is a process for that, a development cycle that starts with "We are here." From this starting place we ask, "Where do you want to go?" and "What are the steps to get there?" There will be action taken followed by learning. "What did we learn? What worked? What didn't work?" And the cycle continues anew with, "We are here now." Without the learning step, this is just busy activity and not development. The goal is progress with each rotation of the cycle.

That development cycle applies in multiple layers and in interconnected time frames. For example, there is a development cycle for the whole team coaching engagement, a beginning, middle, and end over

Figure 9-1: Development Cycle

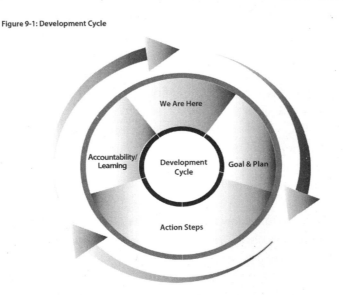

a period of months. There is a time frame and agenda for today's team coaching session. There is a time frame for this particular team conversation currently underway. To be actively present is to be aware of where the team is on the development path in multiple dimensions of scale, simultaneously.

Scanning the Screens

With teams things get complicated quickly, and that simple, efficient cycle we just described can fall apart. Here's an analogy. Maybe you've seen this scene in a movie or TV show: it's the inside of the security office in a large office complex or government building. There are rows of TV screens showing closed circuit TV pictures from multiple cameras mounted throughout the building. Someone is actively scanning these images. For the team coach, that's what it's like working with a team.

As team coach you need to be scanning constantly to track and be ready to respond to:

- The content of the team conversation.
- The energy field, the pace, and the tone of what is happening right now.
- The dynamics of the team. The unique way this team operates and how team members interrelate.
- Individual team members speaking or not speaking. Learning the individual styles. Noticing how individual team members contribute.
- The time line for the session. Are we in danger of not finishing on time? Do we need to make adjustments?
- The unexpected and unplanned; a sudden disruptive course change that wasn't on the agenda.
- The coach's own energy and emotional state.
- The impact of what someone just said. The impact of what the coach just said.
- And much more.

None of this shows up on one monitor in a tidy sequential stream. It all happens at once. One of the differences between individual coaching and team coaching is simply the amount of input you manage with teams.

The Urge to Act Right Now

Teams want answers, especially if things are not working smoothly, or if the team is not hitting expected targets for business performance. When one of those troublesome issues comes up in a team coaching session, teams often want to go straight to fixing, often recycling past ideas and former plans. It is very tempting to move into action right then because it feels like the team is ready, even impatient to get answers. Be aware. Many times this urgent move to action comes too early in the process. If the team moves to action planning too soon, those plans are likely to be made from historical team thinking, doing more of what they've always done and missing the opportunity to approach the issue with fresh eyes and out-of-the-box thinking.

For a team coach it is very tempting to go with the flow and bend to the anxious pressure from the team to move on. It can be challenging to slow down and risk the team's displeasure with the process. One common facilitation option is to capture the good ideas that pop up, save them on a flip chart, and promise to get back to them later. This is reassuring. The team feels they have been heard, their brilliant thoughts are preserved, and there is a promise to plan new action, just not right now.

Also worth noting: sometimes the urge to get into problem solving is simply the more comfortable choice for the team than having what could be an intense, challenging conversation. The discussion of a familiar issue is well practiced. People know where they stand and carrying on is a way to avoid territory that is tricky or uncomfortable. It is often worth asking, "Is this the most important conversation for this team right now?" Sometimes that action-planning or problem-solving conversation is the easy way out.

That deeper, more engaged conversation is typically a slower tempo than the high-speed, pressurized problem-solving drive of everyday work life. That doesn't mean it will be heavy, necessarily, but often slower. Notice that high-productivity teams may get impatient. Even when the tempo is quite upbeat, it is more conscious and typically more deliberate. Change takes time, attention, and practice to get the steps right.

As "dance master," the coach stands in a place that requires both rigor and flexibility. When a new topic comes up out of the blue, a topic that is important to the team, do you abandon the time line and the process you are in or the process you were about to begin? Or do you check with the team and encourage staying in the process on the time line you have been working? There is no field guide that lays out which pathway is the right one to follow. And of course, there will be times too when the most important next step is to stop everything and deal with the critical issue that needs attention before the team can move on. That's the nature of the dance.

Notice the Impact: Internal and External

The coach's attention is focused forward, on the team: listening, watching, sensing, monitoring multiple screens of information. At least a small part of the coach's attention also needs to be on the impact the coach is creating. The coach is not a team member, so in that sense not part of the team system. But the impact of the role itself makes the coach part of the system in the moment. What the coach says or observes, how it is said, the tone of it, the attitude that accompanies the delivery, all have impact; there are submessages being carried on that frequency that go beyond the words.[137,138] There is no place in this picture that is 100 percent neutral, without impact. The team's reaction and perception based on how the coach intervenes will affect the conversation.

Coaches also *receive* impact from whatever is happening in the moment. Coaches can get impatient, frustrated, confused, distracted, anxious—to name a few normal human responses. Any of those might be a fair description of what is going on internally with the coach. Awareness of this personal interior condition is important for effective coaching.

On another level, what the coach is experiencing may also be what the team is experiencing. This is a system experience where the team's impatience, frustration, or confusion are resonating on the coach like a drumhead. The experience the coach is having is like a tuning fork, reverberating in sync or sympathy with the team. This is valuable information about what the team is feeling and experiencing.

The goal is to be actively present with whatever is happening with the team in the moment. There are times when we get hooked or distracted, and it can happen just as easily when things are going swimmingly as when they are coming apart. In the moment we may be feeling a pleasant satisfaction and feeling of pride. But attention on "my brilliant and thoroughly competent performance" is a distraction too. While the coach is celebrating his or her fancy footwork, the dance was moving on and now the coach needs to catch up.

These sorts of disconnections will happen. A thought, an opinion, an emotional response can shift the coach's attention from the team to the coach's personal experience, and it can happen in a flash. When it does turn inward, first notice it, then look to see what can be learned from that experience. Assume there is information there that could be useful in the work with the team. It becomes a clue for something happening in the team. For example, imagine as coach you notice, "I get cranky when Paul speaks. He is such a blowhard egotistical know-it-all." Then, "Okay. If that's not about me and my personal dislike for that kind of self-promotion, get curious: what's happening on the team that creates that? Maybe there's a pattern here." The ability to truly be present depends on being actively aware of the impact of the forces at play.

The System's Pressure to Conform

We have already explored the natural tendency of systems to put unspoken pressure on team members to conform to the team culture. In this competency, we make special note of the fact that the system wants the coach to conform too. The team, as a system, generates a powerful cultural milieu and broadcasts it. It's a magnetic influence, drawing everyone in. Team coaches need to be aware that the system is pulling on the coach to comply with its norms, attitude, and values.

For example, working with a High Productivity—Low Positivity team, we would naturally expect to see that the pressure is always on to move into action, get the problem solved, take the next step. That's the pressure this team exerts on everyone on the team. It will feel impatient. It starts to set up pressure on the coach to drive harder and faster too. A coach may start to feel that the way to be most valuable to the team is to start action steps. It can feel anxious. If the coach's breathing is coming shallow and fast and there's a tightness in the chest, it might be that the system is exerting its influence. Coaches can start to feel that their value to the team and even their professional credibility is at stake if they can't get to action soon. In fact, they are being effectively recruited by the system.

The Essential Ability to Recover

Let's be clear. Things will not go as planned. There will be adjustments needed in that moment when the whole process lurches sideways and the wheels start coming off. As coach, it's easy to get hooked; that's human. The question is, how to recover? That's not a generic question, it's a personal one. How do you, personally, recover? Recovery is what coaches do to get back to ground, and it is an essential step in getting attention back on the team, where it belongs. That's where the work is happening. The true measure of team coaching mastery is not in what coaches do, it's in how they recover.

The Visible Value of Transparency

For coaches, there are times when the most valuable contribution to the process is the obvious: to name, out loud, what everyone is aware of and no one is saying. It's hard for everyone, including the coach, to be present when the experience feels disconnected. More often than not, for coaches, the remedy takes the form of pointing to, or admitting out loud what everyone is aware of.

Team members can sense when there is confusion or things are not working according to plan. If coaches persist blindly, driving on, pushing through, there is a potential for a loss of credibility whether team members articulate it or not. It is certainly tempting to hope no one notices that the boat is sinking and we can continue to row on. After all, it might be embarrassing. For the coach this might happen by simply losing track of the content of the team's conversation and asking a question that sounds out of place; it can happen by facilitating an exercise and forgetting to include an important instruction. Oops.

In actual practice, being transparent, although sometimes humbling, actually builds trust. Team members learn they can count on the coach to tell the truth. There is a sense of relief for the team. They no longer need to smile the fake smile and pretend all is well when it clearly isn't. In most organizations, the more approved practice is to stay silent. By speaking to the obvious you bring a breath of honesty that can generate a team sigh of relief.

Team Coaching Skills

Actively Present

Process Management

> *Awareness of where the team is in the process, adjusting as necessary to stay on course.*

The goal, of course, is progress in team development. There is a destination, and at any moment coach and team are somewhere on that team improvement path. The skill of process management applies in all timeline tiers, at each level of magnification. The skill applies to the big scope of the whole team-engagement project over many months. It applies to the session you are in today and to the activity the team is engaged in right now. Plotting the team's position on the progress map will be based on listening for feedback—sometimes concrete feedback from the team, sometimes from an internal sense based on experience and more subtle signs. That information confirms your view or gives you information about how to adjust to get back on course.

For example, imagine this scenario. In the midst of one of the ongoing coaching sessions, the team leader returns a phone call on the break. When she comes back into the room and shares the news, it starts a conversation in the team that could take—who knows how long? It's an important topic to the team, obviously. There will need to be a few minutes in conversation with the team to sort out whether this is an urgent topic the team needs to address right now, or whether it can be scheduled for a later time. In the context of process management there are two layers here.

One layer is the need to decide about which direction to take. Another layer for the coach is the consideration for how this seeming interruption might be useful material for deeper work with the team. It could be an ideal, in-the-moment opportunity for the team to practice what they are learning about how they listen, or how they make decisions, or whatever that focus is for this team.

Self-management

As management coach, the skill of monitoring your own experience; in the moment, noticing the impact of the team on you and your impact on the team, then adjusting/reconnecting.[139]

So far, we've focused on how to stay upright, riding the wave. Being actively present is clearly about having attention on what is happening out front with the team. It sounds simple enough but it's not always easy. In fact, from time to time the coach's attention will be turned inward, and the coach will disconnect from the team. It's a normal human reaction to something that happened or something that was said. There are a thousand reasons why that might happen and most of those reasons will be personal. Every coach will have a unique set of biases and triggers.[140]

Note that the skill of self-management applies to two dimensions: managing the coach's internal reaction to something that originates with the team or an individual team member, and the coach self-managing his or her impact on the team.[141]

Another way self-management shows up is in awareness that team— as a system—is trying to induct the coach. As a coach who is sensitive to the power of the team's culture, you can feel it. And that impact is present whether the team is on a celebratory high or a depressing low. Being actively present means being aware of the power of the team, as a system, to draw you in—to see the world the way they see it, to share the team beliefs and obey the same taboos. Notice if a team that is feeling helpless has you believing the team is helpless, and you are helpless to do anything about it.

Transparency

The skill of speaking up for the obvious; saying what everyone is aware of but no one is mentioning. This can be a moment of self-disclosure, usually an admission.

Some of the best examples of transparency happen when the coach is modeling it.[142] Here's an example. Imagine, as coach, you are following a team conversation that has started to get chaotic, with many voices chiming in and voices talking over each other. You think you have a bead on an opening for a powerful question. You ask the question—and you are greeted with blank stares. It's a moment for transparency. "Clearly, I am totally lost." Or "Okay, that question landed with a thud. Who can help me get back on track?"

Here is another example. The coach is facilitating an interactive exercise with the team—an exercise the coach has delivered many times with great success. But this time the exercise is utterly failing. The team can clearly tell this is not working. One option at that point is to carry on anyway and maybe accelerate to finish it faster. The other option is to declare it dead on arrival, call a halt and name it. Instead of trying to preserve a facade of professional demeanor, own up to what just happened. In fact, look for a learning opportunity for the team from your own mess.

Transparency can also be the subtle skill of inviting the team to address the topic no one wants to talk about. There is a need for some sensitivity in the use of the invitation; after all, there are reasons why the team is avoiding a difficult or potentially contentious topic. However, it might also be the case that the team is finally ready—even eager—to find a controlled outlet, the team coaching session, to bring to the table this very challenging topic. It's possible that small groups of two or three have taken up the issue in secluded conversation, but not the team as a whole, in a full team forum. The coach may or may not know what the core of the issue is but can sense there is a disturbance in the force and people are walking carefully around the topic, maybe sharing a quick glance to a teammate.

Working with a leadership team several years ago, my colleague and I could feel the vibe of that disturbance and could observe the impact of something that was definitely dampening the energy in the afternoon session. We were scheduled to work with this team the following day as well. The next morning, before the team arrived, we wrote on the flip chart "What is this team tolerating?" and then ignored it when the morning session started. Finally, before the break, one of the team members asked, "Are we ever going to address that question?" That seemed like the perfect cue and led to a breakthrough conversation with more candor than we had experienced with that team.

Recovery

The ability to reconnect with the team and the current process.

As coaches we will stumble over our own feet or stumble over things we didn't see coming. We'll think we have a clear vision of what is happening, feed that back to the team, and learn we are not even in the same postal code. Recovery is how we get back, once we've stumbled. This can be a very individual process. Instead of embarrassment or judgment that takes you away from the work with the team, how do you reconnect? It could be a word or two, or a short phrase—something you say to yourself when you notice the disconnection. It could be a physical movement: sitting up straighter in your chair or standing up. You might use the skill of summarizing to lock back in to the conversation.

Dance with What Shows Up

The agility to blend, flow, lead, and follow as necessary to maintain momentum or alter course for the benefit of the process.

Team coaching can be awkward or elegant, intense or quiet, like walking around on broken glass or sliding on a glassy smooth surface. It will always be unpredictable. The good news is, there is a constant source of rich feedback coming the coach's way at all times—feedback about what's working and what's not, where the process is on track and where it's stuck. In fact, the information about where to go next in the coaching just showed up seconds ago. The dance is afoot, so to speak. Coaching teams requires a high level of agility to work in a complex and changing environment. What will almost certainly get coaches in trouble is rigidly gripping the cherished plan or time line. A key question for this moment is "How can we use what just showed up?" Coaching is rarely linear and sequential except at a metaview level; it is more often improvisation in practice, and that is the skill of dancing with whatever shows up.

Exercise: To Practice the Creative Dance

An improvisation exercise is one way for coaches to build that creative spontaneity and presence muscle. Here is one you can practice with a colleague.[143,144]

The exercise is built on a classic story structure. Kat Koppett in her book *Training to Imagine* calls this the "story spine." The structure should be written on note cards for you and your colleague, or on a flip chart. As initial practice, simply make up a story. You can start with classic archetypes: choose a hero or heroine for the story and the evil adversary. Create a story of struggle, then struggle overcome, the victory completed.

Decide which of you will start, then begin, one sentence at a time, completing these sentence stems by taking turns.

"Once upon a time…"

"Every day…"

"But one day…"

"Because of that… (something happened – repeat this as many times as necessary)

"Until finally…"

"Ever since then…"

"And the moral of the story is…"

Sometimes simply blend and build on your partner's sentence. Sometimes take the story in a new direction or introduce unexpected characters.

This version of the exercise gives you and a colleague practice in the creative process of dancing—instantly—with what shows up. You can also use this exercise with teams. Divide the team into pairs. Have them practice a make-believe story with each other. Then use the story spine for *this* team's story. You might have the team in a circle, even a standing circle, and pass the story around one by one. The debrief of the exercise should be fascinating to hear. The story they create is the team's own narrative.

CHAPTER 10

For the Sake Of

Essential Team Coaching Competency No. 5

The Ability to Be Committed—To Stand in the Fire

What does it mean to be committed as a team coach? It would be easy to assume that the very nature of the work requires the coach to be committed, but as they say, there's committed, and then there's a higher level yet: *Really committed.*

Coaching a team is a demanding assignment. The team coach is working in a complex, often chaotic environment with an unpredictable mix of personalities, priorities, assumptions, and goals, where the choices for the coach come rapidly and the situation changes constantly. To meet this challenge requires a high level of commitment, a willingness to step into the fire for the sake of the team.[145] What's more, it's not just the coach who needs to be committed. To achieve meaningful change requires the team to be committed as well.

Commitment is the fuel that feeds the team coaching process. This is one area where there is an important difference between individual coaching and team coaching. With individuals, the coaching relationship starts with commitment. There are exceptions, of course, but in general the coachee has crossed a threshold and is ready to work with a coach to reach a goal or fulfill a vision. It's a conscious choice for change.

With teams, especially at the beginning, there is typically a range of responses. On one level that range is perfectly understandable. For most teams, team coaching is new territory, different from anything else they've done before. It is certainly different from taking a training class together or the shared experience of a team-building exercise. Team coaching includes ongoing follow-up, and that changes the nature of the work. It's not just a one-time intervention. This is a professional working relationship that will be in place for months.

The ongoing relationship is key to the effectiveness of the process. The interaction between team and coach maintains momentum over the changing terrain of the coaching journey. On days when the elasticity of homeostasis is pulling the team back to old patterns, old behaviors, it is commitment that will keep the process moving forward.[146] It is a mutual commitment by team and coach for the sake of the team working together more effectively, achieving better business results and creating a supportive, engaged team culture.

This competency asks a few simple but essential questions of the coach: "What are you committed to? In practical terms, what does it mean to be committed to the team's development? How far are you willing to go with that commitment?"

The big picture for this competency is this: from the start, the coach is the consistent model of commitment in this ongoing relationship with the team. It is the coach's rigorous and obvious commitment to the process and the team's success that will support the work with the team when the journey is going well, and especially when the ride is bumpy or detours happen.

The Team's Champion

We wrote earlier about the team's tendency to abide by unspoken, limiting beliefs. Those limiting beliefs become the story, the narrative the team tells itself and repeats over time. The refrain goes something like this, "Well, that's the way it is." "You just have to understand, this is what we have to deal with." There is often a tone of resignation and a stepping back from the edge to the comfort zone. "As everyone around here knows..." And there's that limiting belief again.

As a team coach your ears are tuned to those beliefs that undermine the potential in this team—the potential that's in every work team. The coach holds a picture that is built from a view of strengths, even when the team cannot see it for themselves. That's the picture the coach is committed to and the one the coach holds up for the team.

Just to be clear, this is not simply rah-rah cheerleading. To be an authentic champion for this team comes from a place of commitment that is based on strengths the coach has seen expressed and past examples of persevering, excelling. Ultimately, the coach is not telling the team something they don't already know; this picture is a reminder of who they are and who they can be as a team.

Be Willing to Challenge

Commitment to the team can also come in the form of a challenge. Teams may be acutely aware that things are not going well. There may be crippling breakdowns in communication, a tendency for team members to fortify their personal castle walls and ignore each other, lapses in accountability, lack of alignment not getting addressed...Whatever the team issues are, those issues undermine the team's ability to be effective. And yet, that's also the known world. Everyone knows the rules, knows what to expect and how to function in spite of the barriers. It's a trap, a cage, but a familiar one and one they have learned to tolerate and work around.

When the team is vacillating, resisting, or stuck, when the team's commitment is tepid, that may be a time when the coach's commitment needs to be strong enough to raise a challenge. Not for the sake of the coach's plan. It comes from a commitment to the team's improvement and a desire to light a fire that over time will result in a more effective team.

As a team coach, it would be normal to start feeling impatient when watching a team default to old, ineffective ways of operating, or hearing the team back away from courageous conversation to a more comfortable chat as a way to avoid discussing the hard issue. Not impatient *about* the team, but impatient *for* the team. The coach sees both a picture of what is possible for this team when they are at their best and at the same time a picture of the team as they sell themselves short or hold themselves back. At that intersection, the coach needs to be ready to challenge the team, help them see what they are avoiding, and encourage them to see what is within their power and within their grasp. With many senior leadership teams, taking a stand at that moment and challenging the team may require a particular strength of spine. Being challenged may not be an experience they are accustomed to.

This is not always easy. It raises all the normal fears of any coach: "Will this blow up in my face? Will I lose the business? Will they gang up against me?" That's why an essential competency in working with teams is commitment. This might be the moment that truly tests your commitment.

Ability to Wait—Be Patient

You've probably seen the acronym WAIT. It stands for "Why am I talking?" It's a reminder that speaking, or in the case of the team coach, intervening, should be a contribution and have a clear purpose, not just serve as a way to fill up the empty air space. Silence can feel awkward, and for the team coach it can generate a strong desire to say *something*, say anything. There is sometimes a voice in the coach's head whispering, "Do something. They're all looking at you. They didn't understand your question. Ask it again. Ask it a different way."

Resist this temptation. Waiting is a powerful coaching skill. If the silence is uncomfortable for the coach, remember it is uncomfortable for the team as well. At some point, someone will speak up. That silence is also, often, an indication that the team is entering new territory.[147]

It's easy to get a flow of conversation going when the subject is well-trodden ground, when opinions and positions are well known to team members. Everybody has something to say about it. Silence could be a clue that they need a little extra time to reflect. This could be the necessary space the team needs in order to break through, find the courage to say what hasn't been said, or see a new way of looking at an old issue.

Be With/Allow/Amplify

To be committed also includes a commitment to trust the process. There will surely be times when the team is in confusion or conflict, when thunderstorms are brewing, or the conversation feels like it is spiraling into a deep, dark bottomless hole. When the coach senses that, there is a very natural human desire to feel an urge to pull the team back to the light, to a positive platform instead of this shaky ground. There's an urge to escape by looking on the bright side. Be wary of that impulse. It's very possible that the thing this team needs most is to actually explore more deeply what is true, real, and hard to deal with. Trusting the process includes trusting that sufficient safety has been created in the work with the team. The courage to go into that difficult conversation begins with the coach. This could be the moment for the team to have a conversation the team has been avoiding, one that is pent up, and now is the time to go there—ready and willing, or not.

The urge to rescue actually deprives the team of the opportunity to go deeper. And by the way, there is likely to be plenty of desire on the part of team members to pull out of that dive and get to a place that feels easier, safer, more secure. Changing the subject is a predictable escape tactic for teams. As coach, being committed may mean redirecting the team back to the challenging issue when it's clear that that is a more productive place of conversation for the team's development, even if it is uncomfortable.

To trust the process is to trust that there is a bottom and there is an inherent, irrepressible desire for resolution that ultimately will lead to forward movement. The team may need to "marinate" in their own juices until the team is ready for something new. In that case, commitment is the willingness to be with the discomfort for the sake of the team's process.

There is also a flip side to this commitment to "be with" the team experience. The pressure to hit the next target—to keep moving forward—can be so relentless that teams miss the opportunity to celebrate when they meet important goals.[148] Hard work and determination are fine team qualities, *and* a pause to recognize team achievement builds a stronger team identity and reinforces the team's story.

The pause for personal and team recognition can restore energy and rekindle momentum. With some teams this might seem like an unnecessary interruption; it feels like a distraction from the "real work" of the team. In that case, the coach's job might be to challenge the team to celebrate. But it's more than a metaphorical party; celebrate by mining the experience for learning about what was accomplished and how it was accomplished. This helps lay a stronger foundation based on achievement.

Hold the Team Accountable

Teams will make plans and promises they won't keep. They will have reasonable explanations. Out of a sense of compassion and understanding, coaches may be inclined to go easy, forgive, and move on. Actually, moments like these provide a great opportunity to explore what the team is really committed to. Accountability is not about "Did you, or didn't you?" It's not about judgment or shaming. The purpose of holding a high standard for accountability is to maximize the learning from whatever happened. It's about being held to account. "What did you learn? How can this be improved? What support do you need? What requests do you want to make?"

High-performing teams consistently demonstrate a track record for team accountability.[149,150] Not in a nagging way, but with clarity and, when needed, with empathy and support. These teams realize that everyone on the team is responsible for the team's results, every day. Holding the team accountable is a powerful place to model commitment.

Turn It Back to the Team

At some point the team is likely to ask the coach, "What should we do?" The team is looking for answers or advice, and a natural place to go for help is the team coach. In a coaching model, we look first and foremost for a way to turn that question back to the team. There is strong rationale for this. In the four guiding principles, we include one that says, "the team has within it the means to excel." We take a stand for the inherent creativity and ability of teams.[151,152]

We also know that teams understand their business, their situation, and what is possible within their world far better than the coach ever will. We know that the team is more likely to own and follow through on plans the team creates for themselves. The process of finding those solutions also provides deeper learning about the issue and deeper learning for the team about how they work together to address problems. They are also more responsible for the outcome and more motivated to make it work.

When the coach supplies the answer it does two things. One, it reinforces dependency, and our goal is to empower the team; we're working ourselves out of a job. And two, If the coach supplies the answer and things don't work out so well, the team can simply dismiss the failure as somebody else's fault.

Ability to Wear Many Hats

So, absolutely, our "first and foremost" practice is to turn the question back to the team, honoring our coaching modality roots. And this is another area where there is a substantive difference between individual coaching and team coaching. In a traditional coaching model, we say "the client has the answers." In one-on-one coaching, we scrupulously avoid giving advice or problem solving. With teams, in our experience it's a different environment with different expectations.

If, as coach, you simply stonewall the request for help by turning it back to the team, as in, "What would *you* do?" you run the risk of looking like you're unwilling to be helpful. Blend with the request. For example, the coach could ask, "What has worked in the past?" or "What have you seen other teams do in similar situations?" The coach could also propose a brainstorming process to look for solutions; in that context suggestions from the coach would be part of a common contribution rather than a directive from a place of authority.

Being a purist about following a coaching model when the team is struggling for answers and the coach clearly has expertise that could help, but instead withholds it, well, that's just wrong. At least from the point of view of the team. They don't share a purist's commitment to a particular intervention model. They want help and they don't really care what hat the coach is wearing at that moment. So, yes, team coaching is still a coaching modality, *and* there are times when the role will look more like someone with valuable experience and expertise to contribute, a trainer to provide missing team skills, or a facilitator assisting the team in a traditional group process. How will you know when it's time to switch hats? Well, that's the art of the work. You'll have to trust your judgment.

Growing Commitment

Because the coach models commitment, the team becomes more committed too. The ongoing work builds commitment—not just to the process, but commitment to the team's development and commitment to one another. Over time team members increasingly see and make choices for the sake of the team. Commitment is the alchemy that turns independent groups into interdependent teams. When team members are willing to cross the line and be more committed to the team than to their personal agenda, there is extraordinary power at play.

Contracting – Alliance Building

There is an implied contract between coach and team that takes the form of: "We're in this together for the sake of the team's improvement." The clearer and more explicit that contract can be between coach and team, the easier it will be for everyone to be and stay committed. This contracting conversation, conducted early in the work with the team, is enormously valuable as a way to set expectations, clear assumptions, establish the ground rules, and clarify roles. This is a conversation that brings the team and team coach onto common ground. Contracting at its best creates mutual understanding about the common purpose and goals of the collaboration between coach and team.[153]

And if the word "contracting" sounds somehow rigid, or brings up an adversarial tone, another word for this would be "alliance." Crafting an effective alliance implies both agreement by participation and a sense that there is a mutual benefit in which all are invested. An alliance, especially in a coaching model, also has the quality of adaptability. A true alliance can be molded and adjusted over time to continue to fit the needs and changing conditions of the parties involved.

For the Sake Of – This Is Also Personal

For the coach, there is another place of commitment, a personal place. It's the coach's own, "For the sake of..." What is that for you? What is there about working with teams that is compelling, meaningful? Yes, of course, as coaches we want teams to be successful, achieve their goals, get the recognition they deserve. This work with teams can be enormously fulfilling. It can also be enormously draining.

So what motivates you to do this work? What's the reward? Based on conversations with hundreds of coaches over the years, it is clear that this work has meaningful purpose, and that the core answer is unique for every coach. That sense of purpose is where the commitment lives. Complete this sentence in your own words: "I do this for the sake of..."

What are you deeply committed to? And what keeps that commitment alive?

Team Coaching Skills

Committed

Intrude/Take Charge

When necessary, the ability to intervene strongly, to interrupt the conversation and redirect for the sake of a constructive team process.

Earlier in this section of the book we introduced a skill we call "spin and fade." It's the skill of giving the wobbling conversational plate a spin to put it back in motion. Sometimes a gentle spin is not enough. Sometimes it is necessary to courageously step in the middle, intrude in the conversation, and take charge of the moment.

It could be a heated debate starting to spin out of control, or team members' frustration turning to blame and personal attacks. It can also be a time when the topic has clearly drifted off course into trivial territory because it's easier to talk about things like where to add more bicycle parking than it is to deal with the breakdown in team communication and the impact on trust. At times like these, the coach has a responsibility to step in and step in strongly. It's a measure of the coach's commitment to the team.

The style of that intervention will be personal to each coach. It can be done with humor to help de-escalate the electric charge in the room.[154] It can be done with empathy and compassion, as in, "I completely understand the enormous frustration everyone on this team is feeling, given the recent procedural changes—and blaming each other is not productive.[155] You get to express the impact of this new situation on you and your area if ventilating feels useful, but at some point it will be important to move on. How much time do you want for ventilating?"

Ventilating, by the way, is another useful skill when used with care. There are times when teams are flooded or have been carrying the "stuff" of frustration, or unfairness, or perceived disrespect too long.[156] They need to ventilate and blow off some of the accumulated pressure before the team can move on.

Champion

To be the team's number one advocate, especially in challenging situations.

As coach, there is a way that you see what is possible for the team; you see the team's natural ability and resourcefulness. The coach sees it especially on those days when the team can't see it for themselves. As the team's champion, the coach demonstrates a belief in the team's ability to take on the challenges they face.

Imagine this scenario: a project team that is just past midway on the time line but has completed only 25 percent of actual project milestones. The team has been knocked off course by a series of reversals, surprises, and failures. Some of the wounds unfortunately were self-inflicted. There is a pervasive sense of gloom on the team, tossed by the waves of this perfect storm of discouraging news. The team is losing momentum and inching toward a "victim mentality." They are thinking or saying things like, "This project was doomed from the beginning. It was an impossible time line for completion. It was drastically underfunded. What were they thinking?" That victim mentality also breeds criticism of others, blaming, and finding fault. "If those people in R&D would only get their act together—settle on features for the first release . . ." Here is what championing as a skill might sound like:

Sample Dialogue—To Champion:

Coach: It sounds like this is a pretty discouraged team.

Team Member #1: Given the prevailing headwinds, what team wouldn't be?

Coach: Well, let's pause for a moment. Aren't you the same project team that completed Project Romeo last year on time, on budget, against head winds at least as strong. That's the story I heard when we started.

Team Member #2: It was a different set of problems. We didn't have a key supplier go out of business, but yeah, that was basically this same team.

Team Member #3: That was a total team effort.

Coach: And out of that experience came a team value—perseverance I think; is that right?

Team Member #1: Our rugby value.

Coach: What would be different this next week if, as a team, you re-created what it took to be the Project Romeo team again? Because you can, you know. You've done it before.

Challenge

Often takes the form of speaking the hard truth, or making a powerful request—well beyond what the team seems willing to undertake. The ability to go to the edge for the team, then step over the edge.

When the team sounds like they're satisfied with far less than their best, and they're giving weak explanations for giving up, it could be time to put a name to that resignation. When the team is tolerating a bully or circumstances that are clearly damaging to the team or team members, it may be time to challenge the team in strong words. When the team backs down, backs away from a commitment they made, a commitment they said was important, and it looks like they're simply opting to take the easy way out, are you willing to call them on their "stuff"?

There's risk in this. A strong challenge can sound like the coach's judgment. As coach, you likely don't have all the background that led to the decisions that were made. It's possible you could step boldly into it and have the team turn on you. There are many reasons to hold back or be cautious, and there is at least one reason to take a stand: a determined commitment to the team. If the coach models being careful, playing safe, that gives the team permission to do that too.

But when that challenge comes from the place of a true belief in the team—truly caring about the team's success—if it comes from a place of respect, it is more likely to feel like a hard truth to face than a judgment. And by the way, there's no way to predict exactly how team members will respond. This is the skill of standing in the fire. It takes a higher level of commitment to go this far.

Sample Dialogue—To Challenge:

Coach: Sorry. I need to interrupt here. This conversation is making me dizzy. You just keep circling, around and around, and in the last four months of working together I have never seen this team so cautious about something you have declared is uncompromising.

Team Member #1: It's a tricky situation.

Team Member #2: And a situation that got much trickier when Carl Andersen left. He was our number one advocate.

Coach: You need to make a decision as a team. Are you going to take a stand on this or not? Circling, but not landing, is not making a decision. Yes, there's a lot at stake as you have said...

Team Member #3: ...and risky if we do nothing.

Coach: My challenge to you is to make the appointment with the board and be ready to defend your commitment. "Careful" and "compromising" are not words I associate with this team—not on this subject. What's the next step?

Be With/Amplify

To amplify; to stay in the discomfort, even expand into an experience with the team in order to achieve the full value. It may be a disabling experience that is a barrier to progress; it may be an opportunity for celebration and recognition.

Sometimes the road to high-performing team goes down before it goes up. Sometimes it's *essential* that the team have a full experience of what's *not* working before they are willing to find a new way.

Here is an example based on a real team experience. It's a project team that is well behind schedule. Project goals keep shifting. Features and requirements keep changing. Team members are working long hours. The budget is capped. Team members are getting by, earnestly working around issues as they come up, but more and more they are operating solo, head down, "getting my piece handled." This is not the first time the team has addressed the problem of silos and solo operators. In a team coaching session, a number of suggestions are made and people commit to working more collaboratively. Everyone agrees: diligence in communication is important to the project's success. Two weeks later the team is back to the same struggling place again. They have returned once again to a situation that is not working.

This may be the time to have the team really immerse in the dysfunction and have a conversation that explores more deeply the default habits of the team and the consequences of those habits: the impact on individual team members and the impact on the project.[157] It's likely to feel uncomfortable, but until it *does* feel sufficiently uncomfortable, the team can hang on at the edge, making do. As long as the team can get by, that's the likely route the team will take. This is where a deep commitment to the team needs to be invoked.

It's easy to think our job as coaches is to make everything okay. There is an impulse to want to be helpful, which might look like pulling the team out of the mess they're in, but that's not the job. The job is to empower the team, and sometimes that will mean allowing—even helping to amplify—the experience the team is tolerating so that it is no longer tolerable. That experience becomes the nudge that unsticks the team and helps the team over the edge into new, more effective territory.

The upper end of the experience spectrum sometimes needs attention too. On some teams, the focus on moving forward or staying "neutral" is so strong that opportunities to celebrate achievement are ignored or dismissed as trivial. In that case, the team may be missing a powerful infusion of confidence building by moving too fast past this moment. Ultimately there is as much for the team to learn by the successes they achieve as the messes they make.

Structures

The skill of creating action steps that reinforce new behavior.

A structure is any device that helps the team keep its attention on a goal or practice the team has chosen. Awareness is the necessary beginning of change, but sustainable change takes action. Otherwise it is simply a conversational fountain of good ideas and good intentions.

Structures support behavior change. There are two fundamental ways to incorporate change over time. One way is to set a goal: a specific outcome by a specific time. The other way is to establish a new practice or develop a new habit.

There are endless possibilities for structures, limited only by the creativity and commitment of the team. Simple examples include:

- A practice of rereading the team agreements before each team meeting, then reading them again at the end and asking, "What are we learning?"
- The team might design and maintain a tracking log to monitor team performance goals and stepping-stones.
- As part of a regular team meeting, they might add an agenda item to self-report on feedback given and received, and then explore ways to make feedback easier and more effective.

Structures provide a way to monitor progress and a way for the team to hold each other accountable.[158]

An action plan answers the questions "What is the outcome we want?" and "How will we know when we've achieved it?" The structure answers the question "What will keep us on track?" The structure gives the team a grip hold on the way up the ladder of integrating new ways of working together and achieving better business results. It's the structure that turns a good idea into visible action.

This should be familiar territory for teams. Individual performance management goals and key performance indicators are commonplace in organizations. Tracking completion milestones is a structure. It's a structure that is also applied to team outcomes and team KPIs. The skill of creating structures is a way to reinforce change.

Contracting

The intentional design of the working relationship, setting clear expectations, uncovering assumptions.

One of the most common stumbling blocks for teams is the lack of clarity around roles and responsibilities.[159] We hear it often. It's hard to be accountable if team members have different expectations or understanding. This can be a serious ongoing issue for coach and team. The stumbling is the result of misalignment—assumptions made by the two parties that don't match up or expectations that come as a surprise.

Clear contracting is especially important in a team coaching relationship because the team coaching work is not as familiar to teams as traditional team building or consulting. Early in the work with the team, during the discovery and assessment phase, is an ideal time to have a conscious and intentional conversation about the working relationship with the team. This is partly the coach training the team in how the team coaching process works, and it is also a give-and-take negotiation between coach and team, creating the best possible working alliance.

Topics for the conversation will include:

- What to expect from the coaching process
- The role of the coach, or "what the team can expect from me as coach"
- What is expected from the team
- What we do when we're off track or not aligned
- Potential obstacles and what we need to do when they appear
- What are the agreements we need to make to create a safe, encouraging, and supportive environment for the work together?
- What are the team's questions or concerns?

Commitment is easier to draw on when there is clarity and shared understanding.[160] Leaning in to assumptions and expectations is risky and unstable compared to leaning in to what we have agreed to and where we are aligned.

Contracting as a skill provides a stable platform not only for the big-picture ongoing relationship between coach and team but in specific situations as well. Imagine this example: the morning before a team coaching session, the team learns about a reorganization plan that will fundamentally shift reporting relationships between this team and stakeholders. Clearly, the original agenda for the session no longer applies. A conversation about revised goals and outcomes for the session is in order. That would be contracting around the work to be done in a specific instance.

The underlying commitment is to optimize every opportunity for the sake of the team's ongoing development. Instead of skipping over the reactions and emotions caused by the news and trying to move on as if nothing had happened, seize the opportunity to use this to design an effective way of dealing with the changes. Alliance building can happen in a similar way, focused on a particular situation. The team may have agreed that today is the day we talk about that elephant in the room. Rather than just charging in on the topic that has been carefully avoided for so long, it would be wise to acknowledge before starting that this is a difficult, maybe combustible conversation. Then ask, "What agreements do we want to have in place about how we conduct this conversation?"

Exercise: To Practice Creating Structures

Structures come in many different forms. Some will be simple reminders of a goal or commitment; some will be mechanisms to monitor progress or to tally completion steps. Some tracking structures are already familiar and may be in use by the team. For example, a weekly spreadsheet of sales numbers or service calls. The spreadsheet is a structure. The best structures serve two purposes: a functional purpose to maintain attention on action steps and a motivational purpose that inspires or energizes the team.

Working with a team, the practice is to explore structures outside the usual and familiar. The current, everyday structures the team is already using may still serve the functional role but have become too bland to generate team enthusiasm. One more Excel spreadsheet, even with vibrant colors, may not do the trick. For example, look for visual structures: photos or images or video clips. How could they be used as reminders of the important action or commitment by team members? A project team we worked with created a special, handmade milestone award that was given out to a deserving team member with great ceremony every Friday. To an outside observer it might seem silly, but for that team is was a much-coveted prize and an opportunity to shine among team members.

With a team, pick a particular goal or new habit the team wants to acquire and brainstorm six or 10 different structures to support that initiative. Alternatively, for the practice of thinking outside the box, select a personal goal or new habit you want to acquire for yourself and brainstorm a number of creative ways to create structures.

Final Questions

We started this book with one clear question and a clear quest. The question, "What makes great teams great?" And the quest: to describe a repeatable process to transfer that know-how to teams. We believe the team effectiveness model we've detailed provides a credible and proven answer to the question. The team coaching process, thoughtfully implemented, fulfills the quest by providing an established methodology that delivers consistent results. In part 3, we expand on several key areas of the process that deserve special attention, based on the questions we are frequently asked.

The book closes with an exploration of the underlying meaning and purpose this work represents and its potential for impact beyond the performance improvement of teams. The crucial business justification for team coaching is both clear and measurable. In addition, there is a deeper sense of purpose that goes beyond the benefit to the business, without ever minimizing that imperative. There is a very human reason why this work is so important.

CHAPTER 11

Special Considerations

This chapter provides a collection of topics that might have been a list on a flip chart if this were a discussion instead of a book. These are important additional subject areas; we know they're important because they keep coming up in the conversation about team coaching and they have practical, real-world applications. We start with the No. 1 most frequently asked question, "What sorts of teams are the best candidates for this work? What criteria would you apply?"

Best Candidates for Team Coaching

Let's start by addressing the assumption that team coaching is a remedy of last resort for dysfunctional teams. Certainly, there will be times when other attempts have failed to help right the ship of a team in trouble, and team coaching feels like a lifeline. That assumption would be understandable, but it doesn't take into account the vast pool of underperforming teams. Remember, our data shows fewer than one in 10 teams rate themselves high-performing before starting a team coaching process.[161,162,163] As organizations become more familiar with team coaching as a development tool, a track record of success builds momentum for more widespread application of this methodology. In short, best candidates can be found throughout the organization at multiple levels. Having said that, here are a number of criteria to help sort the process of selection.

A Compelling Sense of Urgency

All teams, even high-performing teams, can benefit from this methodology; we've seen the true breadth of that statement in team examples across every imaginable industry segment—in academia, nonprofit, and NGO teams worldwide. But there is one condition that particularly stands out in the definition of best candidates, and that is a compelling sense of urgency.[164]

Here are some typical examples:

- Project teams are typically excellent candidates for team coaching. A successful project is clearly defined by time line, promised outcomes, and budget. Projects and project teams are very visible. The stakes are high and the clock is ticking.
- A merger or acquisition brings together two significant cultures at the macro level and often at the team level as well. There is great pressure to integrate team membership into highly functioning contributors as quickly as possible. In most cases teams are left to sort themselves out over time, with very mixed results. Team coaching can dramatically accelerate the integration process.

  All of the factors in the team effectiveness model will need reorientation in this case, but highlighted among them would be a need for alignment. A rigorous and consistent team coaching program with accountability provides the structure for that initiative. A similar justification supports any internal reorganization as well. Drawing up a new schematic of titles and reporting lines may be the first and only step organizations take in forming a new team and as a consequence, miss the opportunity to take advantage of the opportunity to build team performance practically from a blank page.
- It would be natural to expect that senior leadership teams would have a sense of urgency; after all, they carry the load of responsibility for the organization's direction and performance. They are also the model for other teams in the organization to copy; senior leadership teams set the standard for collaboration and alignment. All eyes are on the team at the top.
- Virtual teams, by virtue of the literal and metaphorical distance between team members, are also typical candidates for team

coaching. So much of team performance depends on often less frequent and less substantial, technology-based frameworks for team interaction. The virtual team environment is growing rapidly, and with it a need to figure out how to perform more effectively in that new environment.

- The need for urgent support for teams can also come from transitions and significant but unexpected changes that affect the team. It could come from a change in team leadership, a new role or mission for the team, or external impact on the team, such as a major announcement in the marketplace. Urgency can come from any change that puts new or increased pressure on the team.

Without a compelling sense of urgency, the coaching process will lack the necessary sustainable motivation that any important change process requires. Short term, changes in how the team interacts may be awkward, requiring energy and attention. Some changes will certainly mean leaving one's comfort zone of the default and automatic. The long-term benefit of the process may seem over the horizon when teams are focused on getting things done on the busy road just ahead. A sense of urgency combined with a commitment to the process maintains the necessary effort.

Leadership Support

In a systems-based model for teams, accountability for staying on track and the drive to maintain momentum is everyone's responsibility. It is also true that the category for "best candidates for team coaching" includes the commitment and support of the team leader. Everyone on the team will take their cues from the action and effort of whoever sits in that chair. Team members will be watching to see how the team leader joins in the process, and that level of engagement will be a standard that team members will measure against in their own behavior. In best cases, the team leader will continue to be an advocate and ally for the team coaching process, even when it reflects on the team leader's leadership.

Leadership support also applies to organizational leadership.[165] It should be clear from the early discovery work that there is strong cultural support from the top of the organization for this work. We have seen exceptions—successful examples of teams that were bucking the system. They were impatient, hard-driving and motivated teams in organization cultures that were satisfied with just-good-enough and a firm commitment not to make waves. Those rogue teams drew energy and persistence from their outsider identity. However, when the question is about "best candidates," the answer is, there are clear advantages for those teams that have sponsorship from the top.

Willingness, Capacity, and Commitment

We can say with absolute confidence that there are three attributes of teams that consistently predict effective results from team coaching. We have that confidence because they are the same three attributes we see in individuals who start a coaching process. Those three are:

Willingness: to embrace change and fully participate in the process

Capacity: to make the change

Commitment: to persist in reaching the goals the coachee has committed to

These three are not easy to define or measure in behavioral terms, but their presence or absence will be key to team coaching success. With accumulated experience working with teams over the years, coaches develop an antenna for these attributes. As much as we take a stand for every team's potential—after all, one of our four guiding principles is "The team has within it the means to excel"—there have been teams that were simply not coachable because they were missing one or more of these three essential attributes. There are times when a team coaching process is not the right intervention. A team stuck in perpetual conflict may need a period of time working on conflict resolution to stabilize the team first. In some cases, individual coaching or relationship coaching between team members may need to happen before work with the whole team is possible. A team under extraordinary deadline pressure may not have the capacity or the willingness to start until the most pressing circumstances are managed. A team with a single clear outcome to achieve might be better served with group facilitation. The time to answer this core question about fit for team coaching is during early discovery conversations.

Keys to a Successful and Sustainable Process

Related to the question about best candidates are questions about how to ensure a successful process once it is launched. Here are the qualities that we have found are important conditions for a successful ongoing team coaching process.

Create a Strong Framework of Trust

The odds of success definitely improve when there is a strong framework of trust within the team and between the team and coach.[166] As we noted earlier, that beneficial framework of trust may not be the case from the start. Regardless of the state of trust in the team at the moment the process begins, consider for a moment the context in which this work is introduced to a team. The territory the team is about to enter is likely to be unfamiliar and potentially risky or uncomfortable. If the truly important conversations were easy, if they were already within the team's comfort zone, those conversations would already be happening. There would likely not be any need for team coaching. That level of uncertainty creates a natural self-protection response that is trust-limiting.

Add to that scenario what the team observes before the work is truly underway. They see that the coach, the one who is in control of this process, has been in private conversation with the team leader and possibly someone from HR as well. The team may be at least wary, maybe even suspicious, of those private conversations. The coach's role may already be tainted, especially if the team is feeling under the microscope. "After all," the team wonders, "why else would the organization want to hire a team coach? There must be something wrong with us." Of course, there will also be some team members who are not surprised, who welcome the opportunity but are uncertain about the process. Clearly an emphasis on building trust is important from the start and important to build on throughout.

Here are keys to building trust and relationship with teams for the purpose of supporting team development.

Be Transparent. To help ensure openness by team members, start by being a model of openness with the team. Be transparent. Be willing to name what everyone is sensing and no one is saying. Tell the truth. When you say to the team, "This process will be most successful when you are open and candid in your team conversations," you can add, "and I know that's not always easy." The team sees they can trust the coach to tell the truth.

Be Inclusive. When working with the team as a system, there is a natural neutrality, a curiosity without judgment. Coaches understand that in order to have a complete picture of what's real on the team, all of the voices need to be accounted for, including the quiet voices and the unpopular or dissenting voices. No one has "the right answer." Everyone has a piece. This is not about trying to achieve consensus, by the way. It is a way to show respect for all of the voices on the team, and it would be normal to have different opinions, different perspectives, and different strategies for action. By paying attention to being inclusive, the team is more likely to stay in the process, knowing there is respect for differences. The coach is seen as trustworthy.

Be Willing to Redesign. Keep in mind that the team-development course that was first laid down on the map may have made perfect sense at the time, but actively present this is, after all, a change process. What the team has learned over the early weeks may be the insight needed for a more effective direction than the one the team started with. The willingness to course correct the process shows a commitment to the team's success. It can be as simple as checking with the team, "Are you getting what you need? How is this working for you? What would make it better?"

Reinforce Relevance. Ultimately, the only viable justification for team coaching is in measurable results that matter to the team and organization. That's why we make such a strong recommendation that teams monitor progress on two tracks during a team engagement: changes and improvement in team dynamics, and impact on business measures. We have built our entire methodology on a premise that high-performing teams excel at both dimensions, Productivity and Positivity. Those two dimensions are inexorably linked to team performance. To develop as a *sustainable,* high-performing team requires putting ample attention on both.

We also know that teams generally place high importance, and therefor heightened attention, on business measures for which they are responsible. They are more likely to be recognized for hitting stretch goals for business KPIs than achieving better scores for communication and trust. So be it. For coaches, this unmistakable preference needs to be honored by reinforcing the impact on the team's selected business metrics. That reinforcement in relevance will pay dividends in resilient team commitment.

Coaching Virtual Teams

The world of teams has changed dramatically over the years, and nowhere is that more obvious than in the proliferation of virtual teams. The availability of communications technology to connect people over global distances instantaneously has made it possible for teams to work together in ways that simply weren't possible a decade ago. From the organization's point of view, creating virtual teams has a number of clear benefits. The choice to assemble a virtual team gives organizations more flexibility to select the right membership for a particular team, regardless of where team members are located. When it comes to a team coaching process, eliminating travel provides significant savings, most importantly in the precious resource of team member time.

Creating virtual teams makes sense, and it comes with significant challenges. Virtual teams, without the in-person connection and the possibility of more spontaneous, less structured meeting opportunities, have a more difficult task when it comes to working together effectively.[167] Reflecting on our team-effectiveness model, virtual teams are often equipped to efficiently handle what we refer to as the Productivity side of the model. It shows up in the functional aspects of being a team: establishing clear goals, holding accountability, maintaining alignment, and so on. But little attention is given to the relationship infrastructure that creates Positivity. For work groups, that balance of emphasis may be perfectly suitable. For true team performance, we believe the same balance applies to virtual teams as we see in high-performing teams that work in-person.

The rapidly expanding world of virtual teams means that more and more, the coaching we do with teams will need to align with the special challenges of that environment. One of the first challenges is the technology itself and all the usual quirks and problems, such as getting the technology to work smoothly for everyone, the impact of local internet availability and signal strength, and the enormous variety of devices to accommodate. In spite of the irksome disruptions that often happen, team members are now reasonably familiar with the form. That's the good news. Unfortunately, it's a form that is well practiced for its functional application, not to create stronger team dynamics.

Team size can be more of an issue for virtual teams partly because of the environment. Gathering more than eight or 10 people on one call is cumbersome and starts to limit the ability to have engaged interaction. Also worth noting: a geographically dispersed team typically means it is also a multicultural team, which brings another layer of potential challenges for the virtual team. With teams spread around the globe, it can also be a challenge simply to find overlapping schedules when people can be awake and reasonably alert.

In spite of the challenges, it is possible to have effective team coaching sessions in this format, but the process requires special considerations, commitment, and training for the team. There needs to be a very conscientious shift in mindset and practice from "conference call," used for everyday information sharing and planning purposes, to "team coaching session," consciously designed to build trust and connection and develop new skills for working together across vast distances.[168]

Assuming the question of reliable technology is answered—not an easy assumption to make—here are seven essentials that will make success of a virtual team coaching session more likely.

1. Train the team: a team coaching session is very different from the standard staff or team meeting. For team coaching, the intention and attention are at a different, more heightened level. This requires being present, tuning in, and listening in ways that may not even be necessary in the typical online meeting where multitasking is commonplace.

2. Emphasize that creating an effective coaching environment is everyone's responsibility. In fact, it is an exercise in team accountability.

3. Create a clear set of team agreements to support the virtual team coaching sessions. Ask the team, "What will help ensure that this

is a valuable use of your time?" Rely on the natural creativity of the team to know what they need in order to be engaged and feel that the time commitment has value.

4. Look for ways to make the session more personal and less simply functional. For example, take a little time at the beginning of each session for a personal check-in. This can be quite short and simple. It's a way to get to know other team members as people with families or hobbies or interesting life experiences. It can also be a purely business inquiry such as, "What is one personal achievement that supports the team since our last session?"

5. Virtual team sessions benefit from changes in format and exercises or activities that shift the pace and focus. Long periods of discussion have the potential for running out of momentum unless there is a conscious break. Look for ways to break up the conversation and engage the team in different ways. Most videoconference systems include features like chat or polls, breakout rooms for small group or pairs conversation, or a white board that replicates the conference room flip chart.

6. As coach, be aware of the power of silence and remember that it is not your job to fill it. There is a natural tendency to want to avoid "dead air," but it can lead a coach to overengage in order to compensate, especially when the coach is missing clues from faces or body language.

7. Check in periodically, especially when you sense people are drifting rather than being present. Be transparent: What do you need? What will help this conversation be more valuable?

This increased organizational emphasis on virtual teams is not going away.[169] The question is how to deal with that phenomenon in a way that maximizes the team's potential. With the team coaching session, because the conversation tends to be broader and deeper than a more standard business meeting, and because it invites a more personal and engaged interaction, it's important to set a different set of guidelines and have different agreements. For the team, doing this process well may take time and practice. For the coach that means the team may need reminding or redirecting when the session starts to waver into more superficial conversation.

Working with the Team Leader

In the team coaching process, the team leader clearly has a special and in some ways complex role. More often than not the team leader takes the initiative to seek out resources to help the team. Even if the initial suggestion comes from HR or another internal source, the focus will be on the team leader. The team coach will first learn about the team and the issues the team is facing from the team leader and occasionally with the added participation of an HR sponsor.

This will be a two-way opportunity for learning: the team coach learning about the team, and the team leader learning about team coaching. There is an opportunity here to set expectations for the team leader and check for assumptions. Many team leaders will hear the words "team coach" and the sports model will quickly come to mind. Organizational team coaching is a similar but different model. In the athletic model, the coach takes a strong authority role, making decisions and setting direction for the team; that will not be the case for an organizational team coach. The team leader's concern about giving up or sharing authority for the direction of the team can be set aside usually with a sense of relief.

In the actual coaching work with the team, there is an important shift in roles for the team leader. In order for the sessions to be as effective as possible, it's important that the team leader participate fully as a member of the team, not just as the boss. The functional role doesn't go away, but the emphasis shifts to the team leader's personal voice. The intent is to recognize every team member's important role and contribution and do that in an environment where every voice counts.

The team leader is not giving up the responsibilities that go with the position. The purpose of the shift in role emphasis is to help create a safe platform for open, candid conversation. A one-on-one conversation between the team coach and the team leader is likely necessary to clarify the importance of this shift for the team's sake. There is an inevitable impact that comes with the leadership position that can have the effect of controlling or dampening conversation. The goal is to minimize that impact. In the end, the team's conversation will only be as honest as it feels safe to be open. The wider the available safe space, the better. The team leader can model and take a stand for that.

Another area where the special role of the team leader may come up is a situation where the coach is already coaching the team leader one-on-one. The question is, can the coach who is coaching the team leader also coach the team? The answer is a personal choice for each coach after considering the potential difficulties.

There is an upside: the team coach already has insight into the team members and team issues; for the coach, the downside is that it could be very difficult to approach this team assignment with neutrality after hearing from the team leader in confidential coaching sessions. Coaching both the team leader and the team also sets up a potential conflict of interest for the coach: "Where is my advocacy rooted?" Even a slight appearance of conflict of interest could derail the team coaching efforts. Team members are likely to start wondering, "What do they talk about in those confidential sessions? Are they talking about me?"

This awkward situation can lead to team members losing a measure of trust for their team leader and may create distrust or holding back in the team coaching process. In a coaching model, the coach is a committed advocate for the client or coachee. When the coach is coaching both the team and team leader, there will naturally be a potential for internal confusion on the part of the coach. "Where is my ultimate commitment?"

A similar situation occurs when the team coach coaches individual team members and the team as a whole. There are team coaches who do mix their team coaching with individual coaching of team members or the team leader. It requires very clear boundaries, faithfully maintained, and clear agreements with the team members around confidentiality that includes a promise on the part of the team coach to not disclose information received from other team members. If all this sounds like a tricky thing to manage and stay in integrity with all parties involved—it is.

The Multiplier Value of Two Coaches

Based on our database of teams, the average size of a team is about 10. Ten may not seem like a very large group to work with compared to a standard training classroom full of participants. But coaching a team and effectively handling all the elements that naturally, and instantly, come up in a session creates a flood of input. It can be enormously challenging to stay engaged, control the process, and be aware of the content and the underlying currents and tides in the flow of team dynamics.

By the time team size gets up to about 12 or above, coaching solo is both daunting and may not be the best way to serve the team. Working solo, a coach can only pay attention to so much. The risk is that coaches can lose track of the threads in the conversation. They can become distracted or hooked by something one team member said, or the way an annoying team member undermines the process, and miss capturing good ideas or topics from the team on the fly.

That's why, with larger teams and teams that have complex or challenging team dynamics, it often makes sense to coach in pairs. The organization is making a substantial investment in time and money for this team; co-coaching helps ensure the best possible outcome for that investment.

This is not a "First me—I'll do this part solo—then you—you'll do that part solo." It is co-coaching. Both coaches are actively engaged; a duet of coaches. This arrangement provides two sets of eyes and two sets of ears, doubling the awareness and experience available in the moment. When one coach takes the primary role in a particular piece of the conversation, the other can be scanning the team, looking for reaction, which might be agreement or disagreement or withdrawal; or as a practical matter, the co-coach can capture key points on a flip chart for the team. This is different from taking turns. It's a sharing, interdependent, seamless process of two coaches in alignment.

In effect, the two coaches are a model of teamwork, not just metaphorically, but literally. The team experiences the best of team interaction. If one of the pair gets temporarily lost, confused, or hooked, the other coach can take the lead while the emotional hook is removed and meaningful conversation stays on track.[170] It's a model of fundamental team-effectiveness skills, like transparency, listening, blending, finding alignment, building on each other, even disagreeing.

Co-coaching is a dance of two that gets easier, more intuitive, and more effective with practice over time. The relationship works best when the two share common values and have a common mindset about the work. That doesn't mean two similar styles; in fact, a partnership of contrasting styles can be especially effective with teams. Introvert/extrovert. Fast pace/deliberate pace. High energy/calm energy. With that breadth, the coaches provide a wider bandwidth for team-member preferences.[171] Where a high-energy extrovert working solo would likely not connect with a portion of the team, a complementary combination makes it possible to engage more effectively with the whole team.

The best examples of co-coaching are the result of a true blend of both coaches, acting together as one coach. Achieving that level of impact and fluid competence starts with spending time to clearly align by consciously designing the co-coaching team alliance. This typically includes a conversation around topics such as "What you can count on me for. Where I often get distracted. What I need from you when that happens. What I know works best for me in co-coaching. How we handle giving feedback to each other in the process."

Co-coaching adds exponential value beyond one plus one in terms of impact with the team and a more accelerated team-development process.

Use of Individual Assessments

The use of individual assessment tools with a team coaching process provides valuable, complementary insight to the systems view of the team. Yes, the team is having a system experience, and at the same time team members are having an individual experience. Both are true. Individual assessments help team members understand their own preferences and how individual styles affect working relationships on the team. For example: how decisions are made, how people engage or don't engage when there is disagreement, how direct to be in feedback, how to process information. The "reasonable" behavior for one person makes common sense. For another, that approach makes no sense.

On high-performing teams, these different perspectives, styles, and ways of working together are highly valued as in, "I have blind spots. You see things I don't see. I'm so glad you're on our team." The differences make for a stronger, more capable team.[172]

There are dozens of individual assessment tools available for creating more clarity and understanding between team members. Some provide a broad view; some are designed for specific purposes. For example, to show different communication styles, how individuals handle conflict, how decisions are made. The individual assessment gives team members a way to understand the motivation behind behavior. This raises awareness for the individual about their own way of working and interacting, and provides a way for team members to understand how others on the team are wired. This new awareness helps to explain why sometimes two people work together easily and smoothly and sometimes it's a very bumpy ride indeed. This new enlightenment can have a very positive effect on working relationships. Worth noting as a caution: for some team members it can also turn into a justification for behavior that is less than collaborative, with the explanation, "Well, I'm a [fill in the blank]. That's me. Get used to it."

Depending on the assessment tool, it is sometimes possible to place all of the team members' individual profiles on the graphic layout of the assessment model. It gives team members a way of seeing the variety of positions on the team and the weight or strength that is present based on what the tool measures. The thing to remember is that these are still individual profiles showing the relationships between individual team members. It is not a portrait of the team; it is a collage of individual pictures. It is also a static picture rather than a way of measuring team performance improvement over time. The individual styles are not likely to change over a six-month coaching engagement, although heightened awareness may help team members communicate and collaborate more effectively. By contrast, a systemic team assessment provides a baseline picture of the team and a way to measure progress over time.

Nurturing the Stakeholder Network

So far, our focus has been on one team more or less in isolation, but teams exist within a network of teams and individual stakeholder relationships. An improvement in team performance will require more than a concentrated focus on the team itself. Performance that matters to the organization will depend on improving stakeholder relationships as well. The same heightened awareness and new behaviors that support team development apply to building stronger stakeholder relationships.[173,174]

The team exists within a network of relationships and can't perform its function in a mindset that reinforces only a nearsighted focus on the team. Those reporting and customer relationships represent a live network of critical information that can help the team excel, but only if there is conscious and intentional attention on stakeholder relationships. The feedback loop is the real world speaking; it is the best reality check a team can get.

This is another area where teams sometimes say, "Yeah, good idea, but who's got time for this?" But the reality is, good stakeholder relationships, up, down, and sideways, can make processes run more smoothly, uncover potential issues before they get to alarming proportions, improve quality, and build a reserve of goodwill for those challenging times that are certain to occur.

How to develop more effective stakeholder relationships is a significant topic all by itself. One way for a team to explore the subject is to look for ways to replicate the team-development practices with stakeholders. For example, a conscious mutual design of the alliance between team and stakeholder, uncovering assumptions and expectations, clarifying roles, looking at patterns and ways to improve communication efficiency. What team members learn about more effective intra-team behavior may also be applied in inter-team behavior.

Systems Within Systems

In the same way that a team is a microsystem, surrounded by and connected to stakeholders, the team is also wired into the organization and that macrosystem. The culture of the organization—including what the organization values, its unique sense of identity or brand, the vision and mission from the organization's point of view, all the way down in detail to commonly held rules of interpersonal behavior—are a constant, inescapable, although invisible force field. No team is an island; it is part of the larger landscape, which includes the organization's cultural norms. Imagine the team as a city, inside a state or province, which is inside a country. There is a national language and local dialects; there are metaphorical mating rituals, an almost religious set of beliefs that people subscribe to as the truth.

The macrosystem exerts tremendous influence—to the point that some teams feel helpless to make changes that might run contrary to the cultural expectations.[175] Imagine for a moment what it is like to be the lone voice on a team advocating for change; taking a stand could be a very visible and unpopular place. Moving up to the next scalable level, the same dynamic is also true. The team risks being marginalized if it takes a new path that doesn't conform to "the way things are done around here." It's a challenge to be different within that cultural world.

Clearly the odds of success for individual teams dramatically improve when the support from the top of the organization is clear, not only clear to the team but to the organization as a whole. When that happens—when it is clear that this work is valued, maybe even that it's ordinary—it becomes a best practice for the organization and part of a strategic commitment to sustainable growth.

For Team Coaches

- What signs tell you that a team is motivated by a strong sense of urgency?
- What would you look for in a team to confirm that they have willingness, capacity, and commitment? What would make you wary?
- How would you handle strong disagreement or conflict in a virtual team setting?
- What advantages could you see in virtual team coaching, apart from the obvious convenience and efficiency?

For Team Leaders

- Where does the urgency come from for the team you lead?
- How would you evaluate your team's willingness, capacity, and commitment to a team-development process?
- As team leader, you will have a unique role in a team coaching process that includes possible tension between your functional role and the responsibilities and authority that go with it and your full participation as a member of the team. What will help you navigate that course?
- What are the current opportunities you see in stakeholder relationships that would benefit from a stronger focus? What is the team's role in that effort?

CHAPTER 12

Why This Work
Is Important

The World Health Organization has called job-related stress a world-wide epidemic.[176] The workplace at every level is a constant pressure cooker. This is not an isolated industry or specific geography issue; it is a well-documented, global issue. The statistics are alarming. According to the US Department of Health and Human Services, over 40 percent of surveyed employees report that yelling and other verbal abuse are common.[177] "Desk rage" and "phone rage" are increasingly common terms. Nearly two-thirds of employees end the day with physical pain related to job stress. The economy may have improved since the worst days of the Great Recession, but job stress, if anything, is worse.

The cost to US business alone is estimated to be $300 billion through absenteeism; turnover; diminished productivity; and medical, legal, and insurance costs.[178] Those are the business costs. And then there are the human costs. Go just beyond the statistics and you will see this is a personal issue. Yes, the pressure to do more with less affects the bottom line, but that stress gets carried home like a bad virus and infects relationships with those we care about most.

It doesn't have to be that way. The scope of the workplace stress problem is widely known because it is people's pervasive experience. The statistics quantify it but the everyday experience at work is the most compelling evidence of the impact. When teams or organizations acknowledge the issue and its impact, they naturally ask the question, "So, what do we *do* about it?"

We believe that the intervention of a team coaching process with competent team coaches is an ideal answer to that question. It's a way to make a difference in the lives of team members and their organizations. This work matters. It provides leverage directly at the point of stress, in the relationships among team members where they interact every day. Effective improvement and sustainable results take adoption and integration of new behavior, and it requires practice over time, but our data shows it works. People can learn to work together in an environment that is free of toxicity, where diversity is valued, where people are aligned on mission and purpose, where they collaborate effectively, where trust and respect are in the air team members breathe every day.

Team coaches play an important role in that shift. They have the opportunity to interact in a meaningful way with people who might not ever seek out a coach or see the need for "personal development." They may have never been down that aisle in the bookstore. But they live the impact of the daily battles and pay the consequences personally. Many times, their families do too, by extension.

The value proposition for this work can be posed in quantitative terms in many convincing ways. In our view, that makes it easier to justify what is clear on human terms.

We believe human beings are wired to be in community. Millions of years of hunting, gathering, barn raising, community building, neighbors helping neighbors, and a thousand other examples demonstrate the nature and importance of interdependence. It's true at work as well. Team members want what all humans want: to feel that they belong, that what they do together matters, that at the end of the day they can say, "Today I made a contribution," and that somebody noticed. If we can create that in our work with teams, we have made a difference.[179]

The world needs this, needs to learn how to pull together, needs to learn how to disagree wholeheartedly and still find ways to be aligned, productive, even energized. That best team experience we highlighted at the beginning of this book is an attainable goal. Imagine going to work every day looking forward to that kind of empowering team culture, achieving results and creating supportive community.

There is no better place to practice that than on teams. Every day, opportunities to learn and practice are present in the very nature of the work people do. Starting with teams is ideal because of the viable size of the team community, the obvious inherent value of collaboration, and the opportunity to practice new behavior and see visible success. In fact, we see this as our mission: to change the quality of life at work.

Endnotes

Introduction

1. Based on data from the TCI Team Diagnostic database. Initial baseline team assessments before a team coaching process has begun.
2. Jim Harter, "Dismal Employee Engagement Is a Sign of Global Mismanagement," *Gallup Blog*, December 20, 2017, https://www.gallup.com/work place/231668/dismal-employee-engagement-sign-global-mismanagement .aspx)
3. Susan Sorenson and Keri Garman, "How to Tackle U.S. Employees' Stagnating Engagement," *Gallup Business Journal*, June 11, 2013, https:// news.gallup.com/businessjournal/162953/tackle-employees-stagnating -engagement.aspx/.

Part 1

4. Erika Herb, Keith Leslie, and Colin Price, "Teamwork at the Top," *McKinsey Quarterly*, May 2001, https://www.mckinsey.com/business-functions/ organization/our-insights/teamwork-at-the-top/.

1

5. Justin Bariso, "Google Spent Years Studying Effective Teams: This Single Quality Contributed Most to Their Success," *Inc.,* January 7, 2018, https:// www.inc.com/justin-bariso/google-spent-years-studying-effective-teams- this-single-quality-contributed-most-to-their-success.html/.
6. Nicky Wakefield, et al., "Leadership Awakened," *Deloitte Insights*, February 29, 2016, https://www2.deloitte.com/insights/us/en/focus/human-capital- trends/2016/identifying-future-business-leaders-leadership.html/.

7. Heather R. Huhman, "How to Properly Prepare First-Time Managers," *Business Insider,* March 22, 2011, https://www.businessinsider.com/how-to-properly-prepare-your-first-time-managers-2011-3/.

8. Aaron De Smet, Gerald Lackey, and Leigh M. Weiss, "Untangling Your Organization's Decision Making," *McKinsey Quarterly*, June 2017, https://www.mckinsey.com/business-functions/organization/our-insights/untangling-your-organizations-decision-making/.

9. Michael Mink, "Making Yourself and Others Accountable Is Business Critical," *Investor's Business Daily,* August 29, 2016, https://www.investors.com/news/management/leaders-and-success/making-yourself-and-others-accountable-is-business-critical/.

10. Erika Herb, Keith Leslie, and Colin Price, "Teamwork at the Top," *McKinsey Quarterly,* May 2001, https://www.mckinsey.com/business-functions/organization/our-insights/teamwork-at-the-top/.

11. Rachel Willard-Grace et al., "Team Structure and Culture Are Associated with Lower Burnout in Primary Care," *Journal of the American Board of Family Medicine* 27, no. 2 (2014): 229–238, http://www.jabfm.org/content/27/2/229.full.pdf.

12. Marc Kaplan et al., "Shape Culture Drive Strategy," *Deloitte Insights*, February 29, 2016, https://www2.deloitte.com/insights/us/en/focus/human-capital-trends/2016/impact-of-culture-on-business-strategy.html.

13. Daniel Goleman, *Emotional Intelligence: Why It Can Matter More than IQ* (New York: Bantam, 2006).

14. "How to Engineer Team Camaraderie and High-Performance," BlueIQ, June 22, 2017, http://getblueiq.com/how-to-engineer-team-camaraderie-and-high-performance/.

15. Jill E. Perry-Smith, "Social Yet Creative: The Role of Social Relationships in Facilitating Individual Creativity," *Academy of Management Journal* 49, no. 1 (2006): 85–101.

16. Scott Keller and Mary Meaney, "High-Performing Teams: A Timeless Leadership Topic," *McKinsey Quarterly*, June 2017, https://www.mckinsey.com/business-functions/organization/our-insights/high-performing-teams-a-timeless-leadership-topic.

17. Scott Keller and Mary Meaney, "Successfully Transitioning to New Leadership Roles," *McKinsey Quarterly*, May 2018, https://www.mckinsey.com/business-functions/organization/our-insights/successfully-transitioning-to-new-leadership-roles.

2

18. Frederick P. Morgeson, D. Scott DeRue, and Elizabeth P. Karam, "Leadership in Teams: A Functional Approach to Understanding Leadership Structures and Processes," *Journal of Management* 36, no. 1 (January 2010): 5–9.

19. Nagaraj Sivasubramaniam, William D. Murry, Bruce J. Avolio, and Dong I. Jung, "A Longitudinal Model of the Effects of Team Leadership and Group Potency on Group Performance," *Group and Organization Management* 27, no. 1 (2002): 66–96.

20. Chris Pick, "Survey: IT Leaders Lack Business Skills and Resources," Apptio, March 15, 2011, https://www.apptio.com/emerge/survey-it-leaders -lack-business-skills-and-resources.

21. J. Øvretveit, "Team Decision-Making," *Journal of Interprofessional Care* 9, no. 1 (1995): 41–51.

22. Michiel Kruyt, Judy Malan, and Rachel Tuffield, "Three Steps to Building a Better Top Team," *McKinsey Quarterly*, February 2011, https://www .mckinsey.com/business-functions/organization/our-insights/three-steps -to-building-a-better-top-team.

23. Ute R. Hülsheger, Neil Anderson, and Jesus F. Salgado, "Team-Level Predictors of Innovation at Work: A Comprehensive Meta-Analysis Spanning Three Decades of Research," *Journal of Applied Psychology* 94, no. 5 (2009): 1128.

24. Michael A. West and Neil R. Anderson, "Innovation in Top Management Teams," *Journal of Applied Psychology* 81, no. 6 (1996): 680.

25. Patricia M. Fandt, "The Relationship of Accountability and Interdependent Behavior to Enhancing Team Consequences," *Group and Organization Studies* 16, no. 3 (1991): 300–12.

26. Eric Sundstrom, Kenneth P. De Meuse, and David Futrell, "Work Teams: Applications and Effectiveness," *American Psychologist* 45, no. 2 (1990): 120.

27. Lucy L. Gilson and Christina E. Shalley, "A Little Creativity Goes a Long Way: An Examination of Teams' Engagement in Creative Processes," *Journal of Management* 30, no. 4 (2004): 453–70.

28. Jon R. Katzenbach and Douglas K. Smith, "The Discipline of Teams," *Harvard Business Review* 71, no. 2 (1993): 111–20.

29. J. Richard Hackman and Ruth Wageman, "A Theory of Team Coaching," *Academy of Management Review* 30, no. 2 (2005): 269–87.

30. Edwin A. Locke and Gary P. Latham, *A Theory of Goal Setting and Task Performance* (Englewood Cliffs, NJ: Prentice Hall, 1990).

31. Dean Tjosvold, Moureen M. Tang, and Michael West, "Reflexivity for Team Innovation in China: The Contribution of Goal Interdependence," *Group and Organization Management* 29, no. 5 (2004): 540–59.

32. Shawn Burke et al., "Understanding Team Adaptation: A Conceptual Analysis and Model," *Journal of Applied Psychology* 91, no. 6 (2006): 1189.

33. Ute R. Hülsheger, Neil Anderson, and Jesus F. Salgado, "Team-Level Predictors of Innovation at Work: A Comprehensive Meta-Analysis Spanning Three Decades of Research," *Journal of Applied Psychology* 94, no. 5 (2009): 1128.

3

34. C. S. Burke et al., "Understanding Team Adaptation: A Conceptual Analysis and Model," *Journal of Applied Psychology* 91, no. 6 (2006): 1189.

35. Amy Edmondson, "Psychological Safety and Learning Behavior In Work Teams," *Administrative Science Quarterly* 44, no. 2 (1999): 350–83.

36. Jon Katzenbach and Douglas K. Smith, "The Discipline of Teams," *Harvard Business Review* 71, no. 2 (1993): 111–20.

37. N. B. Moe and D. Šmite, "Understanding a Lack of Trust in Global Software Teams: A Multiple-Case Study," *Software Process: Improvement and Practice* 13, no. 3 (2008): 217–31.

38. Jody Hoffer Gittell, "A Theory of Relational Coordination," in *Positive Organizational Scholarship: Foundations of a New Discipline*, ed. Kim S. Cameron (San Francisco, CA: Berrett-Koehler, 2003), 279–295.

39. Abraham Carmeli, Jane E. Dutton, and Ashley E. Hardin, "Respect as an Engine for New Ideas: Linking Respectful Engagement, Relational Information Processing, and Creativity among Employees and Teams," *Human Relations* 68, no. 6 (2015): 1021–47.

40. Jane E. Dutton, *Energize Your Workplace: How to Create and Sustain High-Quality Connections at Work* (New York: John Wiley and Sons, 2006).

41. João F. Guassi Moreira, Jay J. Van Bavel, and Eve H. Telzer, "The Neural Development of 'Us and Them,'" *Social Cognitive and Affective Neuroscience* 12, no. 2 (2016): 184–96.

42. Austen Krill and Steven M. Platek, "In-Group and Out-Group Membership Mediates Anterior Cingulate Activation to Social Exclusion," *Frontiers in Evolutionary Neuroscience* 1, no. 1 (2009).

43. Gert-Jan Pepping and Erik J. Timmermans, "Oxytocin and the Biopsychology of Performance in Team Sports," *Scientific World Journal* (2012): 1–10.

44. Paul J. Zak, "How Oxytocin Can Make Your Job More Meaningful," *Greater Good Magazine*, June 6, 2018, https://greatergood.berkeley.edu/article/item/how_oxytocin_can_make_your_job_more_meaningful.

45. Annamarie Mann, "Why We Need Best Friends at Work," Gallup Workplace, January 15, 2018, https://www.gallup.com/workplace/236213/why-need-best-friends-work.aspx.

46. Judith A. Ross, "Team Camaraderie: Can You Have Too Much?" *Harvard Management Update* 10, no. 11 (2005): 3.

47. Sean Wise, "Can a Team Have Too Much Cohesion?: The Dark Side to Network Density," *European Management Journal* 32, no. 5 (2014): 703–11.

48. Svan Lembke and Marie G. Wilson, "Putting the 'Team' into Teamwork: Alternative Theoretical Contributions for Contemporary Management Practice," *Human Relations* 51, no. 7 (1998): 927–44.

49. Blake E. Ashforth and Fred Mael, "Social Identity Theory and the Organization," *Academy of Management Review* 14, no. 1 (1989): 20–39.

50. Günter K. Stahl, Martha L. Maznevski, Andreas Voigt, and Karsten Jonsen, "Unraveling the Effects of Cultural Diversity in Teams: A Meta-Analysis of Research on Multicultural Work Groups," *Journal of International Business Studies* 41, no. 4 (2010): 690–709.

51. Niina Nurmi and Pamela J. Hinds, "Job Complexity and Learning Opportunities: A Silver Lining in the Design of Global Virtual Work," *Journal of International Business Studies* 47, no. 6 (2016): 631–54.

52. Lou Solomon, "The Top Complaints from Employees about Their Leaders," *Harvard Business Review*, June 24, 2015, https://hbr.org/2015/06/the-top-complaints-from-employees-about-their-leaders.

53. Bianca Beersma and Gerben A. Van Kleef, "How the Grapevine Keeps You in Line," *Social Psychological and Personality Science* 2, no. 6 (2011): 642–49.

54. Y. Donchin et al., "A Look into the Nature and Causes of Human Errors in the Intensive Care Unit," *BMJ Quality and Safety in Health Care* 12, no. 2 (2003): 143–47.

55. Kay Lovelace, Debra L. Shapiro, and Laurie R. Weingart, "Maximizing Cross-Functional New Product Teams' Innovativeness and Constraint Adherence: A Conflict Communications Perspective," *Academy of Management Journal* 44, no. 4 (2001): 779–93.

56. Andrew Van de Ven, "Central Problems in the Management of Innovation," *Management Science* 32 (1986): 590–607.

57. Mary O'Hara-Devereaux and Robert Johansen, *Globalwork: Bridging Distance, Culture, and Time* (San Francisco, CA: Jossey-Bass, 1994).

58. Jill E. Perry-Smith and Christina E. Shalley, "The Social Side of Creativity: A Static and Dynamic Social Network Perspective," *Academy of Management Review* 28, no. 1 (2003): 89–106.

59. Ronald Bledow et al., "A Dialectic Perspective on Innovation: Conflicting Demands, Multiple Pathways, and Ambidexterity," *Industrial and Organizational Psychology* 2, no. 3 (2009): 305–37.

60. Carsten K. W. De Dreu and Michael A. West, "Minority Dissent and Team Innovation: The Importance of Participation in Decision Making," *Journal of Applied Psychology* 86, no. 6 (2001): 1191.

61. Christina E. Shalley and Lucy L. Gilson, "What Leaders Need to Know: A Review of Social and Contextual Factors that Can Foster or Hinder Creativity," *Leadership Quarterly* 15, no. 1 (2004): 33–53.

62. Peter J. Carnevale and Tahira M. Probst, "Social Values and Social Conflict in Creative Problem Solving and Categorization," *Journal of Personality and Social Psychology* 74, no. 5 (1998): 1300.

63. Allen C. Amason, "Distinguishing the Effects of Functional and Dysfunctional Conflict on Strategic Decision Making: Resolving a Paradox for Top Management Teams," *Academy of Management Journal* 39, no. 1 (1996): 123–48.

64. Karen A. Jehn, "A Multimethod Examination of the Benefits and Detriments of Intragroup Conflict," *Administrative Science Quarterly* 40, no. 2 (1995): 256–82.

65. Lisa Hope Pelled, "Demographic Diversity, Conflict, and Work Group Outcomes: An Intervening Process Theory," *Organization Science* 7, no. 6 (1996): 615–31.

66. Cristina B. Gibson and Jennifer A. Manuel, "Building Trust: Effective Multicultural Communication Processes in Virtual Teams," in *Virtual Teams That Work: Creating Conditions for Virtual Team Effectiveness* (San Francisco, CA: Jossey-Bass, 2003), 59–86.

67. Atreyi Kankanhalli, Bernard C. Y. Tan, and Kwok-Kee Wei, "Conflict and Performance in Global Virtual Teams," *Journal of Management Information Systems* 23, no. 3 (2006): 237–74.

68. Charles R. Schwenk, "Effects of Devil's Advocacy and Dialectical Inquiry on Decision Making: A Meta-Analysis," *Organizational Behavior and Human Decision Processes* 47, no. 1 (1990): 161–76.

69. Jill E. Perry-Smith, "Social Yet Creative: The Role of Social Relationships in Facilitating Individual Creativity," *Academy of Management Journal* 49, no. 1 (2006): 85–101.

70. Erik Larson, "New Research: Diversity + Inclusion = Better Decision Making at Work," *Forbes*, September 21, 2017, https://www.forbes.com/sites/

eriklarson/2017/09/21/new-research-diversity-inclusion-better-decision
-making-at-work/#7077ee1c4cbf.

71. Carsten K. W. De Dreu and Michael A. West, "Minority Dissent and Team Innovation: The Importance of Participation in Decision Making," *Journal of Applied Psychology* 86, no. 6 (2001): 1191.

72. C. R. Snyder and Howard L. Fromkin, *Uniqueness: The Pursuit of Human Difference* (New York: Plenum, 1980).

73. Marilynn B. Brewer, "The Importance of Being We: Human Nature and Intergroup Relations," *American Psychologist* 62, no. 8 (2007): 728.

74. Bradley J. West, Jaime L. Patera, and Melissa K. Carsten, "Team Level Positivity: Investigating Positive Psychological Capacities and Team Level Outcomes," *Journal of Organizational Behavior: The International Journal of Industrial, Occupational, and Organizational Psychology and Behavior* 30, no. 2 (2009): 249–67.

75. Tal Y. Katz-Navon and Miriam Erez, "When Collective- and Self-Efficacy Affect Team Performance: The Role of Task Interdependence," *Small Group Research* 36, no. 4 (2005): 437–65.

76. Andrew J. Oswald, Eugenio Proto, and Daniel Sgroi, "Happiness and Productivity," *Journal of Labor Economics* 33, no. 4 (2015): 789–822.

4

77. Marcus Goncalves, *Team Building* (New York: ASME, 2006).

78. Alex Palmer, "When Teambuilding Fails," *Successful Meetings*, August 3, 2015, http://www.successfulmeetings.com/Strategy/Meeting-Strategies/When-Teambuilding-Fails/.

79. Charles L. Slater and David L. Simmons, "The Design and Implementation of a Peer Coaching Program," *American Secondary Education* 29, no. 3 (2001): 67–76.

80. David Clutterbuck, *Coaching the Team at Work* (New York: Nicholas Brealey, 2011).

81. David Kirk, "World-Class Teams," *McKinsey Quarterly*, December 1992, https://www.mckinsey.com/business-functions/organization/our-insights/world-class-teams.

82. Ibid.

83. Anita Sarma and André van der Hoek, "A Need Hierarchy for Teams," Department of Informatics, Donald Bren School of Information and Computer Sciences, University of California Irvine, 2004.

84. Marcial Losada and Emily Heaphy, "The Role of Positivity and Connectivity in the Performance of Business Teams: A Nonlinear Dynamics Model," *American Behavioral Scientist* 47, no. 6 (2004): 740–65.

5

85. Stacia Garr, Andrew Liakopoulos, and Lisa Barry, "Performance Management Is Broken: Replace 'Rank and Yank' with Coaching and Development," *Deloitte Insights*, March 4, 2014, https://www2.deloitte.com/insights/us/en/focus/human-capital-trends/2014/hc-trends-2014-performance-management.html.

86. Alex Vincent, "Team Performance: How to Turn Good into Great," Lee Hecht Harrison, June 11, 2018, https://www.lhh.com/our-knowledge/2018/transformation-insights-no-1/team-performance-how-to-turn-good-into-great.

87. Phillippa Lally et al., "How Are Habits Formed: Modelling Habit Formation in the Real World," *European Journal of Social Psychology* 40, no. 6 (2010): 998–1009.

88. Deloitte University Press, *Global Human Capital Trends 2016: The New Organization: Different by Design*, https://www2.deloitte.com/content/dam/Deloitte/global/Documents/HumanCapital/gx-dup-global-human-capital-trends-2016.pdf.

89. Joint Commission on Accreditation of Healthcare Organizations, *Health Care at the Crossroads: Strategies for Improving the Medical Liability System and Preventing Patient Injury* (Oakbrook Terrace, IL: Joint Commission on Accreditation of Healthcare Organizations, 2005), https://www.jointcommission.org/assets/1/18/Medical_Liability.pdf.

90. Holly B. Tompson et al., *Coaching: A Global Study of Successful Practices; Current Trends and Future Possibilities, 2008–2018* (New York: American Management Association, 2008).

91. Mark Colgate, *8 Moments of Power in Coaching: How to Design and Deliver High-Performance Feedback to All Employees* (Boise, ID: Elevate, 2016).

92. Scott Shank, "A Case Study of Professional Coach-Client Communication" (thesis, Western Michigan University, 2015).

93. Holly B. Tompson et al., *Coaching: A Global Study of Successful Practices; Current Trends and Future Possibilities, 2008–2018* (New York: American Management Association, 2008).

94. M. R. Champathes, "Coaching for Performance Improvement: The 'Coach' Model," *Development and Learning in Organizations: An International Journal* 20, no. 2 (2006): 17–18.

95. Nils Brede Moe, Daniela S. Cruzes, Tore Dybå, and Ellen Engebretsen, "Coaching a Global Agile Virtual Team," in *Proceedings of the 2015 IEEE 10th International Conference on Global Software Engineering* (Washington, DC: IEEE Computer Society, 2015), 33–37.

96. Eric K. Shaw et al., "How Team-Based Reflection Affects Quality Improvement Implementation: A Qualitative Study," *Quality Management in Health Care* 21, no. 2 (2012): 104.

Part 2

6

97. George A. Neuman, Stephen H. Wagner, and Neil D. Christiansen, "The Relationship Between Work-Team Personality Composition and the Job Performance of Teams," *Group and Organization Management* 24, no. 1 (1999): 28–45.

98. Anne S. York, Kim A. McCarthy, and Todd C. Darnold, "Building Biotechnology Teams: Personality Does Matter," *Journal of Commercial Biotechnology* 15, no. 4 (2009): 335–46.

99. Bradley J. West, Jaime L. Patera, and Melissa K. Carsten, "Team Level Positivity: Investigating Positive Psychological Capacities and Team Level Outcomes," *Journal of Organizational Behavior: The International Journal of Industrial, Occupational, and Organizational Psychology and Behavior* 30, no. 2 (2009): 249–67.

100. B. Adkins and D. Caldwell, "Firm or Subgroup Culture: Where Does Fitting In Matter Most?" *Journal of Organizational Behavior: The International Journal of Industrial, Occupational, and Organizational Psychology and Behavior* 25, no. 8 (2004): 969–78.

101. S. L. Gaertner et al., "Across Cultural Divides: The Value of a Superordinate Identity," in *Cultural Divides: Understanding and Overcoming Group Conflict*, ed. D. A. Prentice and D. T. Miller (New York: Russell Sage Foundation, 1999), 173–212.

102. Naomi Ellemers, Ed Sleebos, Daan Stam, and Dick de Gilder, "Feeling Included and Valued: How Perceived Respect Affects Positive Team Identity and Willingness to Invest in the Team," *British Journal of Management* 24, no. 1 (2013): 21–37.

103. R. J. Marshak, "Generative Conversations: How to Use Deep Listening and Transforming Talk in Coaching and Consulting," in *Handbook for Strategic HR-Section 3: Use of Self as an Instrument of Change* (Nashville, TN: AMACOM, 2015).

104. D. Randy Garrison, Terry Anderson, and Walter Archer, "Critical Thinking and Computer Conferencing: A Model and Tool to Assess Cognitive Presence," *American Journal of Distance Education* 15, no. 1 (2001): 7–23.

7

105. J. Hu and R.C. Liden, "Antecedents of Team Potency and Team Effectiveness: An Examination of Goal and Process Clarity and Servant Leadership," *Journal of Applied Psychology* 96, no. 4 (2011): 851.

106. David M. Schweiger, William R. Sandberg, and James W. Ragan, "Group Approaches for Improving Strategic Decision Making: A Comparative Analysis of Dialectical Inquiry, Devil's Advocacy, and Consensus," *Academy of Management Journal* 29, no. 1 (1986): 51–71.

107. David M. Schweiger, William R. Sandberg, and Paula L. Rechner, "Experiential Effects of Dialectical Inquiry, Devil's Advocacy, and Consensus Approaches to Strategic Decision Making," *Academy of Management Journal* 32, no. 4 (1989): 745–72.

108. Henning Bang, Synne L. Fuglesang, Mariann R. Ovesen, and Dag Erik Eilertsen, "Effectiveness in Top Management Group Meetings: The Role of Goal Clarity, Focused Communication, and Learning Behavior," *Scandinavian Journal of Psychology* 51, no. 3 (2010): 253–61.

109. K. Gyllensten and S. Palmer, "The Coaching Relationship: An Interpretative Phenomenological Analysis," *International Coaching Psychology Review* 2, no. 2 (2007): 168–77.

110. Harry Weger, Gina Castle Bell, Elizabeth M. Minei, and Melissa C. Robinson, "The Relative Effectiveness of Active Listening in Initial Interactions," *International Journal of Listening* 28, no. 1 (2014): 13–31.

111. Kerryn E. Griffiths and Marilyn A. Campbell, "Regulating the Regulators: Paving the Way for International, Evidence-Based Coaching Standards," *International Journal of Evidence Based Coaching and Mentoring* 6, no. 1 (2008): 19–31.

112. Jonathan Chan and Clifford Mallett, "The Value of Emotional Intelligence for High Performance Coaching," *International Journal of Sports Science and Coaching* 6, no. 3 (2011): 315–28.

113. Robert Baron, "Positive Effects of Conflict: A Cognitive Perspective," *Employee Responsibilities and Rights Journal* 4, no. 1 (1991): 25–36.

114. Karen Jehn, "A Multimethod Examination of the Benefits and Detriments of Intragroup Conflict," *Administrative Science Quarterly* 40, no. 2 (1995): 256–82.

115. Mary E. Zellmer-Bruhn and Cristina B. Gibson, "Metaphors and Meaning: An Intercultural Analysis of the Concept of Teamwork," *Administrative Science Quarterly* 46, no. 2 (2001): 274–303.

116. Janis A. Cannon-Bowers, Eduardo Salas, and Sharolyn Converse, "Shared Mental Models in Expert Team Decision Making," in *Individual and Group*

Decision Making: Current Issues, ed. N. J. Castellan Jr. (Hillsdale, NJ: Lawrence Erlbaum, 1993), 221–46.

8

117. Coleen R. Saylor, "Reflection and Professional Education: Art, Science, and Competency," *Nurse Educator* 15, no. 2 (1990): 8-11.

118. Zoë Knowles, Gareth Tyler, David Gilbourne, and Martin Eubank, "Reflecting on Reflection: Exploring the Practice of Sports Coaching Graduates," *Reflective Practice* 7, no. 2 (2006): 163–79.

119. Jennifer A. Chatman and Francis J. Flynn, "The Influence of Demographic Heterogeneity on the Emergence and Consequences of Cooperative Norms in Work Teams," *Academy of Management Journal* 44, no. 5 (2001): 956–74.

120. Alex Sandy Pentland, "The New Science of Building Great Teams," *Harvard Business Review* 90, no. 4 (2012): 60–70.

121. Michael E. Palanski, Surinder S. Kahai, and Francis J. Yammarino, "Team Virtues and Performance: An Examination of Transparency, Behavioral Integrity, and Trust," *Journal of Business Ethics* 99, no. 2 (2011): 201–16.

122. Amanuel G. Tekleab, Narda R. Quigley, and Paul E. Tesluk, "A Longitudinal Study of Team Conflict, Conflict Management, Cohesion, and Team Effectiveness," *Group and Organization Management* 34, no. 2 (2009): 170–205.

123. James E. Driskell, Eduardo Salas, and Joan Johnston, "Does Stress Lead to a Loss of Team Perspective?" *Group Dynamics: Theory, Research, and Practice* 3, no. 4 (1999): 291–302.

124. Marie Whitney and Harold Christian Schafer, "Maintaining Observer Skills through an Effective Coaching Structure," *Society of Petroleum Engineers* (January 1, 2007), https://www.onepetro.org/conference-paper/SPE-106812-MS.

125. Michael Farrell, Madeline Schmitt, and Gloria Heinemann, "Informal Roles and the Stages of Interdisciplinary Team Development," *Journal of Interprofessional Care* 15, no. 3 (2001): 281–95.

126. "Watch Out for These Dysfunctional Roles in Teams," MTD: Management Training Specialists, December 27, 2012, https://www.mtdtraining.com/blog/watch-out-for-these-dysfunctional-roles-in-your-team.htm.

127. Baden Eunson, *Communicating in the 21st Century* (Milton, Qld, Australia: John Wiley and Sons, 2012).

128. James R. Lincoln and Jon Miller, "Work and Friendship Ties in Organizations: A Comparative Analysis of Relation Networks," *Administrative Science Quarterly* 24, no. 2 (1979): 181–99.

129. Lingtao Yu and Mary Zellmer-Bruhn, "Introducing Team Mindfulness and Considering Its Safeguard Role against Conflict Transformation and Social Undermining," *Academy of Management Journal* 61, no. 1 (2018): 324–47.

130. Elaine Cox, "Coaching Understood: A Pragmatic Inquiry into the Coaching Process," *International Journal of Sports Science and Coaching* 8, no. 1 (2013): 265–70.

131. "The Nine Belbin Team Roles," Belbin, https://www.belbin.com/about/belbin-team-roles/.

132. R. L. Cook, and K. R. Hammond, "Interpersonal Learning and Interpersonal Conflict Reduction in Decision-Making Groups," in *Improving Group Decision Making in Organizations*, ed. R. A. Guzzo (New York: Academic Press, 1982), 13–40.

133. Nagesh Belludi, "The Curse of Teamwork: Groupthink," Right Attitudes, October 11, 2016, http://www.rightattitudes.com/2016/10/11/teamwork-groupthink/.

134. Harvard Business School Staff, "Measure Your Team's Intellectual Diversity," *Harvard Business Review* (May 21, 2015), https://hbr.org/2015/05/measure-your-teams-intellectual-diversity.

135. Taylor H. Cox and Stacy Blake, "Managing Cultural Diversity: Implications for Organizational Competitiveness," *Academy of Management Perspectives* 5, no. 3 (1991): 45–56.

136. Charlan Nemeth, Keith Brown, and John Rogers, "Devil's Advocate versus Authentic Dissent: Stimulating Quantity and Quality," *European Journal of Social Psychology* 31, no. 6 (2001): 707–20.

9

137. Alison Carter, Anna Blackman, and Rachel Hay, "What Makes a Coach Effective?" Institute for Employment Studies, April 11, 2016, https://www.employment-studies.co.uk/system/files/resources/files/mp116.pdf.

138. Charalambos Vlachoutsicos, "Your Body Language Speaks for You in Meetings," *Harvard Business Review* (blog), September 19, 2012, https://hbr.org/2012/09/your-body-language-speaks-for.

139. "Self-Management and Coaching," NovoEd, September 24, 2015, https://novoed.com/blog/1006/self-management-and-coaching/.

140. Travis Kemp, "Is Coaching an Evolved Form of Leadership? Building a Transdisciplinary Framework for Exploring the Coaching Alliance," *International Coaching Psychology Review* 4, no. 1 (2009): 105–10.

141. Tuire Havia, "How Do Coaches Establish Trust in Team Sports?: A Qualitative Research of Coaching Leadership" (thesis, University of Jyväskylä, 2017), https://jyx.jyu.fi/bitstream/handle/123456789/56523/URN: NBN:fi:jyu-201712214851.pdf.

142. Daniel Goleman, *Primal Leadership: Realizing the Power of Emotional Intelligence* (Boston, MA: Harvard Business School, 2002).

143. Tom Yorton, "3 Improv Exercises that Can Change the Way Your Team Works," *Harvard Business Review*, March 9, 2015, https://hbr.org/2015/03/3-improv-exercises-that-can-change-the-way-your-team-works.

144. Dusya Vera and Mary Crossan, "Improvisation and Innovative Performance in Teams," *Organization Science* 16, no. 3 (2005): 203–24.

10

145. Thomas D. Raedeke, Anne H. Warren, and Tracy L Granzyk, "Coaching Commitment and Turnover: A Comparison of Current and Former Coaches," *Research Quarterly for Exercise and Sport* 73, no. 1 (2002): 73–86.

146. Glenn M. Parker, *Cross-Functional Teams: Working with Allies, Enemies, and Other Strangers* (New York: John Wiley and Sons, 2003).

147. Andy Rankin, "The Use of 'Silence' in Coaching," *International Journal of Mentoring and Coaching* 1 (2008): 1–5.

148. John P. Kotter and Dan Cohen, *The Heart of Change: Real Life Stories of How People Change Their Organization* (Boston, MA: Harvard Business School, 2001).

149. Joseph Grenny, "The Best Teams Hold Themselves Accountable," *Harvard Business Review* (blog), May 30, 2014, https://hbr.org/2014/05/the-best-teams-hold-themselves-accountable.

150. Patricia M. Fandt, "The Relationship of Accountability and Interdependent Behavior to Enhancing Team Consequences," *Group and Organization Studies* 16, no. 3 (1991): 300–12.

151. Cheryl Stein, "Cheryl Stein on Coaching versus Consulting," Monster, accessed on October 17, 2018, https://www.monster.ca/career-advice/article/cheryl-stein-on-coaching-versus-consulting-canada.

152. Forbes Coaches Council, "Key Differences between Coaching and Consulting (and How to Decide What Your Business Needs)," *Forbes*, June 14, 2018, https://www.forbes.com/sites/forbescoachescouncil/2018/06/14/key-differences-between-coaching-and-consulting-and-how-to-decide-what-your-business-needs/#73c49f2e3d71.

153. Javier Abarca et al., "Teamwork and Working in Teams," in *Introductory Engineering Design: A Projects-Based Approach*, ed. Janet Yowell and Denise Carlson (Boulder: University of Colorado, 2000), https://itll.colorado.edu/images/uploads/courses_workshops/geen1400/textbook/ch06teamwork_and_working_in_teams.pdf.

154. J. L. Thompson, "Building Collective Communication Competence in Interdisciplinary Research Teams," *Journal of Applied Communication Research* 37, no. 3 (2009): 278–97.

155. Richard E. Boyatzis, Melvin L. Smith, and Alim J. Beveridge, "Coaching with Compassion: Inspiring Health, Well-Being, and Development in Organizations," *Journal of Applied Behavioral Science* 49, no. 2 (2013): 153–78.

156. Michelle Gielan, "You Can Deliver Bad News to Your Team without Crushing Them," *Harvard Business Review*, March 21, 2016, https://hbr.org/2016/03/you-can-deliver-bad-news-to-your-team-without-crushing-them.

157. Patrick Lencioni, "Conquering Team Dysfunction," Table Group, 2014, https://www.tablegroup.com/imo/media/doc/Conquer_Team_Dysfunction.pdf.

158. M. A. Marks and F. J. Panzer, "The Influence of Team Monitoring on Team Processes and Performance," *Human Performance* 17, no. 1 (2004): 25–41.

159. Steven Bray and Lawrence Brawley, "Role Efficacy, Role Clarity, and Role Performance Effectiveness," *Small Group Research* 33, no. 2 (2002): 233–53.

160. Ferdinand F. Fournies, *Coaching for Improved Work Performance, Revised Edition* (New York: McGraw Hill, 2000).

Part 3

11

161. Behnam Tabrizi, "Cross-Functional Dysfunctional" (unpublished paper), https://www.dropbox.com/s/515i3fow8qrdoeh/CFDFv4.doc?dl=0.

162. University of Phoenix, "University of Phoenix Survey Reveals Nearly Seven-in-Ten Workers Have Been Part of Dysfunctional Teams" (news release), January 16, 2013, https://www.phoenix.edu/news/releases/2013/01/university-of-phoenix-survey-reveals-nearly-seven-in-ten-workers-have-been-part-of-dysfunctional-teams.html.

163. Josh Bersin, Jason Geller, Nicky Wakefield, and Brett Walsh, "Introduction: The New Organization, Different by Design," *Deloitte Insights*, February 29, 2016, https://www2.deloitte.com/insights/us/en/focus/human-capital-trends/2016/human-capital-trends-introduction.html.

164. Connie J. Gersick, "Time and Transition in Work Teams: Toward a New Model of Group Development," *Academy of Management Journal* 31, no. 1 (1988): 9–41.

165. M. R. Bashshur, A. Hernández, and V. González-Romá, "When Managers and Their Teams Disagree: A Longitudinal Look at the Consequences of Differences in Perceptions of Organizational Support," *Journal of Applied Psychology* 96, no. 3 (2011): 558.

166. P. Kanawattanachai and Y. Yoo, "Dynamic Nature of Trust In Virtual Teams," *Journal of Strategic Information Systems* 11, no. 3 (2002): 187–213.

167. Hayward Andres, "Technology-Mediated Collaboration Shared Mental Model and Task Performance," *Journal of Organizational and End User Computing* 24 (2012): 64–81.

168. Bradley Kirkman et al., "Five Challenges to Virtual Team Success: Lessons from Sabre, Inc.," *Academy of Management Perspectives* 16, no. 3 (2002): 67–79.

169. "Employment Trends," World Economic Forum, accessed on October 17, 2018, http://reports.weforum.org/future-of-jobs-2016/employment-trends/.

170. Judith Kapustin Katz, Sally Rosen, and Page Morahan, "What Is Team Coaching, and Why Use Co-coaches?" *Academic Physician and Scientist* (2009): 4–5.

171. Ibid.

172. Tricia Varvel, Stephanie G. Adams, Shelby J. Pridie, and Bianey C. Ruiz Ulloa, "Team Effectiveness and Individual Myers-Briggs Personality Dimensions," *Journal of Management in Engineering* 20, no. 4 (2004): 141–46.

173. Cathy Powell and Sharon Toye, "The Power and Process of Team Coaching," Heidrick & Struggles, December 31, 2015, https://www.heidrick.com/Knowledge-Center/Article/The-power-and-process-of-team-coaching.

174. Gretchen M. Spreitzer, "Social Structural Characteristics of Psychological Empowerment," *Academy of Management Journal* 39, no. 2 (1996): 483–504.

175. Steve W. J. Kozlowski and Bradford S. Bell, "Work Groups and Teams in Organizations," Cornell University ILR School (2001), https://digitalcommons.ilr.cornell.edu/cgi/viewcontent.cgi?referer=https://scholar.google.com/&httpsredir=1&article=1396&context=articles.

12

176. "Stress at the Workplace," World Health Organization, accessed on October 17, 2018, http://www.who.int/occupational_health/topics/stressatwp/en/.

177. "Attitudes in the American Workplace VII: The Seventh Annual Labor Day Survey," American Institute of Stress, accessed on October 17, 2018,

https://www.stress.org/wp-content/uploads/2011/08/2001Attitude-in -the-Workplace-Harris.pdf.

178. UMass Lowell, "Financial Costs of Job Stress," https://www.uml.edu/ research/cph-new/worker/stress-at-work/financial-costs.aspx.

179. Charles Duhigg, "What Google Learned from Its Quest to Build the Perfect Team," *New York Times*, February 25, 2016, https://www.nytimes .com/2016/02/28/magazine/what-google-learned-from-its-quest-to -build-the-perfect-team.html.

Bibliography

Ancona, Deborah G., and Henrik Bresman. *X-Teams: How to Build Teams that Lead, Innovate, and Succeed*. Boston, MA: Harvard Business School Press, 2007.

Bader, Gloria E., Audrey E. Bloom, Richard Y. Chang, and Richard V. Chang. *Measuring Team Performance: A Practical Guide to Tracking Team Success*. San Francisco, CA: Pfeiffer, 1994.

Belbin, Meredith. *Team Roles at Work*. Woburn, MA: Butterworth-Heinemann, 1993.

Bellman, Geoffrey M., and Kathleen D. Ryan. *Extraordinary Groups: How Ordinary Teams Achieve Amazing Results*. San Francisco, CA: Jossey-Bass, 2009.

Beyerlein, Michael Martin, Sue Freedman, Craig McGee, and Linda Moran. *Beyond Teams: Building the Collaborative Organization*. San Francisco: Jossey-Bass, 2002.

Biech, Elaine, ed. *The Pfeiffer Book of Successful Team-Building Tools: Best of the Annuals*. San Francisco, CA: Pfeiffer, 2007.

Brannick, Michael T., Eduardo Salas, and Carolyn W. Prince, eds. *Team Performance Assessment and Measurement: Theory, Methods, and Applications*. Mahwah, NJ: Lawrence Erlbaum, 1997.

Brenner, Dean M. *Sharing the Sandbox: Building and Leading World-Class Teams in the 21st Century*. Wallingford, CT: Latimer, 2012.

Britton, Jennifer J. *From One to Many: Best Practices for Team and Group Coaching*. Hoboken, NJ: John Wiley and Sons, 2013.

Burruss, James A., J. Richard Hackman, Debra A. Nunes, and Ruth Wageman. *Senior Leadership Teams: What It Takes to Make Them Great*. Boston, MA: Harvard Business School Press, 2008.

Bushe, Gervase R. *Clear Leadership: Sustaining Real Collaboration and Partnership at Work*. Mountain View, CA: Davies-Black, 2009.

Cain, James, and Barry Jolliff. *Teamwork and Teamplay*. Dubuque, IA: Kendall/Hunt, 1998.

Clutterbuck, David. *Coaching the Team at Work*. London: Nicholas Brealey, 2007.

Cobb, Anthony T. *Leading Project Teams: The Basics of Project Management and Team Leadership*. 2nd ed. London: SAGE, 2011.

Covey, Stephen R. *The Speed of Trust: The One Thing that Changes Everything*. With Rebecca R. Merrill. New York: Free Press, 2008.

Deeprose, Donna. *The Team Coach: Vital New Skills for Supervisors and Managers in a Team Environment*. New York: American Management Association, 1995.

DeRosa, Darleen M., and Richard Lepsinger. *Virtual Team Success: A Practical Guide for Working and Leading from a Distance*. San Francisco, CA: Jossey-Bass, 2010.

Dyer, William G., W. Gibb Dyer, Jeffrey H. Dyer, and Edgar H. Schein. *Team Building: Proven Strategies for Improving Team Performance*. San Francisco: Jossey-Bass, 2007.

Fiore, Stephen M., and Eduardo Salas. *Team Cognition: Understanding the Factors that Drive Process and Performance*. Washington, DC: American Psychological Association, 2004.

Frontiera, Joe, and Daniel Leidl. *Team Turnarounds: A Playbook for Transforming Underperforming Teams*. San Francisco, CA: Jossey-Bass, 2012.

Guttman, Howard. *Great Business Teams: Cracking the Code for Standout Performance*. Hoboken, NJ: John Wiley and Sons, 2008.

Hackman, J. Richard, ed. *Groups that Work (and Those that Don't): Creating Conditions for Effective Teamwork*. San Francisco, CA: Jossey-Bass, 1990.

Harvard Business Review on Building Better Teams. Boston, MA: Harvard Business Review Press, 2011.

Hawkins, Peter. *Leadership Team Coaching: Developing Collective Transformational Leadership*. 2nd ed. Philadelphia, PA: Kogan Page, 2014.

Huszczo, Gregory E. *Tools for Team Leadership: Delivering the X-Factor in Team Excellence*. Palo Alto, CA: Davies-Black, 2004.

Isaacs, William. *Dialogue and the Art of Thinking Together: A Pioneering Approach to Communicating in Business and in Life*. New York: Currency, 1999.

Jones, Steven D., and Don J. Schilling. *Measuring Team Performance: A Step-by-Step, Customizable Approach for Managers, Facilitators, and Team Leaders*. San Francisco: Jossey-Bass, 2000.

Katzenbach, Jon R., and Douglas K. Smith. *The Discipline of Teams*. Boston, MA: Harvard Business School Press, 2009.

Katzenbach, Jon R., and Douglas K. Smith. *The Wisdom of Teams: Creating the High-Performance Organization*. New York: HarperCollins, 1993.

Kayser, Thomas A. *Building Team Power: How to Unleash the Collaborative Genius of Teams for Increased Engagement, Productivity, and Results.* New York: McGraw-Hill, 2010.

Kegan, Robert, and Lisa Laskow Lahey. *How the Way We Talk Can Change the Way We Work: Seven Languages for Transformation.* San Francisco: Jossey-Bass, 2001.

Koppett, Kat. *Training to Imagine: Practical Improvisational Theatre Techniques for Trainers and Managers to Enhance Creativity, Teamwork, Leadership, and Learning.* Sterling, VA: Stylus, 2013.

LaFasto, Frank M. J., and Carl E. Larson. *When Teams Work Best: 6,000 Team Members and Leaders Tell What It Takes to Succeed.* Thousand Oaks, CA: SAGE, 2001.

Lencioni, Patrick M. *The Advantage: Why Organizational Health Trumps Everything Else in Business.* Hoboken, NJ: John Wiley and Sons, 2012.

Lencioni, Patrick. *The Five Dysfunctions of a Team: A Leadership Fable.* New York: Random House, 2002.

Levi, Daniel. *Group Dynamics for Teams.* 3rd ed. Thousand Oaks, CA: SAGE, 2010.

Lewis, Richard D. *When Teams Collide: Managing the International Team Successfully.* Boston, MA: Nicholas Brealey, 2012.

Maravelas, Anna. *How to Reduce Workplace Conflict and Stress: How Leaders and Their Employees Can Protect Their Sanity and Productivity from Tension and Turf Wars.* Franklin Lakes, NJ: Career, 2005.

Martinelli, Russ J., Tim Rahschulte, and James M. Waddell. *Leading Global Project Teams: The New Leadership Challenge.* Oshawa, ON, Canada: Multi-Media, 2010.

Maxwell, John C., and Sean Runnette. *Teamwork 101: What Every Leader Needs to Know.* New York: HarperCollins, 2009.

Nadler, Reldan S. *Leading with Emotional Intelligence: Hands-on Strategies for Building Confident and Collaborative Star Performers.* New York: McGraw-Hill, 2010.

Parker, Glenn M. *Team Players and Team Work: New Strategies for Developing Successful Collaboration.* San Francisco, CA: Jossey-Bass, 2008.

Patterson, Kerry, Joseph Grenny, Ron McMillan, and Al Switzler. *Crucial Conversations: Tools for Talking When Stakes Are High.* New York: McGraw-Hill, 2002.

Pellerin, Charles J. *How NASA Builds Teams: Mission Critical Soft Skills for Scientists, Engineers, and Project Teams.* Hoboken, NJ: John Wiley and Sons, 2009.

Phillips, Patricia Pulliam, Jack J. Phillips, and Lisa Edwards. *Measuring the Success of Coaching: A Step-by-Step Guide for Measuring Impact and Calculating ROI*. Alexandria, VA: ASTD Press, 2012.

Pritchard, Kevin, and John Eliot. *Help the Helper: Building a Culture of Extreme Teamwork*. New York: Portfolio/Penguin, 2012.

Ray, Darrel, and Howard Bronstein. *Teaming Up: Making the Transition to a Self-Directed, Team-Based Organization*. New York: McGraw-Hill, 1995.

Sawyer, R. Keith. *Group Genius: The Creative Power of Collaboration*. New York: Basic Books, 2007.

Schwarz, Roger M. *Smart Leaders, Smarter Teams: How You and Your Team Get Unstuck to Get Results*. New York: John Wiley and Sons, 2013.

Scott, Susan. *Fierce Conversations: Achieving Success at Work and in Life, One Conversation at a Time*. New York: Berkley, 2002.

Stanier, Michael Bungay. *The Coaching Habit: Say Less, Ask More and Change the Way You Lead Forever*. Toronto, ON, Canada: Box of Crayons, 2016.

Stowell, Steven J., and Stephanie S. Mead. *The Team Approach: With Teamwork Anything Is Possible*. Sandy, UT: CMOE Press, 2007.

Wellins, Richard S., Jeanne M. Wilson, and William C. Byham. *Empowered Teams: Creating Self-Directed Work Groups that Improve Quality, Productivity, and Participation*. San Francisco, CA: Jossey-Bass, 1991.

Whitney, Diana, Jay Cherney, Amanda Trosten-Bloom, and Ron Fry. *Appreciative Team Building: Positive Questions to Bring Out the Best of Your Team*. Lincoln, NE: iUniverse, 2004.

What the TCI Team Performance Data Reveals

Overview

The TCI Team Diagnostic™ is an assessment tool initially created by Alexis Phillips, cofounder of Team Coaching International (TCI). The model on which the assessment is based was created over a period of several years by surveying the available literature focusing on the competencies necessary for teams to be both highly productive and highly collaborative. The ultimate goal of this initiative was the creation of tools to support teams and team coaches in an effective process for delivering improved business results in a sustainable, engaged team culture.

The Model

After collecting a long list of attributes for team performance, Phillips saw that the list could be divided into two categories: team competencies necessary to get the job done—the Productivity dimension—and competencies necessary for team members to work together to get the job done—the Positivity dimension.

The Productivity dimension includes the following seven team competencies:

- Team Leadership
- Resources

- Decision making
- Proactive
- Accountability
- Goals and Strategies
- Alignment

The Positivity dimension includes these seven competencies:

- Trust
- Respect
- Camaraderie
- Communication
- Constructive Interaction
- Diversity
- Optimism

Data Analysis Using the TCI Team Diagnostic

This is a systems-based assessment tool using a nine-point Likert scale and 80 standard statements for team member scoring that range from "Does not describe our team" to "Completely describes our team." All items are written from the team perspective. For example, "On our team we have clear goals." or, "On our team we tend to avoid conflict."

The assessment is delivered via an online, individualized link to ensure anonymity for team members. In addition to the standard 80 items, there is an option to add three to five survey-style, open-ended questions for written responses.

When team members have completed the assessment, the data is aggregated and downloaded into a coaching report. The report has five graphic layers, each layer showing a finer level of detail.

The TCI Team Diagnostic is in 23 languages as of this writing. Team members on multinational teams have the option to select a language of their preference from that list. Reports can be published in all languages.

Arabic	French (EU)	Portuguese (Brazil)
Chinese	German	Portuguese (Portugal)
Danish	Greek	Russian
Dutch	Hebrew	Spanish (EU)

English	Italian	Spanish (Latin America)
English (UK)	Japanese	Swedish
Finnish	Norwegian	Turkish
French (Canadian)	Polish	

What the Data Shows

The results we show in this appendix are based on an analysis of 3,307 team assessments from the years 2008 to 2017.

Rank Order of the 14 Team Performance Indicators

For all teams in the data set, here is the rank order from highest score to lowest score for all 14 factors:

Figure A-1: For all teams in the data set, here is the rank order from highest score to lowest score for all 14 factors. Data from the TCI Team Diagnostic™ database, based on more than 3,000 teams, 2008-2017.

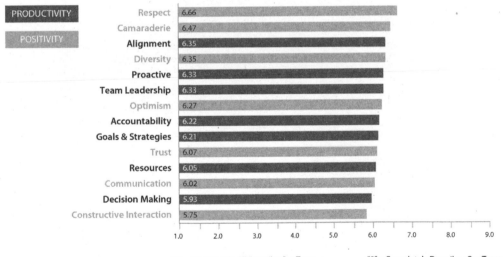

PRODUCTIVITY

POSITIVITY

Respect	6.66
Camaraderie	6.47
Alignment	6.35
Diversity	6.35
Proactive	6.33
Team Leadership	6.33
Optimism	6.27
Accountability	6.22
Goals & Strategies	6.21
Trust	6.07
Resources	6.05
Communication	6.02
Decision Making	5.93
Constructive Interaction	5.75

"1" = Does Not At All Describe Our Team   "9" = Completely Describes Our Team

Here is the same set for High Productivity—High Positivity teams:

Figure A-2: For High Productivity—High Positivity teams, here is the rank order from highest score. Data from the TCI Team Diagnostic™ database, based on more than 3,000 teams, 2008-2017.

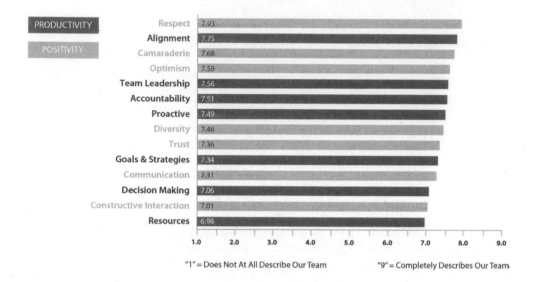

"1" = Does Not At All Describe Our Team   "9" = Completely Describes Our Team

And the scores for the 14 factors for Low-Low teams:

Figure A-3: For Low Productivity—Low Positivity teams, here is the rank order from highest score. Data from the TCI Team Diagnostic™ database, based on more than 3,000 teams, 2008-2017.

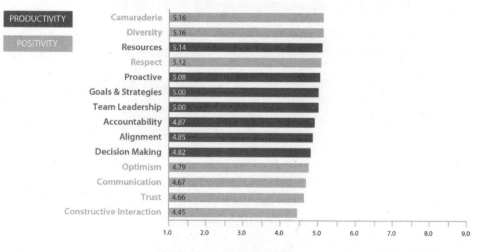

"1" = Does Not At All Describe Our Team   "9" = Completely Describes Our Team

There are some general consistencies between the three scales. For example, Constructive Interaction is either at the bottom or next to it. Team Leadership tends to land about in the middle. There are also notable exceptions. Optimism scores about midway with all teams, ranks fourth with High-High teams, and ranks eleventh with Low-Low teams. The data also shows that, as expected, high-performing teams do everything better.

It is also instructive to separate the factors into the two dimensions and look at the rank order in that configuration. The differences between the three categories are more visible.

Productivity Seven

Figure A-4: Rank order by dimension: Productivity. Data from the TCI Team Diagnostic™ database, based on more than 3,000 teams, 2008-2017.

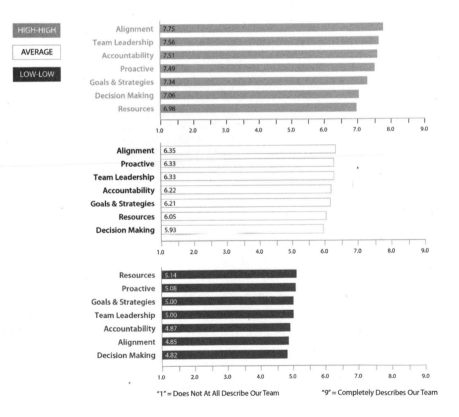

"1" = Does Not At All Describe Our Team   "9" = Completely Describes Our Team

Positivity Seven

Figure A-5: Rank order by dimension: Positivity. Data from the TCI Team Diagnostic™ database, based on more than 3,000 teams, 2008-2017.

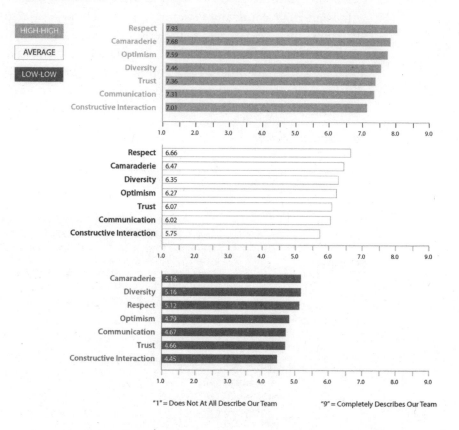

There are some areas where high-performing teams especially excel compared to other teams. The size of the gap between High-High and Low-Low gives us a way to see that comparison. This graphic shows what the best teams do exceptionally well. Notice that four of the top five are Positivity factors. Top teams create a collaborative culture.

Figure A-6: Spread between High-High and Low-Low teams in rank order from highest spread. Data from the TCI Team Diagnostic™ database, based on more than 3,000 teams, 2008-2017.

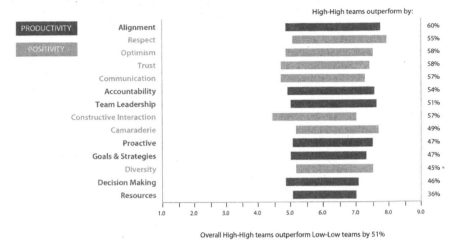

Overall High-High teams outperform Low-Low teams by 51%

How the Analysis of the Data Can Be Used

Team members are often curious to know where they stand compared to other teams. The TCI Team Diagnostic is a self-assessment, so technically speaking the comparison would not be based on normative data. However, the results from thousands of team assessments provide a reasonably stable baseline for that comparison and a way to satisfy the team's curiosity. As team coach, it is important to remember and perhaps remind the team that what is more important than the data scores and the comparison with other teams is the unique opportunity the data reveals for *this* team. A thousand teams might score Trust or Decision Making 4.5, and there would be a thousand different reasons for that score depending on the team.

Yes, it would be possible to simply review the data from 3,000 teams and choose the lower scoring factors for team development. As a coaching methodology, however, we have a strong reluctance to let the data be too directive. The agenda for team improvement will be most effective when it is clearly owned by the team based on team conversation and reflects unique team changes in behavior.

For more detailed review of the data, including pre– and post– team coaching results, go to: teamcoachinginternational.com/data.

Team Coaching Toolkit

The following collection of team exercises provides experiential tools based on the TCI team-effectiveness model designed to be used by coaches and teams. The exercises are all online and available for download: teamcoachinginternational.com/toolkit/.

The goal of the toolkit exercises is to create a learning experience for the team that naturally leads to a team conversation to harvest the team's insights about the topic, and more especially, how that topic applies to this team at this time. In addition to a description of the exercise and instructions for facilitation, each exercise also includes sample questions the coach can use in the debrief with the team.

Quad Exercise

An interactive exercise to familiarize team members with the quad matrix and the two basic dimensions in the model, Productivity and Positivity. Team members experience the different cultures and underlying behavioral norms characteristic of each of the four quadrants.

Productivity Game

The seven Productivity Team Performance Indicators are described on a deck of seven cards. The cards are distributed among the team members. Team members enthusiastically take a stand for the one they received.

Positivity Wheel

Team members thoughtfully review and experience the essential importance of each of the seven Positivity factors. At the end of the exercise team members choose one to be advocate for on the team.

Team Purpose

This exercise answers the question, "What are we here for?" Every team has a unique purpose in the organization, a role only this team can fill. This exercise is designed to help teams clarify and align behind their unique team purpose. It takes about 30 minutes.

Diminishing Resources

Teams are under relentless pressure to do more with less. This exercise reminds teams of the stress, the resulting behaviors, and the key to repeatable team success (almost always overlooked).

Three Short Stories and Introductions

One way teams build trust over time is by the simple process of getting to know one another on a human, personal level. This exercise provides teams with a structure to hear those stories in a way that helps ensure a safe environment for the storytelling.

Best Team

This is an exercise we learned from Appreciative Inquiry, David Cooperrider's work.[1] Team members recall a really great team they have been on and look for the attributes that set great teams apart from all the rest.

---

[1] For more information about Appreciative Inquiry go to: https://www.centerforappreciativeinquiry.net/more-on-ai/what-is-appreciative-inquiry-ai/.

Constellation Gallery

One of the consistent areas of frustration on teams is lack of clarity around roles and responsibilities. This powerful diversity and alignment exercise can help teams graphically picture roles and accountability on a project or process.

Least Agreement / Most Agreement

This exercise uses the team's own assessment results from this graphic layer in the coaching report to explore areas where team members are having the most diverse experience and areas of most common experience.

Team Toxins

Research shows[2] there are four communication styles that over time are toxic to working relationships. This exercise raises team awareness of those four and gives teams a way to address the impact when they show up. The exercise also includes a description of team antidotes to the team toxins.

---

[2] For more information about the research work of John Gottman go to: https://www.gottman.com/.

TCI Four Integrated Assessment Tools

There are four assessments in the suite of tools for teams, team leaders, and organizations. All four are based on the same TCI team-effectiveness model. For each of the assessments, the standard 80 items for scoring are modified so that the language shift is appropriate for the different perspectives. Several of the graphics in the coaching report are common to all four assessments, which makes it possible to show comparisons easily; for example, showing the team leader's view of the team compared to the whole team's view. This gives team and coach the ability to measure team progress over time. Here are brief descriptions of the four. For a more detailed description and information about applications, please go to https://teamcoachinginternational.com/programs/.

TCI Team Diagnostic™

The original, first used with teams in 2004

Today the assessment is available in more than 20 languages and has been used with thousands of teams worldwide. With the TCI Team Diagnostic, the perspective is the whole team, as in, "There is a high level of accountability and follow-through on our team." The result is a self-portrait of the team drawn by the team, which leads to a team conversation, and that leads to an action plan that leads to team development. With the TCI Team Diagnostic, every voice counts and every voice counts equally. In this systems-based approach, the attention is on the team rather than individual relationships on the team.

Team 360 View™

A candid view of the target team by stakeholders who interact with the team on a regular basis

The team decides who to invite to give feedback. That list might include the team's direct reports, the senior team or board the team reports to, plus internal or external customers. The result is new insight into how the team is perceived; in addition, the process of inviting stakeholders and gathering feedback naturally opens a stakeholder conversation. We find that the application leads to stronger, more effective stakeholder relationships. With the Team 360 View the perspective shifts to an outsider's view looking in, as in, "The team (I am assessing) seeks sufficient input in decision making."

Organization View™

Broad view of the organization as a whole or a significant sample

The Organization View is typically used in conjunction with a large-scale initiative, such as a change management project. The Organization View provides feedback to senior leadership about conditions and perceptions widely held in the organization. Data can be sliced vertically (for example, sales regions), or horizontally (such as all project managers). The Organization View is also a reflection of the senior team's values and priorities. People in the organization take their cue from the team at the top.

Team Leader View™

The team leader's perspective on the team he or she leads

Items are modified so the team leader is viewing the team through a personal lens. This assessment is often used in one-on-one executive and leadership coaching. It provides a language set for the team leader to use in evaluating his or her perception of team strengths and areas for development. The Team Leader View is often used by team coaches to introduce the model, assessment process, and methodology to the team leader. The confidential debrief of assessment results builds relationship and trust and frequently piques the team leader's interest in seeing the whole team's results.

Because the graphic format is similar for all four assessment reports, it is possible to create comparison reports where the results of two assessments can be overlapped. In this case, showing the team leader's Team Leader View polar diagram and the team's TCI Team Diagnostic graphic.

Figure A-7: Sample comparison graphic showing Team Diagnostic™ results and Team Leader View™ results.

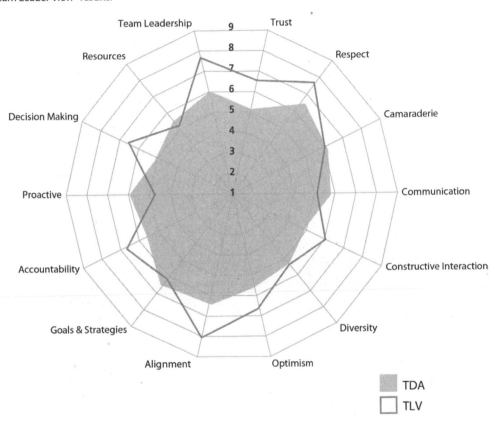

About the Authors

Phillip Sandahl,
Chief Coaching Officer

Cofounder of Team Coaching International (TCI) in 2004, Phil is an internationally recognized consultant/coach, trainer, and author. Phil has worked with teams in North America, Europe, and Asia. He has been training coaches internationally for more than 20 years. Phil is a former senior faculty member for the Co-Active Training Institute (CTI), the world's largest coaching training organization. In his role as curriculum designer and principal trainer for TCI, Phil has trained more than 1,500 team coaches from 50 countries. He has spoken at international coaching and HR conferences in Europe, Scandinavia, Canada, the United States, and Australia. Phil is also coauthor of *Co-Active Coaching,* considered the leading textbook on individual coaching, now in its fourth edition with 120,000 copies in print and in 10 languages.

Alexis Phillips
Chief Coaching Technology Officer

A founding partner of Team Coaching International, Alexis is the creative architect of the TCI Team Diagnostic model and the suite of four assessments based on that model. Her vision and commitment to effective, engaged teams have been the driving energy behind this work. She saw the need for the transformative balance of Productivity and Positivity, and identified the key team competencies for those two dimensions.

She also saw the need for a congruent methodology to convert the measurable data into team conversation, action, and learning. As team coach, she has worked with a wide range of leadership teams in a variety of industry sectors, including IT, manufacturing, pharmaceutical, financial services, and nonprofit organizations. Alexis is a passionate pioneer in the field of team coaching and gave this coaching niche credible, measurable tools for sustainable team improvement.

Index